THE CHEQUE BOOK

OF

THE BANK OF FAITH

By the same author

THE TREASURY OF THE BIBLE

LECTURES TO MY STUDENTS

MORNING AND EVENING DAILY READINGS

JOHN PLOUGHMAN'S TALK

JOHN PLOUGHMAN'S PICTURES

THE CHEQUE BOOK
OF THE BANK OF FAITH

Precious Promises for Daily Readings

C. H. SPURGEON

MARSHALL, MORGAN & SCOTT
London

Marshall, Morgan & Scott
a member of the Pentos group
1 Bath Street, London EC1V 9LB

This edition 1971
Fourth impression 1979

ISBN 0 551 05027 6

Printed in Great Britain
by J. W. Arrowsmith Ltd., Bristol
9760M30

PREFACE.

A PROMISE from God may very instructively be compared to a cheque payable to order. It is given to the believer with the view of bestowing upon him some good thing. It is not meant that he should read it over comfortably, and then have done with it. No, he is to treat the promise as a reality, as a man treats a cheque.

He is to take the promise, and endorse it with his own name by personally receiving it as true. He is by faith to *accept* it as his own. He sets to his seal that God is true, and true as to this particular word of promise. He goes further, and believes that he has the blessing in having the sure promise of it, and therefore he puts his name to it to testify to the receipt of the blessing.

This done, he must believingly *present* the promise to the Lord, as a man presents a cheque at the counter of the Bank. He must plead it by prayer, expecting to have it fulfilled. If he has come to heaven's bank at the right date, he will receive the promised amount at once. If the date should happen to be further on, he must patiently wait till its arrival; but meanwhile he may count the promise as money, for the Bank is sure to pay when the due time arrives.

Some fail to place the endorsement of faith upon the cheque, and so they get nothing; and others are slack in presenting it, and these also receive nothing. This is not the fault of the promise, but of those who do not act with it in a common-sense, business-like manner.

God has given no pledge which he will not redeem, and encouraged no hope which he will not fulfil. To help my brethren to believe this, I have prepared this little volume. The sight of the promises themselves is good for the eyes of faith : the more we study the words of grace, the more grace shall we derive from the words. To the cheering Scriptures I have added testimonies of my own, the fruit of trial and experience. I believe all the promises of God, but many of them I have personally tried and proved. I have seen that they are true, for they have been fulfilled to me. This, I trust, may be cheering to the young ; and not without solace to the older sort. One man's experience may be of the utmost use to another ; and this is why the man of God of old wrote, "I sought the Lord, and he heard me"; and again, "This poor man cried, and the Lord heard him."

I commenced these daily portions when I was wading in the surf of controversy. Since then I have been cast into "waters to swim in", which, but for God's upholding hand, would have proved waters to drown in. I have endured tribulation from many flails. Sharp bodily pain succeeded mental depression, and this was accompanied both by bereavement, and affliction in the person of one dear as life. The waters rolled in continually, wave upon wave. I do not mention this to exact sympathy, but simply to let the reader see that I am no dry-land sailor. I have traversed those oceans which are not Pacific full many a time : I know the roll of the billows, and the rush of the winds. Never were the promises of Jehovah so precious to me ·as at this hour. Some of them I never understood till now ; I had not reached the date at which they matured, for I was not myself mature enough to perceive their meaning.

How much more wonderful is the Bible to me now than it was a few months ago! In obeying the Lord, and bearing his reproach outside the camp, I have not received new promises; but the result to me is much the same as if I had done so, for the old ones have opened up to me with richer stores. Specially has the Word of the Lord to his servant Jeremiah sounded exceedingly sweet in mine ears. His lot it was to speak to those who would not hear, or hearing, would not believe. His was the sorrow which comes of disappointed love, and resolute loyalty; he would have turned his people from their errors, but he would not himself quit the way of the Lord. For him there were words of deep sustaining power, which kept his mind from failing where nature unaided must have sunk. These and such like golden sentences of grace I have loved more than my necessary food, and with them I have enriched these pages.

Oh, that I might comfort some of my Master's servants! I have written out of my own heart with the view of comforting their hearts. I would say to them in their trials— My brethren, God is good. He will not forsake you: he will bear you through. There is a promise prepared for your present emergencies; and if you will believe and plead it at the mercy-seat through Jesus Christ, you shall see the hand of the Lord stretched out to help you. Everything else will fail, but his word never will. He has been to me so faithful in countless instances that I must encourage you to trust him. I should be ungrateful to God and unkind to you if I did not do so.

May the Holy Spirit, the Comforter, inspire the people of the Lord with fresh faith! I know that, without his divine power, all that I can say will be of no avail; but, under his quickening influence, even the humblest testimony will confirm feeble knees, and strengthen weak hands. God is glorified when his servants trust him implicitly. We cannot be too much of children with our heavenly Father. Our young ones ask no question about our will or our power, but having once received a promise from father, they rejoice in the prospect of its fulfilment, never doubting that it is sure as the sun. May many readers, whom I may never see, discover the duty and delight of such child-like trust in God while they are reading the little bit which I have prepared for each day in the year.

C. H. Spurgeon

"And I will put enmity between thee and the woman, and between thy seed and her seed; it shall bruise thy head, and thou shalt bruise his heel."—Gen. iii. 15.

THIS is the first promise to fallen man. It contains the whole gospel, and the essence of the covenant of grace. It has been in great measure fulfilled. The seed of the woman, even our Lord Jesus, was bruised in his heel, and a terrible bruising it was. How terrible will be the final bruising of the serpent's head! This was virtually done when Jesus took away sin, vanquished death, and broke the power of Satan; but it awaits a still fuller accomplishment at our Lord's Second Advent, and in the day of Judgment. To us the promise stands as a prophecy that we shall be afflicted by the powers of evil in our lower nature, and thus bruised in our heel: but we shall triumph in Christ, who sets his foot on the old serpent's head. Throughout this year we may have to learn the first part of this promise by experience, through the temptations of the devil, and the unkindness of the ungodly who are his seed. They may so bruise us that we may limp with our sore heel; but let us grasp the second part of the text, and we shall not be dismayed. By faith let us rejoice that we shall still reign in Christ Jesus, the woman's seed.

"And the God of peace shall bruise Satan under your feet shortly."—ROM. xvi. 20.

THIS promise follows well upon that of yester-day. We are evidently to be conformed to our covenant Head, not only in his being bruised in his heel, but in his conquest of the evil one. Even under *our* feet is the old dragon to be bruised. The Roman believers were grieved with strife in the church; but their God was "the God of peace," and gave them rest of soul. The arch-enemy tripped up the feet of the unwary, and deceived the hearts of the simple; but he was to get the worst of it, and to be trodden down by those whom he had troubled. This victory would not come to the people of God through their own skill or power; but God himself would bruise Satan. Though it would be under their feet, yet the bruising would be of the Lord alone.

Let us bravely tread upon the tempter! Not only inferior spirits, but the Prince of darkness himself must go down before us. In unquestioning confidence in God, let us look for speedy victory. "SHORTLY." Happy word! *Shortly* we shall set our foot on the old serpent! What a joy to crush evil! What dishonour to Satan to have his head bruised by human feet! Let us by faith in Jesus tread the tempter down.

> *"The land whereon thou liest, to thee will I give it."*
> Gen. xxviii. 13.

NO promise is of private interpretation: it belongs not to one saint, but to all believers. If, my brother, thou canst in faith lie down upon a promise, and take thy rest thereon, it is thine. Where Jacob "lighted," and tarried, and rested, there he took possession. Stretching his weary length upon the ground, with the stones of that place for his pillows, he little fancied that he was thus entering into ownership of the land; and yet so it was. He saw in his dream that wondrous ladder which for all true believers unites earth and heaven; and surely where the foot of the ladder stood he must have a right to the soil, for otherwise he could not reach the divine stairway. All the promises of God are Yea and Amen in Christ Jesus; and as he is ours, every promise is ours if we will but lie down upon it in restful faith.

Come, weary one, use thy Lord's words as thy pillows. Lie down in peace. Dream only of Him. Jesus is thy ladder of light. See the angels coming and going upon him between thy soul and thy God; and be sure that the promise is thine own God-given portion, and that it will not be robbery for thee to take it to thyself, as spoken *specially to thee.*

"I will make them to lie down safely."—Hosea ii. 18.

YES, *the Saints are to have peace.* The passage from which this gracious word is taken speaks of peace "with the beasts of the field, and with the fowls of heaven, and with the creeping things of the ground." This is peace with earthly enemies, with mysterious evils, and with little annoyances! Any of these might keep us from lying down, but none of them shall do so. The Lord will quite destroy those things which threaten his people: "I will break the bow and the sword, and the battle out of the earth." Peace will be profound indeed when all the instruments of disquiet are broken to pieces.

With this peace will come rest. "So he giveth his beloved sleep." Fully supplied and divinely quieted, believers lie down in calm repose.

This rest will be a safe one. It is one thing to lie down, but quite another "to lie down safely." We are brought to the land of promise, the house of the Father, the chamber of love, and the bosom of Christ: surely we may now "lie down safely." It is safer for a believer to lie down in peace than to sit up and worry.

"He maketh me to lie down in green pastures." We never rest till the Comforter makes us lie down.

" I will strengthen thee."—Isa. xli. 10.

WHEN called to serve or to suffer, we take stock of our strength, and we find it to be less than we thought, and less than we need. But let not our heart sink within us while we have such a word as this to fall back upon, for it guarantees us all that we can possibly need. God has strength omnipotent; that strength he can communicate to us; and his promise is that he will do so. He will be the food of our souls, and the health of our hearts; and thus he will give us strength. There is no telling how much power God can put into a man. When divine strength comes, human weakness is no more a hindrance.

Do we not remember seasons of labour and trial in which we received such special strength that we wondered at ourselves? In the midst of danger we were calm, under bereavement we were resigned, in slander we were self-contained, and in sickness we were patient. The fact is, that God gives unexpected strength when unusual trials come upon us. We rise out of our feeble selves. Cowards play the man, foolish ones have wisdom given them, and the silent receive in the self-same hour what they shall speak. My own weakness makes me shrink, but God's promise makes me brave. Lord, strengthen me "according to thy word."

"Yea, I will help thee."—Isa. xli. 10.

YESTERDAY'S promise secured us strength for what we have to do, but this guarantees us aid in cases where we cannot act alone. The Lord says, "I will help thee." Strength within is supplemented by help without. God can raise us up allies in our warfare if so it seems good in his sight; and even if he does not send us human assistance, he himself will be at our side, and this is better still. "Our August Ally" is better than legions of mortal helpers.

His help is timely: he is a very present help in time of trouble. His help is very wise: he knows how to give each man help meet and fit for him. His help is most effectual, though vain is the help of man. His help is more than help, for he bears all the burden, and supplies all the need. "The Lord is my helper, I will not fear what man can do unto me."

Because he has already been our help, we feel confidence in him for the present and the future. Our prayer is, "Lord, be thou my helper"; our experience is, "The Spirit also helpeth our infirmities"; our expectation is, "I will lift up mine eyes unto the hills, whence cometh my help"; and our song soon will be, "Thou, Lord, hast holpen me."

"Thou shalt see greater things than these."—John i. 50.

THIS is spoken to a childlike believer, who was ready to accept Jesus as the Son of God, the King of Israel, upon one convincing piece of argument. Those who are willing to see shall see: it is because we shut our eyes that we become so sadly blind.

We have seen much already. Great things and unsearchable has the Lord showed unto us, for which we praise his name; but there are greater truths in his Word, greater depths of experience, greater heights of fellowship, greater works of usefulness, greater discoveries of power, and love, and wisdom. These we are yet to see if we are willing to believe our Lord. The faculty of inventing false doctrine is ruinous, but power to see the truth is a blessing. Heaven shall be opened to us, the way thither shall be made clear to us in the Son of man, and the angelic commerce which goes on between the upper and the lower kingdoms shall be made more manifest to us. Let us keep our eyes open towards spiritual objects, and expect to see more and more. Let us believe that our lives will not drivel down into nothing, but that we shall be always on the growing hand, seeing greater and still greater things, till we behold the Great God himself, and never again lose the sight of him.

"Blessed are the pure in heart: for they shall see God."
Matt. v. 8.

PURITY, even purity of heart, is the main thing to be aimed at. We need to be made clean within through the Spirit and the Word, and then we shall be clean without by consecration and obedience. There is a close connection between the affections and the understanding: if we love evil, we cannot understand that which is good. If the heart is foul, the eye will be dim. How can those men see a holy God who love unholy things?

What a privilege it is to see God here! A glimpse of him is heaven below! In Christ Jesus the pure in heart behold the Father. We see him, his truth, his love, his purpose, his sovereignty, his covenant character, yea, we see himself in Christ. But this is only apprehended as sin is kept out of the heart. Only those who aim at godliness can cry, "Mine eyes are ever towards the Lord." The desire of Moses, "I beseech thee, show me thy glory," can only be fulfilled in us as we purify ourselves from all iniquity. We shall "see him as he is"; and "every one that hath this hope in him purifieth himself." The enjoyment of present fellowship and the hope of the beatific vision are urgent motives for purity of heart and life. Lord, make us pure in heart, that we may see thee!

"The liberal soul shall be made fat."—Prov. xi. 25.

IF I desire to flourish in soul, I must not hoard up my stores, but must distribute to the poor. To be close and niggardly is the world's way to prosperity, but it is not God's way, for he saith. "There is that scattereth, and yet increaseth; and there is that withholdeth more than is meet, and it tendeth to poverty." Faith's way of gaining is giving. I must try this again and again; and I may expect that as much of prosperity as will be good for me will come to me as a gracious reward for a liberal course of action.

Of course, I may not be sure of growing rich. I shall be fat, but not too fat. Too great riches might make me as unwieldy as corpulent persons usually are, and cause me the dyspepsia of worldliness, and perhaps bring on a fatty degeneration of the heart. No, if I am fat enough to be healthy, I may well be satisfied; and if the Lord grants me a competence, I may be thoroughly content.

But there is a mental and spiritual fatness which I would greatly covet; and these come as the result of generous thoughts towards my God, his church, and my fellow-men. Let me not stint, lest I starve my heart. Let me be bountiful, and liberal; for so shall I be like my Lord. He gave himself for me: shall I grudge him anything?

"He that watereth shall be watered also himself."
Prov. xi. 25.

I F I carefully consider others, God will consider me; and in some way or other he will recompense me. Let me consider the poor, and the Lord will consider me. Let me look after little children, and the Lord will treat me as his child. Let me feed his flock, and he will feed me. Let me water his garden, and he will make a watered garden of my soul. This is the Lord's own promise; be it mine to fulfil the condition, and then to expect its fulfilment.

I may care about myself till I grow morbid; I may watch over my own feelings till I feel nothing; and I may lament my own weakness till I grow almost too weak to lament. It will be far more profitable for me to become unselfish, and out of love to my Lord Jesus begin to care for the souls of those around me. My tank is getting very low; no fresh rain comes to fill it; what shall I do? I will pull up the plug, and let its contents run out to water the withering plants around me. What do I see? My cistern seems to fill as it flows. A secret spring is at work. While all was stagnant, the fresh spring was sealed; but as my stock flows out to water others the Lord thinketh upon me. Hallelujah!

"And it shall come to pass, when I bring a cloud over the earth, that the bow shall be seen in the cloud."
Gen. ix. 14.

JUST now clouds are plentiful enough, but we are not afraid that the world will be destroyed by a deluge. We see the rainbow often enough to prevent our having any such fears. The covenant which the Lord made with Noah stands fast, and we have no doubts about it. Why, then, should we think that the clouds of trouble, which now darken our sky, will end in our destruction? Let us dismiss such groundless and dishonouring fears.

Faith always sees the bow of covenant promise whenever sense sees the cloud of affliction. God has a bow with which he might shoot out his arrows of destruction; but see! it is turned upward. It is a bow without an arrow or a string; it is a bow hung out for show, no longer used for war. It is a bow of many colours, expressing joy and delight, and not a bow blood-red with slaughter, or black with anger. Let us be of good courage. Never does God so darken our sky as to leave his covenant without a witness; and even if he did, we would trust him, since he cannot change, or lie, or in any other way fail to keep his covenant of peace. Until the waters go over the earth again, we shall have no reason for doubting our God.

"For the Lord will not cast off for ever."—Lament. iii. 31.

HE may cast away for a season, but not for ever. A woman may leave off her ornaments for a few days, but she will not forget them, nor throw them upon the dunghill. It is not like the Lord to cast off those whom he loves : for, "having loved his own which were in the world, he loved them unto the end." Some talk of our being in grace and out of it, as if we were like rabbits that run in and out of their burrows : but, indeed, it is not so. The Lord's love is a far more serious and abiding matter than this.

He chose us from eternity, and he will love us throughout eternity. He loved us so as to die for us, and we may therefore be sure that his love will never die. His honour is so wrapt up in the salvation of the believer, that he can no more cast him off than he can cast off his own robes of office as King of glory. No, no ! The Lord Jesus, as a Head, never casts off his members ; as a Husband, he never casts off his bride.

Did you think you were cast off? Why did you think so evil of the Lord who has betrothed you to himself? Cast off such thoughts, and never let them lodge in your soul again. "The Lord hath not cast away his people which he foreknew" (Rom. xi. 2). "He hateth putting away" (Mal. ii. 16).

> *"Him that cometh to me I will in no wise cast out."*
> John vi. 37.

IS there any instance of our Lord's casting out a coming one? If there be so, we would like to know of it; but there has been none, and there never will be. Among the lost souls in hell there is not one that can say, "I went to Jesus, and he refused me." It is not possible that you or I should be the first to whom Jesus shall break his word. Let us not entertain so dark a suspicion.

Suppose we go to Jesus now about the evils of to-day. Of this we may be sure—he will not refuse us audience, or cast us out. Those of us who have often been, and those who have never gone before—let us go together, and we shall see that he will not shut the door of his grace in the face of any one of us.

"This man receiveth sinners," but he repulses none. We come to him in weakness and sin, with trembling faith, and small knowledge, and slender hope; but he does not cast us out. We come by prayer, and that prayer broken; with confession, and that confession faulty; with praise, and that praise far short of his merits; but yet he receives us. We come diseased, polluted, worn out, and worthless; but he doth in no wise cast us out. Let us come again to-day to him who never casts us out.

"Come unto me, all ye that labour and are heavy laden, and I will give you rest."—Matt. xi. 28.

WE who are saved find rest in Jesus. Those who are not saved will receive rest if they come to him, for here he promises to "give" it. Nothing can be freer than a gift; let us gladly accept what he gladly gives. You are not to buy it, nor to borrow it; but to receive it as a gift. You labour under the lash of ambition, covetousness, lust, or anxiety: he will set you free from this iron bondage, and give you rest. You are "laden"— yes, "*heavy* laden" with sin, fear, care, remorse, fear of death; but if you come to him, he will unload you. He carried the crushing mass of our sin, that we might no longer carry it. He made himself the great Burden-bearer, that every heavy laden one might cease from bowing down under the enormous pressure.

Jesus gives rest. It is so. Will you believe it? Will you put it to the test? Will you do so at once? Come to Jesus, by quitting every other hope, by thinking of him, believing God's testimony about him, and trusting everything with him. If you thus come to him, the rest which he will give you will be deep, safe, holy, and everlasting. He gives a rest which develops into heaven, and he gives it this day to all who come to him.

"For the needy shall not alway be forgotten: the expectation of the poor shall not perish for ever."—Ps. ix. 18.

POVERTY is a hard heritage; but those who trust in the Lord are made rich by faith. They know that they are not forgotten of God; and though it may seem that they are overlooked in his providential distribution of good things, they look for a time when all this shall be righted. Lazarus will not always lie among the dogs at the rich man's gate, but he will have his recompense in Abraham's bosom.

Even now the Lord remembers his poor but precious sons. "I am poor and needy; yet the Lord thinketh upon me," said one of old; and it is even so. The godly poor have great expectations. They expect the Lord to provide them all things necessary for this life and godliness; they expect to see all things working for their good; they expect to have all the closer fellowship with their Lord, who had not where to lay his head; they expect his Second Advent, and to share its glory. This expectation cannot perish, for it is laid up in Christ Jesus, who liveth for ever; and because he lives, it shall live also. The poor saint singeth many a song which the rich sinner cannot understand. Wherefore, let us, when we have short commons below, think of the royal table above.

"And it shall come to pass, that whosoever shall call on the name of the Lord shall be delivered."—Joel ii. 32.

WHY do I not call on his name? Why do I run to this neighbour and that, when God is so near and will hear my faintest call? Why do I sit down, and devise schemes, and invent plans? Why not at once roll myself and my burden upon the Lord? Straightforward is the best runner—why do I not run at once to the living God? In vain shall I look for deliverance anywhere else; but with God I shall find it; for here I have his royal SHALL to make it sure.

I need not ask whether I *may* call on him or not, for that word "Whosoever" is a very wide and comprehensive one. Whosoever means *me*, for it means anybody and everybody who calls upon God. I will therefore follow the leading of the text, and at once call upon the glorious Lord who has made so large a promise.

My case is urgent, and I do not see how I am to be delivered; but this is no business of mine. He who makes the promise will find out ways and means of keeping it. It is mine to obey his commands; it is not mine to direct his counsels. I am his servant, not his solicitor. I call upon him, and he will deliver me.

"And he said, Certainly I will be with thee."—Ex. iii. 12.

OF course, if the Lord sent Moses on an errand, he would not let him go alone. The tremendous risk which it would involve, and the great power it would require, would render it ridiculous for God to send a poor lone Hebrew to confront the mightiest king in all the world, and then leave him to himself. It could not be imagined that a wise God would match poor Moses with Pharaoh and the enormous forces of Egypt. Hence he says, "Certainly I will be with thee," as if it were out of the question that he would send him alone.

In my case, also, the same rule will hold good. If I go upon the Lord's errand, with a simple reliance upon his power, and a single eye to his glory, it is certain that he will be with me. His sending me binds him to back me up. Is not this enough? What more can I want? If all the angels and archangels were with me, I might fail; but if HE is with me, I must succeed. Only let me take care that I act worthily towards this promise. Let me not go timidly, half-heartedly, carelessly, presumptuously. What manner of person ought he to be who has God with him! In such company it behoveth me to play the man. and like Moses go in unto Pharaoh without fear.

"When thou shalt make his soul an offering for sin, he shall see his seed."—Isa. liii. 10.

OUR Lord Jesus has not died in vain. His death was sacrificial: he died as our substitute, because death was the penalty of our sins; and because his substitution was accepted of God, he has saved those for whom he made his soul a sacrifice. By death he became like the corn of wheat which bringeth forth much fruit. There must be a succession of children unto Jesus; he is, "the Father of the everlasting age." He shall say, "Behold, I and the children whom thou hast given me."

A man is honoured in his sons, and Jesus hath his quiver full of these arrows of the mighty. A man is represented in his children, and so is the Christ in Christians. In his seed a man's life seems to be prolonged and extended; and so is the life of Jesus continued in believers.

Jesus lives, for he sees his seed. He fixes his eye on us, he delights in us, he recognizes us as the fruit of his soul travail. Let us be glad that our Lord does not fail to enjoy the result of his dread sacrifice, and that he will never cease to feast his eyes upon the harvest of his death. Those eyes which once wept for us, are now viewing us with pleasure. Yes, he looks upon those who are looking unto him. Our eyes meet! What a joy is this!

"If thou shalt confess with thy mouth the Lord Jesus, and shalt believe in thine heart that God hath raised him from the dead, thou shalt be saved."—Rom. x. 9.

THERE must be confession with the mouth. Have I made it? Have I openly avowed my faith in Jesus as the Saviour whom God has raised from the dead, and have I done it in God's way? Let me honestly answer this question.

There must also be belief with the heart. Do I sincerely believe in the risen Lord Jesus? Do I trust in Him as my sole hope of salvation? Is this trust from my heart? Let me answer as before God.

If I can truly claim that I have both confessed Christ and believed in him, then *I am saved.* The text does not say it may be so, but it is plain as a pikestaff, and clear as the sun in the heavens: "Thou shalt be saved." As a believer and a confessor, I may lay my hand on this promise, and plead it before the Lord God at this moment, and throughout life, and in the hour of death, and at the day of judgment.

I must be saved from the guilt of sin, the power of sin, the punishment of sin, and ultimately from the very being of sin. God hath said it—"Thou shalt be saved." I believe it. I shall be saved: I am saved. Glory be to God for ever and ever!

"To him that overcometh will I give to eat of the tree of life, which is in the midst of the paradise of God."—Rev. ii. 7.

NO man may turn his back in the day of battle, or refuse to go to the holy war. We must fight if we would reign, and we must carry on the warfare till we overcome every enemy, or else this promise is not for us, since it is only for "him that overcometh." We are to overcome the false prophets who have come into the world, and all the evils which accompany their teaching. We are to overcome our own faintness of heart, and tendency to decline from our first love. Read the whole of the Spirit's word to the church at Ephesus.

If by grace we win the day, as we shall if we truly follow our conquering Leader, then we shall be admitted to the very centre of the paradise of God, and shall be permitted to pass by the cherub and his flaming sword, and come to that guarded tree, whereof if a man eat, he shall live for ever. We shall thus escape that endless death which is the doom of sin, and gain that everlasting life which is the seal of innocence, the outgrowth of immortal principles of God-like holiness. Come, my heart, pluck up courage! To flee the conflict will be to lose the joys of the new and better Eden; to fight unto victory is to walk with God in Paradise.

"The Egyptians shall know that I am the Lord."—Ex. vii. 5.

THE ungodly world is hard to teach. Egypt does not know Jehovah, and therefore dares to set up its idols, and even ventures to ask—"Who is the Lord?" Yet the Lord means to break proud hearts, whether they will or not. When his judgments thunder over their heads, darken their skies, destroy their harvests, and slay their sons, they begin to discern somewhat of Jehovah's power. There will yet be such things done in the earth as shall bring sceptics to their knees. Let us not be dismayed because of their blasphemies, for the Lord can take care of his own name, and he will do so in a very effectual manner.

The salvation of his own people was another potent means of making Egypt know that the God of Israel was Jehovah, the living and true God. No Israelite died by any one of the ten plagues. None of the chosen seed were drowned in the Red Sea. Even so, the salvation of the elect, and the sure glorification of all true believers, will make the most obstinate of God's enemies acknowledge that Jehovah he is the God.

Oh, that his convincing power would go forth by his Holy Spirit in the preaching of the gospel, till all nations shall bow at the name of Jesus, and call him Lord!

*"Blessed is he that considereth the poor : the Lord will
deliver him in time of trouble."*—Ps. xli. 1.

TO think about the poor and let them lie on
our hearts is a Christian man's duty ; for
Jesus put them with us and near us when he said,
" The poor ye have always with you."

Many give their money to the poor in a hurry,
without thought ; and many more give nothing at
all. This precious promise belongs to those who
" consider " the poor, look into their case, devise
plans for their benefit, and considerately carry
them out. We can do more by care than by cash,
and most with the two together. To those who
consider the poor the Lord promises his own consideration in times of distress. He will bring us
out of trouble if we help others when they are
in trouble. We shall receive very singular providential help if the Lord sees that we try to
provide for others. We shall have a time of
trouble, however generous we may be; but if we
are charitable, we may put in a claim for peculiar
deliverance, and the Lord will not deny his own
word and bond. Miserly curmudgeons may help
themselves, but considerate and generous believers
the Lord will help. As you have done unto
others, so will the Lord do unto you. Empty your
pockets.

"And he shall put his hand upon the head of the burnt offering; and it shall be accepted for him to make atonement for him."—Lev. i. 4.

IF by that laying on of his hand the bullock became the offerer's sacrifice, how much more shall Jesus become ours by the laying on of the hand of faith?

> " My faith doth lay her hand
> On that dear head of thine,
> While like a penitent I stand,
> And there confess my sin."

If a bullock could be accepted for him to make atonement for him, how much more shall the Lord Jesus be our full and all-sufficient propitiation? Some quarrel with the great truth of substitution; but as for us, it is our hope, our joy, our boast, our all. Jesus is accepted for us to make atonement for us, and we are "accepted in the Beloved."

Let the reader take care at once to lay his hand on the Lord's completed sacrifice, that by accepting it he may obtain the benefit of it. If he has done so once, let him do it again. If he has never done so, let him put out his hand without a moment's delay. Jesus is yours now if you will have him. Lean on him; lean hard on him; and he is yours beyond all question; you are reconciled to God, your sins are blotted out, and you are the Lord's.

"He will keep the feet of his saints."—1 Sam. ii. 9.

THE way is slippery, and our feet are feeble, but the Lord will keep our feet. If we give ourselves up by obedient faith to be his holy ones, he will himself be our guardian. Not only will he charge his angels to keep us, but he himself will preserve our goings.

He will keep our feet from falling, so that we do not defile our garments, wound our souls, and cause the enemy to blaspheme.

He will keep our feet from wandering, so that we do not go into paths of error, or ways of folly, or courses of the world's custom.

He will keep our feet from swelling through weariness, or blistering because of the roughness and length of the way.

He will keep our feet from wounding: our shoes shall be iron and brass, so that even though we tread on the edge of the sword, or on deadly serpents, we shall not bleed, or be poisoned.

He will also pluck our feet out of the net. We shall not be entangled by the deceit of our malicious and crafty foes.

With such a promise as this, let us run without weariness, and walk without fear. He who keeps our feet will do it effectually.

"He looketh upon men, and if any say, I have sinned, and perverted that which was right, and it profited me not; he will deliver his soul from going into the pit, and his life shall see the light."—Job xxxiii. 27, 28.

THIS is a word of truth, gathered from the experience of a man of God, and it is tantamount to a promise. What the Lord has done, and is doing, he will continue to do while the world standeth. The Lord will receive into his bosom all who come to him with a sincere confession of their sin; in fact, he is always on the look-out to discover any that are in trouble because of their faults.

Can we not endorse the language here used? Have we not sinned, sinned personally so as to say, "I have sinned"? Sinned wilfully, having perverted that which is right? Sinned so as to discover that there is no profit in it, but an eternal loss? Let us, then, go to God with this honest acknowledgment. He asks no more. We can do no less.

Let us plead his promise in the name of Jesus. He will deliver us from the pit of hell which yawns for us; he will grant us life and light. Why should we despair? Why should we even doubt? The Lord does not mock humble souls. He means what he says. The guilty can be forgiven. Those who deserve execution can receive free pardon. Lord, we confess, and we pray thee to forgive!

"Surely there is no enchantment against Jacob, neither is there any divination against Israel."—Num. xxiii. 23.

HOW this should cut up root and branch all silly, superstitious fears! Even if there were any truth in witchcraft and omens, they could not affect the people of the Lord. Those whom God blesses devils cannot curse.

Ungodly men, like Balaam, may cunningly plot the overthrow of the Lord's Israel; but with all their secrecy and policy they are doomed to fail. Their powder is damp, the edge of their sword is blunted. They gather together; but as the Lord is not with them, they gather together in vain. We may sit still, and let them weave their nets, for we shall not be taken in them. Though they call in the aid of Beelzebub, and employ all his serpentine craft, it will avail them nothing: the spells will not work, the divination will deceive them. What a blessing this is! How it quiets the heart! God's Jacobs wrestle with God, but none shall wrestle with *them* and prevail. God's Israels have power with God and prevail, but none shall have power to prevail against them. We need not fear the fiend himself, nor any of those secret enemies whose words are full of deceit, and whose plans are deep and unfathomable. They cannot hurt those who trust in the living God. We defy the devil and all his legions.

"And there shall ye remember your ways, and all your doings, wherein ye have been defiled; and ye shall loathe yourselves in your own sight for all your evils that ye have committed."—Ez. xx. 43.

WHEN we are accepted of the Lord, and are standing in the place of favour, and peace, and safety, then we are led to repent of all our failures and miscarriages towards our gracious God. So precious is repentance, that we may call it a diamond of the first water, and this is sweetly promised to the people of God as one most sanctifying result of salvation. He who accepts repentance, also gives repentance; and he gives it not out of "the bitter box," but from among those "wafers made with honey" on which he feeds his people. A sense of blood-bought pardon and of undeserved mercy, is the best means of dissolving a heart of stone. Are we feeling hard? Let us think of covenant love, and then we shall leave sin, lament sin, and loathe sin; yea, we shall loathe ourselves for sinning against such infinite love. Let us come to God with this promise of penitence, and ask him to help us to remember, and repent, and regret, and return. Oh, that we could enjoy the meltings of holy sorrow! What a relief would a flood of tears be! Lord, smite the rock, or speak to the rock, and cause the waters to flow!

"And God shall wipe away all tears from their eyes."
Rev. xxi. 4.

YES, we shall come to this if we are believers. Sorrow shall cease, and tears shall be wiped away. This is the world of weeping, but it passes away. There shall be a new heaven, and a new earth, so says the first verse of this chapter; and therefore there will be nothing to weep over concerning the fall and its consequent miseries. Read the second verse, and note how it speaks of the bride and her marriage. The Lamb's wedding is a time for boundless pleasure, and tears would be out of place. The third verse says that God himself will dwell among men; and surely at his right hand there are pleasures for evermore, and tears can no longer flow.

What will our state be when there will be no more sorrow, nor crying, neither shall there be any more pain? This will be more glorious than we can as yet imagine. O eyes that are red with weeping, cease your scalding flow, for in a little while ye shall know no more tears! None can wipe tears away like the God of love, but he is coming to do it. "Weeping may endure for a night, but joy cometh in the morning." Come, Lord, and tarry not; for now both men and women must weep!

"Observe and hear all these words which I command thee, that it may go well with thee, and with thy children after thee for ever, when thou doest that which is good and right in the sight of the Lord thy God."—Deut. xii. 28.

THOUGH salvation is not by the works of the law, yet the blessings which are promised to obedience are not denied to the faithful servants of God. The curses our Lord took away when he was made a curse for us, but no clause of blessing has been abrogated.

We are to note and listen to the revealed will of the Lord, giving our attention not to portions of it, but to "all these words." There must be no picking and choosing, but an impartial respect to all that God has commanded. This is the road of blessedness for the father and for his children. The Lord's blessing is upon his chosen to the third and fourth generation. If they walk uprightly before him, he will make all men know that they are a seed which the Lord has blessed.

No blessing can come to us or ours through dishonesty or double dealing. The ways of worldly conformity and unholiness cannot bring good to us or ours. It will go well with us when we go well before God. If integrity does not make us prosper, knavery will not. That which gives pleasure to God will bring pleasure to us.

"And, behold, I am with thee, and will keep thee in all places whither thou goest."—Gen. xxviii. 15.

DO we need journeying mercies? Here are choice ones—God's presence and preservation. In all places we need both of these, and in all places we shall have them if we go at the call of duty, and not merely according to our own fancy. Why should we look upon removal to another country as a sorrowful necessity when it is laid upon us by the divine will? In all lands the believer is equally a pilgrim and a stranger; and yet in every region the Lord is his dwelling-place, even as he has been to his saints in all generations. We may miss the protection of an earthly monarch, but when God says, "I will keep thee," we are in no real danger. This is a blessed passport for a traveller, and a heavenly escort for an emigrant.

Jacob had never left his father's room before: he had been a mother's boy, and not an adventurer like his brother. Yet he went abroad, and God went with him. He had little luggage, and no attendants; yet no prince ever journeyed with a nobler body-guard. Even while he slept in the open field, angels watched over him, and the Lord God spoke to him. If the Lord bids us go, let us say with our Lord Jesus, "Arise, let us go hence."

"My God will hear me."—Micah vii. 7.

FRIENDS may be unfaithful, but the Lord will not turn away from the gracious soul; on the contrary, he will hear all its desires. The prophet says, "Keep the doors of thy mouth from her that lieth in thy bosom. A man's enemies are the men of his own house." This is a wretched state of affairs; but even in such a case the Best Friend remains true, and we may tell him all our grief.

Our wisdom is to look unto the Lord, and not to quarrel with men or women. If our loving appeals are disregarded by our own relatives, let us wait upon the God of our salvation, for he will hear us. He will hear us all the more because of the unkindness and oppression of others, and we shall soon have reason to cry, "Rejoice not against me, O mine enemy!"

Because God is the living God, he can hear; because he is a loving God, he will hear; because he is our covenant God, he has bound himself to hear us. If we can each one speak of him as "My God," we may with absolute certainty say, "My God will hear me." Come, then, O bleeding heart, and let thy sorrows tell themselves out to the Lord thy God! I will bow the knee in secret, and inwardly whisper, "My God will hear me."

"But unto you that fear my name shall the Sun of righteousness arise with healing in his wings."—Mal. iv. 2.

FULFILLED once in the first advent of our glorious Lord, and yet to have a fuller accomplishment in his second advent, this gracious word is also for daily use. Is it dark with the reader? Does the night deepen into a denser blackness? Still let us not despair: the sun will yet rise. When the night is darkest, dawn is nearest.

The sun which will arise is of no common sort. It is THE sun—the Sun of Righteousness, whose every ray is holiness. He who comes to cheer us, comes in the way of justice as well as of mercy, comes to violate no law even to save us. Jesus as much displays the holiness of God as his love. Our deliverance, when it comes, will be safe because righteous.

Our one point of inquiry should be—" Do we fear the name of the Lord? Do we reverence the living God, and walk in his ways?" Then for us the night must be short; and when the morning cometh, all the sickness and sorrow of our soul will be over for ever. Light, warmth, joy, and clearness of vision will come, and healing of every disease and distress will follow after.

Has Jesus risen upon us? Let us sit in the sun. Has he hidden his face? Let us wait for his rising. He will shine forth as surely as the sun.

"And ye shall go forth, and grow up as calves of the stall."—Mal. iv. 2.

YES, when the sun shines, the sick quit their chambers, and walk abroad to breathe the fresh air. When the sun brings spring and summer the cattle quit their stalls, and seek pasture on the higher Alps. Even thus, when we have conscious fellowship with our Lord, we leave the stall of despondency, and walk abroad in the fields of holy confidence. We ascend to the mountains of joy, and feed on sweet pasturage which grows nearer heaven than the provender of carnal men.

To "go forth" and to "grow up" is a double promise. O my soul, be thou eager to enjoy both blessings! Why shouldst thou be a prisoner? Arise, and walk at liberty. Jesus saith that his sheep shall go in and out and find pasture ; go forth, then, and feed in the rich meadows of boundless love.

Why remain a babe in grace? Grow up. Young calves grow fast, especially if they are stall-fed ; and thou hast the choice care of thy Redeemer. Grow, then, in grace, and in the knowledge of thy Lord and Saviour. Be neither straitened nor stunted. The Sun of Righteousness has risen upon thee. Answer to his beams, as the buds to the natural sun. Open thine heart, expand and grow up into him in all things.

"He that spared not his own Son, but delivered him up for us all, how shall he not with him also freely give us all things?"—Rom. viii. 32.

IF this is not a promise in form, it is in fact. Indeed, it is more than one promise, it is a conglomerate of promises. It is a mass of rubies, and emeralds, and diamonds, with a nugget of gold for their setting. It is a question which can never be answered so as to cause us any anxiety of heart. What can the Lord deny us after giving us Jesus? If we need all things in heaven and earth, he will grant them to us: for if there had been a limit anywhere, he would have kept back his own Son.

What do I want to-day? I have only to ask for it. I may seek earnestly, but not as if I had to use pressure, and extort an unwilling gift from the Lord's hand; for he will give *freely*. Of his own will, he gave us his own Son. Certainly no one would have proposed such a gift to him. No one would have ventured to ask for it. It would have been too presumptuous. He freely gave his Only-begotten; and, O my soul, canst thou not trust thy heavenly Father to give thee anything, to give thee everything? Thy poor prayer would have no force with Omnipotence if force were needed; but his love, like a spring, rises of itself, and overflows for the supply of all thy needs.

> *"I will not leave you comfortless : I will come to you.'*
> John xiv. 18.

HE left us, and yet we are not left orphans. He is our comfort, and he is gone; but we are not comfortless. Our comfort is that he will come to us, and this is consolation enough to sustain us through his prolonged absence. Jesus is already on his way : he says, "I come quickly" : he rides post-haste towards us. He says, "I will come": and none can prevent his coming, or put it back for a quarter of an hour. He specially says, "I will come *to you*"; and so he will. His coming is specially to and for his own people. This is meant to be their present comfort while they mourn that the Bridegroom doth not yet appear.

When we lose the joyful sense of his presence we mourn ; but we may not sorrow as if there were no hope. Our Lord in a little wrath has hid himself from us for a moment ; but he will return in full favour. He leaves us in a sense, but only in a sense. When he withdraws, he leaves a pledge behind that he will return. O Lord, come quickly ! There is no life in this earthly existence if thou be gone. We sigh for the return of thy sweet smile When wilt thou come unto us ? We are sure th wilt appear; but be thou like a roe, or a yo hart Make no tarrying, O our God !

"When I see the blood, I will pass over you."—Ex. xii. 13.

MY own sight of the precious blood is for my comfort; but it is the Lord's sight of it which secures my safety. Even when I am unable to behold it, the Lord looks at it, and passes over me because of it. If I am not so much at ease as I ought to be, because my faith is dim, yet I am equally safe, because the Lord's eye is not dim, and he sees the blood of the great Sacrifice with steady gaze. What a joy is this!

The Lord sees the deep inner meaning, the infinite fulness of all that is meant by the death of his dear Son. He sees it with restful memory of justice satisfied, and all his matchless attributes glorified. He beheld creation in its progress, and said, "It is very good"; but what does he say of redemption in its completeness? What does he say of the obedience even unto death of his Well-beloved Son? None can tell his delight in Jesus, his rest in the sweet savour which Jesus presented when he offered himself without spot unto God.

Now rest we in calm security. We have God's Sacrifice and God's Word to create in us a sense of perfect security. He will, he must, pass over us, because he spared not our glorious Substitute. Justice joins hands with love to provide everlasting salvation for all the blood-besprinkled ones.

"If thou shalt hearken unto the voice of the Lord thy God, blessed shalt thou be in the city."—Deut. xxviii. 2, 3.

THE city is full of care, and he who has to go there from day to day finds it to be a place of great wear and tear. It is full of noise, and stir, and bustle, and sore travail : many are its temptations, losses, and worries. But to go there with the divine blessing takes off the edge of its difficulty ; to remain there with that blessing is to find pleasure in its duties, and strength equal to its demands.

A blessing in the city may not make us great, but it will keep us good ; it may not make us rich, but it will preserve us honest. Whether we are porters, or clerks, or managers, or merchants, or magistrates, the city will afford us opportunities for usefulness. It is good fishing where there are shoals of fish, and it is hopeful to work for our Lord amid the thronging crowds. We might prefer the quiet of a country life ; but if called to town, we may certainly prefer it because there is room for our energies.

To-day let us expect good things because of this promise, and let our care be to have an open ear to the voice of the Lord, and a ready hand to execute his bidding. Obedience brings the blessing. " In keeping his commandments there is great reward."

" If thou return to the Almighty, thou shalt be built up."
Job xxii. 23.

ELIPHAZ, in this utterance, spoke a great truth, which is the summary of many an inspired Scripture. Reader, has sin pulled you down? Have you become like a ruin? Has the hand of the Lord gone out against you, so that in estate you are impoverished, and in spirit you are broken down? Was it your own folly which brought upon you all this dilapidation? Then the first thing to be done is to return to the Lord. With deep repentance and sincere faith find your way back from your backsliding. It is your duty, for you have turned away from him whom you professed to serve. It is your wisdom, for you cannot strive against him and prosper. It is your immediate necessity, for what he has done is nothing compared to what he may do in the way of chastisement, since he is Almighty to punish.

See what a promise invites you! You shall be " built up." None but the Almighty can set up the fallen pillars, and restore the tottering walls of your condition; but he can and he will do it if you return to him. Do not delay. Your crushed mind may quite fail you if you go on to rebel; but hearty confession will ease you, and humble faith will console you. Do this, and all will be well

"I will uphold thee with the right hand of my right-eousness."—Isa. xli. 10.

FEAR of falling is wholesome. To be venture-some is no sign of wisdom. Times come to us when we feel that we must go down unless we have very special support. Here we have it. God's right hand is a grand thing to lean upon. Mind, it is not only his hand, though it keepeth heaven and earth in their places, but his *right* hand : his power united with skill, his power where it is most dexterous. Nay, this is not all, it is written, "I will uphold thee with the right hand *of my righteousness.*" That hand which he uses to maintain his holiness, and to execute his royal sentences—this shall be stretched out to hold up his trusting ones. Fearful is our danger, but joyful is our security. The man whom God upholds, devils cannot throw down.

Weak may be our feet, but almighty is God's right hand. Rough may be the road, but Omni-potence is our upholding. We may boldly go forward. We shall not fall. Let us lean continually where all things lean. God will not withdraw his strength, for his righteousness is there as well : he will be faithful to his promise, and faithful to his Son, and therefore faithful to us. How happy we ought to be ! Are we not so ?

"And I will bring the third part through the fire, and will refine them as silver is refined, and will try them as gold is tried : they shall call on my name, and I will hear them : I will say, It is my people : and they shall say, The Lord is my God."—Zech. xiii. 9.

GRACE transmutes us into precious metal, and then the fire and the furnace follow as a necessary consequence. Do we start at this ? Would we sooner be accounted worthless, that we might enjoy repose, like the stones of the field ? This would be to choose the viler part : like Esau, to take the pottage, and give up the covenant portion. No, Lord; we will gladly be cast into the furnace rather than be cast out from thy presence !

The fire only refines, it does not destroy. We are to be brought through the fire, not left in it. The Lord values his people as silver, and therefore he is at pains to purge away their dross. If we are wise, we shall rather welcome the refining process than decline it. Our prayer will be that our alloy may be taken from us rather than that we should be withdrawn from the crucible.

O Lord, thou triest us indeed ! We are ready to melt under the fierceness of the flame. Still, this is thy way, and thy way is the best. Sustain us under the trial, and complete the process of our purifying, and we will be thine for ever and ever.

"For thou shalt be his witness unto all men of what thou hast seen and heard."—Acts xxii. 15.

PAUL was chosen to see and hear the Lord speaking to him out of heaven. This divine election was a high privilege for himself; but it was not intended to end with him, it was meant to have an influence upon others; yea, upon all men. It is to Paul that Europe owes the gospel at this hour.

It is ours in our measure to be witnesses of that which the Lord has revealed to us, and it is at our peril that we hide the precious revelation. First, we must see and hear, or we shall have nothing to tell; but when we have done so, we must be eager to bear our testimony. It must be personal: "Thou shalt be." It must be for Christ: "Thou shalt be *his* witness." It must be constant and all absorbing; we are to be this above all other things, and to the exclusion of many other matters. Our witness must not be to a select few who will cheerfully receive us; but to "all men"—to all whom we can reach, young or old, rich or poor, good or bad. We must never be silent like those who are possessed by a dumb spirit; for the text before us is a command, and a promise, and we must not miss it—" *Thou shalt be his witness.*" "Ye are my witnesses, saith the Lord."

Lord, fulfil this word to me also!

"I will pour my spirit upon thy seed, and my blessing upon thine offspring."—Isa. xliv. 3.

OUR dear children have not the Spirit of God by nature, as we plainly see. We see much in them which makes us fear as to their future, and this drives us to agonizing prayer. When a son becomes specially perverse, we cry with Abraham, "Oh, that Ishmael might live before thee!" We would sooner see our daughters Hannahs than empresses. This verse should greatly encourage us. It follows upon the words, "Fear not, O Jacob, my servant," and it may well banish our fears.

The Lord will give his Spirit; will give it plentifully, pouring it out; will give it effectually, so that it shall be a real and eternal blessing. Under this divine outpouring our children shall come forward, and "one shall say, I am the Lord's; and another shall call himself by the name of Jacob."

This is one of those promises concerning which the Lord will be enquired of. Should we not, at set times, in a distinct manner, pray for our offspring? We cannot give them new hearts, but the Holy Spirit can; and he is easily to be entreated of. The great Father takes pleasure in the prayers of fathers and mothers. Have we any dear ones outside of the ark? Let us not rest till they are shut in with us by the Lord's own hand.

"And the Lord said unto Abram, after that Lot was separated from him, Lift up now thine eyes, and look from the place where thou art northward, and southward, and eastward, and westward: for all the land which thou seest, to thee will I give it, and to thy seed for ever."—Gen. xiii. 14, 15.

A SPECIAL blessing for a memorable occasion. Abram had settled a family dispute. He had said, "Let there be no strife, I pray thee, between thee and me, for we be brethren"; and hence he received the blessing which belongs to peace-makers. The Lord and giver of peace delights to manifest his grace to those who seek peace and pursue it. If we desire closer communion with God, we must keep closer to the ways of peace.

Abram had behaved very generously to his kins-man, giving him his choice of the land. If we deny ourselves for peace sake, the Lord will more than make it up to us. As far as the patriarch can see, he can claim, and we may do the like by faith. Abram had to wait for the actual possession, but the Lord entailed the land upon him and his posterity. Boundless blessings belong to us by covenant gift. All things are ours. When we please the Lord, he makes us to look everywhere, and see all things our own, whether things present, or things to come, all are ours, and we are Christ's, and Christ is God's.

"Blessed shalt thou be in the field."—Deut. xxviii. 3.

SO was Isaac blessed when he walked therein at eventide to meditate. How often has the Lord met us when we have been alone! The hedges and the trees can bear witness to our joy. We look for such blessedness again.

So was Boaz blessed when he reaped his harvest, and his workmen met him with benedictions. May the Lord prosper all who drive the plough! Every farmer may urge this promise with God, if indeed he obeys the voice of the Lord God.

We go to the field to labour as father Adam did; and since the curse fell on the soil through the sin of Adam the first, it is a great comfort to find a blessing through Adam the second.

We go to the field for exercise, and we are happy in the belief that the Lord will bless that exercise, and give us health, which we will use to his glory.

We go to the field to study nature, and there is nothing in a knowledge of the visible creation which may not be sanctified to the highest uses by the divine benediction.

We have at last to go to the field to bury our dead; yea, others will in their turn take us to God's acre in the field: but we are blessed, whether weeping at the tomb, or sleeping in it.

"He that trusteth in the Lord, mercy shall compass him about."—Ps. xxxii. 10.

O FAIR reward of trust! My Lord, grant it me to the full! The truster above all men feels himself to be a sinner; and lo, mercy is prepared for him: he knows himself to have no deservings, but mercy comes in, and keeps house for him on a liberal scale. O Lord, give me this mercy, even as I trust in thee!

Observe, my soul, what a body-guard thou hast! As a prince is compassed about with soldiery, so art thou compassed about with mercy. Before and behind, and on all sides, ride these mounted guards of grace. We dwell in the centre of the system of mercy, for we dwell in Christ Jesus.

O my soul, what an atmosphere dost thou breathe! As the air surrounds thee, even so does the mercy of thy Lord. To the wicked there are many sorrows, but to thee there are so many mercies that thy sorrows are not worth mentioning. David says, "Be glad in the Lord, and rejoice, ye righteous; and shout for joy, all ye that are upright in heart." In obedience to this precept my heart shall triumph in God, and I will tell out my gladness. As thou hast compassed me with mercy, I will also compass thine altars, O my God, with songs of thanksgiving!

" The Lord hath been mindful of us : he will bless us."
Ps. cxv. 12.

I CAN set my seal to that first sentence. Cannot
you ? Yes, Jehovah has thought of us, provided for us, comforted us, delivered us, and guided
us. In all the movements of his providence he has
been mindful of us, never overlooking our mean
affairs. His mind has been full of us—that is the
other form of the word "mindful." This has been
the case all along, and without a single break. At
special times, however, we have more distinctly seen
this mindfulness, and we would recall them at this
hour with overflowing gratitude. Yes, yes, " the
Lord hath been mindful of us."

The next sentence is a logical inference from the
former one. Since God is unchangeable, he will
continue to be mindful of us in the future as he has
been in the past ; and his mindfulness is tantamount
to blessing us. But we have here, not only the
conclusion of reason but the declaration of inspira-
tion : we have it on the Holy Ghost's authority—
" HE WILL BLESS US." This means great things
and unsearchable. The very indistinctness of the
promise indicates its infinite reach. He will bless
us after his own divine manner, and that for ever
and ever. Therefore, let us each say, " Bless the
Lord, O my soul ! "

"I will not execute the fierceness of mine anger, I will not return to destroy Ephraim: for I am God, and not man."—Hos. xi. 9.

THE Lord thus makes known his sparing mercies. It may be that the reader is now under heavy displeasure, and everything threatens his speedy doom. Let the text hold him up from despair. The Lord now invites you to consider your ways, and confess your sins. If he had been man, he would long ago have cut you off. If he were now to act after the manner of men, it would be a word and a blow, and then there would be an end of you : but it is not so, for "as high as the heavens are above the earth, so high are his ways above your ways."

You rightly judge that he is angry, but he keepeth not his anger for ever: if you turn from sin to Jesus, God will turn from wrath. Because God is God, and not man, there is still forgiveness for you, even though you may be steeped up to your throat in iniquity. You have a God to deal with, and not a hard man, nor even a merely just man. No human being could have patience with you : you would have wearied out an angel, as you have wearied your sorrowing father ; but God is longsuffering. Come and try him at once. Confess, believe, and turn from your evil way, and you shall be saved.

"Be ye strong therefore, and let not your hands be weak: for your work shall be rewarded."—2 Chron. xv. 7.

GOD had done great things for King Asa and Judah, but yet they were a feeble folk. Their feet were very tottering in the ways of the Lord, and their hearts very hesitating, so that they had to be warned that the Lord would be with them while they were with him, but that if they forsook him he would leave them. They were also reminded of the sister kingdom, how ill it fared in its rebellion, and how the Lord was gracious to it when repentance was shown. The Lord's design was to confirm them in his way, and make them strong in righteousness. So ought it to be with us. God deserves to be served with all the energy of which we are capable.

If the service of God is worth anything, it is worth everything. We shall find our best reward in the Lord's work if we do it with determined diligence. Our labour is not in vain in the Lord, and we know it. Half-hearted work will bring no reward ; but, when we throw our whole soul into the cause, we shall see prosperity. This text was sent to the author of these notes in a day of terrible storm, and it suggested to him to put on all steam, with the assurance of reaching port in safety with a glorious freight.

"He will fulfil the desire of them that fear him: he also will hear their cry, and will save them."—Ps. cxlv. 19.

HIS own Spirit has wrought this desire in us, and therefore he will answer it. It is his own life within which prompts the cry, and therefore he will hear it. Those who fear him are men under the holiest influence, and, therefore, their desire is to glorify God, and enjoy him for ever. Like Daniel, they are men of desires, and the Lord will cause them to realize their aspirations.

Holy desires are grace in the blade, and the heavenly Husbandman will cultivate them till they come to the full corn in the ear. God-fearing men desire to be holy, to be useful, to be a blessing to others, and so to honour their Lord. They desire supplies for their need, help under burdens, guidance in perplexity, deliverance in distress; and sometimes this desire is so strong, and their case so pressing, that they cry out in agony, like little children in pain, and then the Lord works most comprehensively, and does all that is needful, according to this word—" and will save them."

Yes, if we fear God, we have nothing else to fear; if we cry to the Lord, our salvation is certain.

Let the reader lay this text on his tongue, and keep it in his mouth all the day, and it will be to him as " a wafer made with honey."

"Though I have afflicted thee, I will afflict thee no more."
Nahum i. 12.

THERE is a limit to affliction. God sends it
and God removes it. Do you sigh, and say
"When will the end be?" Remember that our
griefs will surely and finally end when this poor
earthly life is over. Let us quietly wait, and
patiently endure the will of the Lord till he cometh.

Meanwhile, our Father in heaven takes away the
rod when his design in using it is fully served.
When he has whipped away our folly, there will
be no more strokes. Or, if the affliction is sent for
testing us, that our graces may glorify God, it
will end when the Lord has made us bear witness
to his praise. We would not wish the affliction to
depart till God has gotten out of us all the honour
which we can possibly yield him.

There may to-day be "a great calm." Who knows
how soon those raging billows will give place to a
sea of glass, and the sea birds sit on the gentle waves?
After long tribulation the flail is hung up, and the
wheat rests in the garner. We may, before many
hours are past, be just as happy as now we are sorrowful. It is not hard for the Lord to turn night into
day. He that sends the clouds can as easily clear
the skies. Let us be of good cheer. It is better
on before. Let us sing Hallelujah by anticipation.

"The Lord shall guide thee continually."—Isa. lviii. 11.

WHAT aileth thee? Hast thou lost thy way? Art thou entangled in a dark wood, and canst thou not find thy paths? Stand still, and see the salvation of God. He knows the way, and he will direct thee in it if thou cry unto him.

Every day brings its own perplexity. How sweet to feel that the guidance of the Lord is continual! If we choose our own way, or consult with flesh and blood, we cast off the Lord's guidance; but if we abstain from self-will, then he will direct every step of our road, every hour of the day, and every day of the year, and every year of our life. If we will but be guided, we shall be guided. If we will commit our way unto the Lord, he will direct our course so that we shall not lose ourselves.

But note to whom this promise is made. Read the previous verse: "If thou draw out thy soul to the hungry." We must feel for others, and give them, not a few dry crusts, but such things as we ourselves would wish to receive. If we show a tender care for our fellow-creatures in the hour of their need, then will the Lord attend to our necessities, and make himself our continual Guide. Jesus is the Leader, not of misers, nor of those who oppress the poor, but of the kind and tender-hearted. Such persons are pilgrims, who shall never miss their way.

"He will bless them that fear the Lord, both small and great."—Ps. cxv. 13.

THIS is a word of cheer to those who are of humble station and mean estate. Our God has a very gracious consideration for those of small property, small talent, small influence, small weight. God careth for the small things in creation, and even regards sparrows in their lighting upon the ground. Nothing is small to God, for he makes use of insignificant agents for the accomplishment of his purposes. Let the least among men seek of God a blessing upon his littleness, and he shall find his contracted sphere to be a happy one.

Among those who fear the Lord there are little and great. Some are babes, and others are giants. But these are all blessed. Little faith is blessed faith. Trembling hope is blessed hope. Every grace of the Holy Spirit, even though it be only in the bud, bears a blessing within it. Moreover, the Lord Jesus bought both the small and the great with the same precious blood, and he has engaged to preserve the lambs as well as the full-grown sheep. No mother overlooks her child because it is little; nay, the smaller it is, the more tenderly does she nurse it. If there be any preference with the Lord, he does not arrange them as "great and small," but as "small and great."

"David said moreover, The Lord that delivered me out of the paw of the lion, and out of the paw of the bear, he will deliver me out of the hand of this Philistine."
1 Sam. xvii. 37.

THIS is not a promise if we consider only the words, but it is truly so as to its sense; for David spoke a word which the Lord endorsed by making it true. He argued from past deliverances that he should receive help in a new danger. In Jesus all the promises are Yea and Amen to the glory of God by us, and so the Lord's former dealings with his believing people will be repeated.

Come, then, let us recall the Lord's former loving-kindnesses. We could not have hoped to be delivered aforetime by our own strength; yet the Lord delivered us. Will he not again save us? We are sure he will. As David ran to meet his foe, so will we. The Lord has been with us, he is with us, and he has said, "I will never leave thee, nor forsake thee." Why do we tremble? Was the past a dream? Think of the dead bear and lion. Who is this Philistine? True, he is not quite the same, and is neither bear nor lion; but then God is the same, and his honour is as much concerned in the one case as in the other. He did not save us from the beasts of the forest to let a giant kill us. Let us be of good courage.

"If ye abide in me, *and my words abide in you, ye shall ask what ye will, and it shall be done unto you.*"
John xv. 7.

O F necessity we must be in Christ to live unto him, and we must abide in him to be able to claim the largesse of this promise from him. To abide in Jesus is never to quit him for another love, or another object, but to remain in living, loving, conscious, willing union with him. The branch is not only ever near the stem, but ever receiving life and fruitfulness from it. All true believers abide in Christ in a sense; but there is a higher meaning, and this we must know before we can gain unlimited power at the throne. "Ask what ye will" is for Enochs who walk with God, for Johns who lie in the Lord's bosom, for those whose union with Christ leads to constant communion.

The heart must remain in love, the mind must be rooted in faith, the hope must be cemented to the Word, the whole man must be joined unto the Lord, or else it would be dangerous to trust us with power in prayer. The *carte blanche* can only be given to one whose very life is, "Not I, but Christ liveth in me." O you who break your fellowship, what power you lose! If you would be mighty in your pleadings, the Lord himself must abide in you, and you in him.

"If ye abide in me, and my words abide in you, *ye shall ask what ye will, and it shall be done unto you."*
John xv. 7.

NOTE well, that we must hear Jesus speak if we expect him to hear us speak. If we have no ear for Christ, he will have no ear for us. In proportion as we hear we shall be heard.

Moreover, what is heard must remain, must live in us, and must abide in our character as a force and a power. We must receive the truths which Jesus taught, the precepts which he issued, and the movements of his Spirit within us; or we shall have no power at the mercy-seat.

Suppose our Lord's words to be received, and to abide in us, what a boundless field of privilege is opened up to us! We are to have our will in prayer, because we have already surrendered our will to the Lord's command. Thus are Elijahs trained to handle the keys of heaven, and lock or loose the clouds. One such man is worth a thousand common Christians. Do we humbly desire to be intercessors for the church and the world, and like Luther to be able to have what we will of the Lord? Then we must bow our ear to the voice of the Well-beloved, and treasure up his words, and carefully obey them. He had need "hearken diligently" who would pray effectually.

"Ye shall be named the priests of the Lord."—Isa. lxi. 6.

THIS literal promise to Israel belongs spiritually to the seed after the Spirit, namely, to all believers. If we live up to our privileges, we shall live unto God so clearly and distinctly, that men shall see that we are set apart for holy service, and shall name us the priests of the Lord. We may work, or trade, as others do, and yet we may be solely and wholly the ministering servants of God. Our one occupation shall be to present the perpetual sacrifice of prayer, and praise, and testimony, and self-consecration, to the living God by Jesus Christ.

This being our one aim, we may leave distracting concerns to those who have no higher calling. "Let the dead bury their dead." It is written, "Strangers shall stand and feed your flocks, and the sons of the alien shall be your plowmen and your vine-dressers." They may manage politics, puzzle out financial problems, discuss science, and settle the last new quibbles of criticism; but we will give ourselves unto such service as becomes those who, like the Lord Jesus, are ordained to a perpetual priesthood.

Accepting this honourable promise as involving a sacred duty, let us put on the vestments of holiness, and minister before the Lord all day long.

"The lip of truth shall be established for ever: but a lying tongue is but for a moment."—Prov. xii. 19.

TRUTH wears well. Time tests it, but it right well endures the trial. If, then, I have spoken the truth, and have for the present to suffer for it, I must be content to wait. If also I believe the truth of God, and endeavour to declare it, I may meet with much opposition, but I need not fear, for ultimately the truth must prevail.

What a poor thing is the temporary triumph of falsehood! "A lying lip is but for a moment"! It is a mere gourd, which comes up in a night, and perishes in a night; and the greater its development the more manifest its decay. On the other hand, how worthy of an immortal being is the avowal and defence of that truth which can never change; the everlasting gospel, which is established in the immutable truth of an unchanging God! An old proverb saith, "He that speaks truth shames the devil." Assuredly he that speaks the truth of God will put to shame all the devils in hell, and confound all the seed of the serpent which now hiss out their falsehoods.

O my heart, take care that thou be in all things on the side of truth, both in small things and great; but, specially, on the side of him by whom grace and truth have come among men!

c

"He shall not be afraid of evil tidings: his heart is fixed, trusting in the Lord."—Ps. cxii. 7.

SUSPENSE is dreadful. When we have no news from home, we are apt to grow anxious, and we cannot be persuaded that "no news is good news." Faith is the cure for this condition of sadness: the Lord by his Spirit settles the mind in holy serenity, and all fear is gone as to the future as well as the present.

The fixedness of heart spoken of by the Psalmist is to be diligently sought after. It is not believing this or that promise of the Lord, but the general condition of unstaggering trustfulness in our God, the confidence which we have in him that he will neither do us ill himself, nor suffer anyone else to harm us. This constant confidence meets the unknown as well as the known of life. Let the morrow be what it may, our God is the God of to-morrow. Whatever events may have happened which to us are unknown, our Jehovah is God of the unknown as well as of the known. We are determined to trust the Lord, come what may. If the very worst should happen, our God is still the greatest and best. Therefore will we not fear though the postman's knock should startle us, or a telegram wake us at midnight. The Lord liveth, and what can his children fear?

"Knowing in yourselves that ye have in heaven a better and an enduring substance."—Heb. x. 34.

THIS is well. Our substance here is very unsubstantial; there is no substance in it. But God has given us a promise of real estate in the glory-land, and that promise comes to our hearts with such full assurance of its certainty, that we know in ourselves that we have an enduring substance there. Yes, "we have" it even now. They say, "A bird in the hand is worth two in the bush"; but we have our bird in the bush and in the hand too. Heaven is even now our own. We have the title-deeds of it, we have the earnest of it, we have the first-fruits of it. We have heaven in price, in promise, and in principle : this we know not only by the hearing of the ear, but "in ourselves."

Should not the thought of the better substance on the other side of Jordan reconcile us to present losses? Our spending-money we may lose, but our treasure is safe. We have lost the shadows, but the substance remains, for our Saviour lives, and the place which he has prepared for us abides. There is a better land, a better substance, a better promise; and all this comes to us by a better covenant; wherefore, let us be in better spirits, and say unto the Lord, "Every day will I bless thee; and praise thy name for ever and ever."

"Surely goodness and mercy shall follow me all the days of my life."—Ps. xxiii. 6.

A DEVOUT poet sings—

> " Lord, when thou
> Puttest in my time a day, as thou dost now,
> Unknown in other years, grant, I entreat,
> Such grace illume it, that whate'er its phase
> It add to holiness, and lengthen praise !"

This day comes but once in four years. Oh, that we could win a fourfold blessing upon it ! Up till now goodness and mercy, like two guards, have followed us from day to day, bringing up the rear, even as grace leads the van ; and as this out-of-the-way day is one of the days of our life, the two guardian angels will be with us to-day also. Goodness to supply our needs, and mercy to blot out our sins—these twain shall attend our every step this day, and every day till days shall be no more. Wherefore, let us serve the Lord on this peculiar day with special consecration of heart, and sing his praises with more zest and sweetness than ever. Could we not to-day make an unusual offering to the cause of God, or to the poor? By inventiveness of love let us make this twenty-ninth of February a day to be remembered for ever.

"Hear the word of the Lord, ye that tremble at his word; Your brethren that hated you, that cast you out for my name's sake, said, Let the Lord be glorified: but he shall appear to your joy, and they shall be ashamed."—Isa. lxvi. 5.

POSSIBLY this text may not apply to one in a thousand of the readers of this little book of promises; but the Lord cheers that one in such words as these. Let us pray for all such as are cast out wrongfully from the society which they love. May the Lord appear to their joy!

The text applies to truly gracious men who tremble at the word of the Lord. These were hated of their brethren, and at length cast out because of their fidelity and their holiness. This must have been very bitter to them; and all the more so because their casting out was done in the name of religion, and professedly with the view of glorifying God. How much is done for the devil in the name of God! The use of the name of Jehovah to add venom to the bite of the old serpent is an instance of his subtilty.

The appearing of the Lord for them is the hope of his persecuted people. He appears as the advocate and defender of his elect; and when he does so, it means a clear deliverance for the God-fearing and shame for their oppressors. O Lord, fulfil this word to those whom men are deriding!

"But when thou doest alms, let not thy left hand know what thy right hand doeth: that thine alms may be in secret: and thy Father which seeth in secret himself shall reward thee openly."—Matt. vi. 3, 4.

NO promise is made to those who give to the poor to be seen of men. They have their reward at once, and cannot expect to be paid twice.

Let us hide away our charity ;—yes, hide it even from ourselves. Give so often and so much as a matter of course, that you no more take note that you have helped the poor than that you have eaten your regular meals. Do your alms without even whispering to yourself, "How generous I am!" Do not thus attempt to reward yourself. Leave the matter with God, who never fails to see, to record, and to reward. Blessed is the man who is busy in secret with his kindness : he finds a special joy in his unknown benevolences. This is the bread, which eaten by stealth, is sweeter than the banquets of kings. How can I indulge myself to-day with this delightful luxury? Let me have a real feast of tenderness and flow of soul.

Here and hereafter the Lord, himself, will personally see to the rewarding of the secret giver of alms. This will be in his own way and time ; and he will choose the very best. How much this promise means it will need eternity to reveal.

"For thou wilt not leave my soul in hell; neither wilt thou suffer thine Holy One to see corruption."—Ps. xvi. 10.

THIS word has its proper fulfilment in the Lord Jesus; but it applies also, with a variation, to all who are in him. Our soul shall not be left in the separate state, and our body, though it see corruption, shall rise again. The general meaning, rather than the specific application, is that to which we would call our readers' thoughts at this particular time.

We may descend in spirit very low till we seem to be plunged in the abyss of hell; but we shall not be left there. We may appear to be at death's door in heart, and soul, and consciousness; but we cannot remain there. Our inward death as to joy and hope may proceed very far; but it cannot run on to its full consequences, so as to reach the utter corruption of black despair. We may go very low, but not lower than the Lord permits; we may stay in the lowest dungeon of doubt for a while, but we shall not perish there. The star of hope is still in the sky when the night is blackest. The Lord will not forget us and hand us over to the enemy. Let us rest in hope. We have to deal with one whose mercy endureth for ever. Surely, out of death, and darkness, and despair we shall yet arise to life, light, and liberty.

"Them that honour me I will honour."—I Sam. ii. 30.

DO I make the honour of God the great object of my life and the rule of my conduct? If so, he will honour me. I may for a while receive no honour from man, but God will himself put honour upon me in the most effectual manner. In the end it will be found the surest way to honour to be willing to be put to shame for conscience sake.

Eli had not honoured the Lord by ruling his household well, and his sons had not honoured the Lord by behaviour worthy of their sacred office, and therefore the Lord did not honour *them*, but took the high-priesthood out of their family, and made young Samuel to be ruler in the land instead of any of their line. If I would have my family ennobled, I must honour the Lord in all things. God may allow the wicked to win worldly honours; but the dignity which he himself gives, even glory, honour, and immortality, he reserves for those who by holy obedience take care to honour *him*.

What can I do this day to honour the Lord? I will promote his glory by my spoken testimony, and by my practical obedience. I will also honour him with my substance, and by offering to him some special service. Let me sit down and think how I can honour him, since he will honour me.

"He blesseth the habitation of the just."—Prov. iii. 33.

HE fears the Lord, and therefore he comes under the divine protection even as to the roof which covers himself and his family. His home is an abode of love, a school of holy training, and a place of heavenly light. In it there is a family altar where the name of the Lord is daily had in reverence. Therefore the Lord blesses his habitation. It may be a humble cottage or a lordly mansion; but the Lord's blessing comes because of the character of the inhabitant, and not because of the size of the dwelling.

That house is most blest in which the master and mistress are God-fearing people; but a son or daughter or even a servant may bring a blessing on a whole household. The Lord often preserves, prospers, and provides for a family for the sake of one or two in it, who are "just" persons in his esteem, because his grace has made them so. Beloved, let us have Jesus for our constant guest, even as the sisters of Bethany had, and then we shall be blessed indeed.

Let us look to it that in all things we are just— in our trade, in our judgment of others, in our treatment of neighbours, and in our own personal character. A just God cannot bless unjust transactions.

"In thee the fatherless findeth mercy."—Hosea xiv. 3.

THIS is an excellent reason for casting away all other confidences and relying upon the Lord alone. When a child is left without its natural protector, our God steps in and becomes his guardian: so also when a man has lost every object of dependence, he may cast himself upon the living God and find in him all that he needs. Orphans are cast upon the fatherhood of God, and he provides for them. The writer of these pages knows what it is to hang on the bare arm of God, and he bears his willing witness that no trust is so well warranted by facts, or so sure to be rewarded by results, as trust in the invisible but ever living God.

Some children who have fathers are not much the better off because of them, but the fatherless with God are rich. Better have God and no other friend than all the patrons on the earth and no God. To be bereaved of the creature is painful, but so long as the Lord remains the fountain of mercy to us, we are not truly orphaned. Let fatherless children plead the gracious word for this morning, and let all who have been bereaved of visible support do the same. Lord, let me find mercy in thee! The more needy and helpless I am, the more confidently do I appeal to thy loving heart.

"The Lord looseth the prisoners."—Ps. cxlvi. 7.

HE has done it. Remember Joseph, Israel in Egypt, Manasseh, Jeremiah, Peter, and many others. He can do it still. He breaks the bars of brass with a word, and snaps the fetters of iron with a look. He is doing it. In a thousand places troubled ones are coming forth to light and enlargement. Jesus still proclaims the opening of the prison to them that are bound. At this moment doors are flying back and fetters are dropping to the ground.

He will delight to set you free, dear friend, if at this time you are mourning because of sorrow, doubt, and fear. It will be a joy to Jesus to give you liberty. It will give him as great a pleasure to loose you as it will be a pleasure to you to be loosed. No, you have not to snap the iron band: the Lord himself will do it. Only trust him, and he will be your Emancipator. Believe in him in spite of the stone walls, or the manacles of iron. Satan cannot hold you, sin cannot enchain you, even despair cannot bind you, if you will now believe in the Lord Jesus, and in the freeness of his grace, and in the fulness of his power to save.

Defy the enemy, and let the word now before you be your song of deliverance: "Jehovah looseth the prisoners."

"Blessed shall be thy basket and thy store."—Deut. xxviii. 5.

OBEDIENCE brings a blessing on all the provisions which our industry earns for us. That which comes in and goes out at once, like fruit in the basket which is for immediate use, shall be blest; and that which is laid by with us for a longer season shall equally receive a blessing. Perhaps ours is a hand-basket portion. We have a little for breakfast, and a scanty bite for dinner in a basket when we go out to our work in the morning. This is well, for the blessing of God is promised to the basket. If we live from hand to mouth, getting each day's supply in the day, we are as well off as Israel; for when the Lord entertained his favoured people he only gave them a day's manna at a time. What more did *they* need? What more do *we* need?

But if we have a store, how much we need the Lord to bless it! For there is the care of getting, the care of keeping, the care of managing, the care of using; and, unless the Lord bless it, these cares will eat into our hearts, till our goods become our gods, and our cares prove cankers.

O Lord, bless our substance. Enable us to use it for thy glory. Help us to keep worldly things in their proper places, and never may our savings endanger the saving of our souls.

"And seek the peace of the city whither I have caused you to be carried away captives, and pray unto the Lord for it: for in the peace thereof shall ye have peace."—Jer. xxix. 7.

THE principle involved in this text would suggest to all of us who are the Lord's strangers and foreigners that we should be desirous to promote the peace and prosperity of the people among whom we dwell. Specially should our nation and our city be blest by our constant intercession. An earnest prayer for Great Britain and Ireland is well becoming in the mouth of every English believer.

Eagerly let us pray for the great boon of peace, both at home and abroad. If strife should cause bloodshed in our streets, or if foreign battle should slay our brave soldiers, we should all bewail the calamity; let us therefore pray for peace, and diligently promote those principles by which the classes at home and the races abroad may be bound together in bonds of amity.

We ourselves are promised quiet in connection with the peace of the nation, and this is most desirable; for thus we can bring up our families in the fear of the Lord, and also preach the gospel without let or hindrance. To-day let us be much in prayer for our country, confessing national sins, and asking for national pardon and blessing, for Jesus' sake.

"I am come a light into the world, that whosoever believeth on me should not abide in darkness."—John xii. 46.

THIS world is dark as midnight; Jesus has come that by faith we may have light, and may no longer sit in the gloom which covers all the rest of mankind.

Whosoever is a very wide term: it means you and me. If we trust in Jesus we shall no more sit in the dark shadow of death, but shall enter into the warm light of a day which shall never end. Why do we not come out into the light at once?

A cloud may sometimes hover over us, but we shall not abide in darkness if we believe in Jesus. He has come to give us broad daylight. Shall he come in vain? If we have faith we have the privilege of sunlight: let us enjoy it. From the night of natural depravity, of ignorance, of doubt, of despair, of sin, of dread, Jesus has come to set us free; and all believers shall know that he no more comes in vain than the sun rises and fails to scatter his heat and light.

Shake off thy depression, dear brother. Abide not in the dark, but abide in the light. In Jesus is thy hope, thy joy, thy heaven. Look to him, to him only, and thou shalt rejoice as the birds rejoice at sunrise, and as the angels rejoice before the throne.

"And all this assembly shall know that the Lord saveth not with sword and spear: for the battle is the Lord's, and he will give you into our hands."—1 Sam. xvii. 47.

LET this point be settled, that the battle is the Lord's, and we may be quite sure of the victory, and of the victory in such a way as will best of all display the power of God. The Lord is too much forgotten by all men, yea, even by the assemblies of Israel; and when there is an opportunity to make men see that the Great First Cause can achieve his purposes without the power of man, it is a priceless occasion which should be well employed. Even Israel looks too much to sword and spear. It is a grand thing to have no sword in the hand of David, and yet for David to know that his God will overthrow a whole army of aliens.

If we are indeed contending for truth and righteousness, let us not tarry till we have talent, or wealth, or any other form of visible power at our disposal; but with such stones as we find in the brook, and with our own usual sling, let us run to meet the enemy. If it were our own battle we might not be confident; but if we are standing up for Jesus, and warring in his strength alone, who can withstand us? Without a trace of hesitancy let us face the Philistines; for the Lord of Hosts is with us, and who can be against us?

"And of Zebulun he said, Rejoice, Zebulun, in thy going out."—Deut. xxxiii. 18.

THE blessings of the tribes are ours; for we are the true Israel who worship God in the spirit, and have no confidence in the flesh. Zebulun is to rejoice because Jehovah will bless his "going out"; we also see a promise for ourselves lying latent in this benediction. When we go out we will look out for occasions of joy.

We go out to travel, and the providence of God is our convoy. We go out to emigrate, and the Lord is with us both on land and sea. We go out as missionaries, and Jesus saith, "Lo, I am with you unto the end of the world." We go out day by day to our labour, and we may do so with pleasure, for God will be with us from morn till eve.

A fear sometimes creeps over us when starting, for we know not what we may meet with; but this blessing may serve us right well as a word of good cheer. As we pack up for moving, let us put this verse into our travelling trunk; let us drop it into our hearts, and keep it there; yea, let us lay it on our tongue to make us sing. Let us weigh anchor with a song, or jump into the carriage with a psalm. Let us belong to the rejoicing tribe, and in our every movement praise the Lord with joyful hearts.

"Then said I, Ah, Lord God! behold, I cannot speak: for I am a child. But the Lord said unto me, Say not, I am a child: for thou shalt go to all that I shall send thee, and whatsoever I command thee thou shalt speak."

Jer. i. 6, 7.

JEREMIAH was young and felt a natural shrinking when sent upon a great errand by the Lord; but he who sent him would not have him say, "I am a child." What he was in himself must not be mentioned, but lost in the consideration that he was chosen to speak for God. He had not to think out and invent a message, nor to choose an audience: he was to speak what God commanded, and speak where God sent him, and this he would be enabled to do in strength not his own.

Is it not so with some young preacher, or teacher who may read these lines? God knows how young you are, and how slender are your knowledge and experience; but if he chooses to send you, it is not for you to shrink from the heavenly call. God will magnify himself in your feebleness. If you were as old as Methuselah, how much would your years help you? If you were as wise as Solomon, you might be equally as wilful as he. Keep you to your message and it will be your wisdom; follow your marching orders and they will be your discretion.

"As one whom his mother comforteth, so will I comfort you."—Isa. lxvi. 13.

A MOTHER'S comfort! Ah, this is tenderness itself. How she enters into her child's grief! How she presses him to her bosom, and tries to take all his sorrow into her own heart! He can tell her all, and she will sympathize as nobody else can. Of all comforters the child loves best his mother, and even full-grown men have found it so.

Does Jehovah condescend to act the mother's part? This is goodness indeed. We readily perceive how he is a father ; but will he be as a mother also? Does not this invite us to holy familiarity, to unreserved confidence, to sacred rest ? When God himself becomes " the Comforter " no anguish can long abide. Let us tell out our trouble, even though sobs and sighs should become our readiest utterance. He will not despise us for our tears ; our mother did not. He will consider our weakness as she did, and he will put away our faults, only in a surer, safer way than our mother could do. We will not try to bear our grief alone : that would be unkind to one so gentle and so kind. Let us begin the day with our loving God, and wherefore should we not finish it in the same company, since mothers weary not of their children ?

"Therefore say, Thus saith the Lord God; Although I have cast them far off among the heathen, and although I have scattered them among the countries, yet will I be to them as a little sanctuary in the countries where they shall come."—Ezek. xi. 16.

BANISHED from the public means of grace, we are not removed from the grace of the means. The Lord who places his people where they feel as exiles will himself be with them, and be to them all that they could have had at home, in the place of their solemn assemblies. Take this to yourselves, O ye who are called to wander!

God is to his people a place of *refuge.* They find sanctuary with him from every adversary. He is their place of *worship* too. He is with them as with Jacob when he slept in the open field, and rising, said, "Surely God was in this place." To them also he will be a sanctuary of *quiet,* like the Holy of Holies, which was the noiseless abode of the Eternal. They shall be quiet from fear of evil.

God himself, in Christ Jesus, is the sanctuary of *mercy.* The ark of the covenant is the Lord Jesus, and Aaron's rod, the pot of manna, the tables of the law, all are in Christ our sanctuary. In God we find the shrine of *holiness* and of *communion.* What more do we need? O Lord, fulfil this promise, and be ever to.us as a little sanctuary!

"Those things, which ye have both learned, and received, and heard, and seen in me, do: and the God of peace shall be with you."—Phil. iv. 9.

IT is well when a man can with advantage be so minutely copied as Paul might have been. Oh, for grace to imitate him this day and every day!

Should we, through divine grace, carry into practice the Pauline teaching, we may claim the promise which is now open before us; and what a promise it is! God, who loves peace, makes peace, and breathes peace, will be with us. "Peace be with you" is a sweet benediction; but for the God of peace to be with us is far more. Thus we have the fountain as well as the streams, the sun as well as his beams. If the God of peace be with us, we shall enjoy the peace of God which passeth all understanding, even though outward circumstances should threaten to disturb. If men quarrel, we shall be sure to be peace-makers, if the Maker of peace be with us.

It is in the way of truth that real peace is found. If we quit the faith or leave the path of righteousness under the notion of promoting peace, we shall be greatly mistaken. First pure, then peaceable, is the order of wisdom and of fact. Let us keep to Paul's line, and we shall have the God of peace with us as he was with the apostle.

"Be not afraid of their faces: for I am with thee to deliver thee, saith the Lord."—Jer. i. 8.

WHENEVER fear comes in and makes us falter, we are in danger of falling into sin. Conceit is to be dreaded, but so is cowardice. "Dare to be a Daniel." Our great Captain should be served by brave soldiers.

What a reason for bravery is here. God is with those who are with him. God will never be away when the hour of struggle comes. Do they threaten you? Who are you that you should be afraid of a man that shall die? Will you lose your situation? Your God whom you serve will find bread and water for his servants. Can you not trust him? Do they pour ridicule upon you? Will this break your bones or your heart? Bear it for Christ's sake, and even rejoice because of it.

God is with the true, the just, the holy, to deliver them; and he will deliver you. Remember how Daniel came out of the lions' den, and the three holy children out of the furnace. Yours is not so desperate a case as theirs; but if it were, the Lord would bear you through, and make you more than a conqueror. Fear to fear. Be afraid to be afraid. Your worst enemy is within your own bosom. Get to your knees and cry for help, and then rise up saying, "I will trust, and not be afraid."

"The prayer of the upright is his delight."—Prov. xv. 8.

THIS is as good as a promise, for it declares a present fact, which will be the same throughout all ages. God takes great pleasure in the prayers of upright men; he even calls them his delight. Our first concern is to be upright. Neither bending this way nor that, continue upright: not crooked with policy, nor prostrate by yielding to evil, be you upright in strict integrity and straightforwardness. If we begin to shuffle and shift, we shall be left to shift for ourselves. If we try crooked ways, we shall find that we cannot pray, and if we pretend to do so, we shall find our prayers shut out of heaven.

Are we acting in a straight line and thus following out the Lord's revealed will? Then let us pray much and pray in faith. If our prayer is God's delight, let us not stint him in that which gives him pleasure. He does not consider the grammar of it, nor the metaphysics of it, nor the rhetoric of it; in all these men might despise it. He, as a Father, takes pleasure in the lispings of his own babes, the stammerings of his new-born sons and daughters. Should we not delight in prayer since the Lord delights in it? Let us make errands to the throne. The Lord finds us enough reasons for prayer, and we ought to thank him that it is so.

"The Lord will give grace and glory."—Ps. lxxxiv. 11.

GRACE is what we need just now, and it is to be had freely. What can be freer than a gift? To-day we shall receive sustaining, strengthening, sanctifying, satisfying grace. He has given daily grace until now, and as for the future, that grace is still sufficient. If we have but little grace, the fault must lie in ourselves; for the Lord is not straitened, neither is he slow to bestow it in abundance. We may ask for as much as we will and never fear a refusal. He giveth liberally and upbraideth not.

The Lord may not give gold, but he will give grace: he may not give gain, but he will give grace. He will certainly send us trial, but he will give grace in proportion thereto. We may be called to labour, and to suffer, but with the call there will come all the grace required.

What an AND is that in the text—"and glory"! We do not need glory yet, and we are not yet fit for it; but we shall have it in due order. After we have eaten the bread of grace, we shall drink the wine of glory. We must go through the holy —which is grace, to the holiest of all—which is glory. These words "and glory" are enough to make a man dance for joy. A little while—a little while, and then glory for ever!

"Wherefore, if God so clothe the grass of the field, which to-day is, and to-morrow is cast into the oven, shall he not much more clothe you, O ye of little faith?"—Matt. vi. 30.

CLOTHES are expensive, and poor believers may be led into anxiety as to where their next suit will come from. The soles are thin; how shall we get new shoes? See how our thoughtful Lord has provided against this care. Our heavenly Father clothes the grass of the field with a splendour such as Solomon could not equal: will he not clothe his own children? We are sure he will. There may be many a patch and a darn, but raiment we shall have.

A poor minister found his clothes nearly threadbare, and so far gone that they would hardly hold together; but as a servant of the Lord he expected his Master to find him his livery. It so happened that the writer on a visit to a friend had the loan of the good man's pulpit, and it came into his mind to make a collection for him, *and there was his livery.* Many other cases we have seen in which those who have served the Lord have found him considerate of their wardrobe. He who made man so that when he had sinned he needed garments, also in mercy supplied him with them; and those which the Lord gave to our first parents were far better than those they made for themselves.

"Then shalt thou walk in thy way safely, and thy foot shall not stumble."—Prov. iii. 23.

THAT is to say, if we follow the ways of wisdom and holiness we shall be preserved in them. He who travels by daylight along the highway is under the king's protection. There is a way for every man, namely, his own proper calling in life, and if we devoutly walk therein in the fear of God he will preserve us from evil. We may not travel luxuriously, but we shall walk safely. We may not be able to run like young men, but we shall be able to walk like good men.

Our greatest danger lies in ourselves : our feeble foot is so sadly apt to stumble. Let us ask for more moral strength that our tendency to slip may be overcome. Some stumble because they do not see the stone in the way : divine grace enables us to perceive sin, and so to avoid it. Let us plead this promise, and trust in him who upholds his chosen.

Alas! our worst peril is our own carelessness, but against this the Lord Jesus has put us on our guard, saying, " Watch and pray."

Oh for grace to walk this day without a single stumble! It is not enough that we do not actually fall; our cry should be that we may not make the smallest slip with our feet, but may at the last adore him " who is able to keep us from stumbling."

"He giveth grace unto the humble."—James iv. 6.

HUMBLE hearts seek grace, and therefore they get it. Humble hearts yield to the sweet influences of grace, and so it is bestowed on them more and more largely. Humble hearts lie in the valleys where streams of grace are flowing, and hence they drink of them. Humble hearts are grateful for grace and give the Lord the glory of it, and hence it is consistent with his honour to give it to them.

Come, dear reader, take a lowly place. Be little in thine own esteem, that the Lord may make much of thee. Perhaps the sigh breaks out, "I fear I am not humble." It may be that this is the language of true humility. Some are proud of being humble, and this is one of the very worst sorts of pride. We are needy, helpless, undeserving, hell-deserving creatures, and if we are not humble we ought to be. Let us humble ourselves because of our sins against humility, and then the Lord will give us to taste of his favour. It is grace which makes us humble, and grace which finds in this humility an opportunity for pouring in more grace. Let us go down that we may rise. Let us be poor in spirit that God may make us rich. Let us be humble that we may not need to be humbled, but may be exalted by the grace of God.

"I will bring the blind by a way that they knew not."
Isa. xlii. 16.

THINK of the infinitely glorious Jehovah acting as a Guide to the blind! What boundless condescension does this imply! A blind man cannot find a way which he does not know. Even when he knows the road, it is hard for him to traverse it; but a road which he has not known is quite out of the question for his unguided feet. Now, we are by nature blind as to the way of salvation, and yet the Lord leads us into it, and brings us to himself, and then opens our eyes. As to the future, we are all of us blind, and cannot see an hour before us; but the Lord Jesus will lead us even to our journey's end. Blessed be his name!

We cannot guess in which way deliverance can possibly come to us, but the Lord knows, and he will lead us till we shall have escaped every danger. Happy are those who place their hand in that of the great Guide, and leave their way and themselves entirely with him. He will bring them all the way; and when he has brought them home to glory and has opened their eyes to see the way by which he has led them, what a song of gratitude will they sing unto their great Benefactor! Lord, lead thy poor blind child this day, for I know not my way!

"But the Lord is faithful, who shall stablish you, and keep you from evil."—2 Thess. iii. 3.

MEN are often as devoid of reason as of faith. There are with us still "unreasonable and wicked men." There is no use in arguing with them or trying to be at peace with them : they are false at heart, and deceitful in speech. Well, what of this ? Shall we worry ourselves with them ? No ; let us turn to the Lord, for he is faithful. No promise from his word will ever be broken. He is neither unreasonable in his demands upon us, nor unfaithful to our claims upon him. We have a faithful God. Be this our joy.

He will stablish us so that wicked men shall not cause our downfall, and he will keep us so that none of the evils which now assail us shall really do us damage. What a blessing for us that we need not contend with men, but are allowed to shelter ourselves in the Lord Jesus, who is in truest sympathy with us. There is one true heart, one faithful mind, one never changing Love ; there let us repose. The Lord will fulfil the purpose of his grace to us, his servants, and we need not allow a shadow of a fear to fall upon our spirits. Not all that men or devils can do can hinder us of the divine protection and provision. This day let us pray the Lord to stablish and keep us.

> "*When thou liest down, thou shalt not be afraid: yea,
> thou shalt lie down, and thy sleep shall be sweet.*"
> Prov. iii. 24.

IS the reader likely to be confined for a while to the bed by sickness? let him go upstairs without distress with this promise upon his heart— "When thou liest down, thou shalt not be afraid."

When we go to bed at night, let this word smooth our pillow. We cannot guard ourselves in sleep, but the Lord will keep us through the night. Those who lie down under the protection of the Lord are as secure as kings and queens in their palaces, and a great deal more so. If with our lying down there is a laying down of all cares and ambitions, we shall get refreshment out of our beds such as the anxious and covetous never find in theirs. Ill dreams shall be banished, or even if they come, we shall wipe out the impression of them, knowing that they are only dreams.

If we sleep thus we shall do well. How sweetly Peter slept when even the angel's light did not wake him, and he needed a hard jog in the side to wake him up. And yet he was sentenced to die on the morrow. Thus have martyrs slept before their burning. "So he giveth his beloved sleep."

To have sweet sleep we must have sweet lives, sweet tempers, sweet meditations, and sweet love.

"The Lord will strengthen him upon the bed of languishing."—Ps. xli. 3.

REMEMBER that this is a promise to the man who considers the poor. Are you one of these? Then take home the text, but not else.

See how in the hour of sickness the God of the poor will bless the man who cares for the poor! The everlasting arms shall stay up his soul as friendly hands and downy pillows stay up the body of the sick. How tender and sympathizing is this image; how near it brings our God to our infirmities and sicknesses! Whoever heard this of the old heathen Jove, or of the gods of India, or China? This is language peculiar to the God of Israel; he it is who deigns to become nurse and attendant upon good men. If he smites with one hand, he sustains with the other. Oh, it is blessed fainting when one falls upon the Lord's own bosom, and is borne thereon! Grace is the best of restoratives; divine love is the safest stimulant for a languishing patient; it makes the soul strong as a giant, even when the bones are breaking through the skin. No physician like the Lord, no tonic like his promise, no wine like his love.

If the reader has failed in his duty to the poor, let him see what he is losing, and at once become their friend and helper.

"Draw nigh to God, and he will draw nigh to you."
James iv. 8.

THE nearer we come to God, the more graciously will he reveal himself to us. When the prodigal comes to his father, his father runs to meet him. When the wandering dove returns to the ark, Noah puts out his hand to pull her in unto him. When the tender wife seeks her husband's society, he comes to her on wings of love. Come then, dear friend, let us draw nigh to God who so graciously awaits us, yea, comes to meet us.

Did you ever notice that passage in Isaiah lviii. 9? There the Lord seems to put himself at the disposal of his people, saying to them, " Here I am." As much as to say—" What have you to say to me? What can I do for you? I am waiting to bless you." How can we hesitate to draw near?' God is nigh to forgive, to bless, to comfort, to help, to quicken, to deliver. Let it be the main point with us to get near to God. This done, all is done. If we draw near to others, they may before long grow weary of us and leave us; but if we seek the Lord alone, no change will come over his mind, but he will continue to come nearer and yet nearer to us by fuller and more joyful fellowship.

"The Lord shall make thee the head, and not the tail."
Deut. xxviii. 13.

IF we obey the Lord, he will compel our adversaries to see that his blessing rests upon us.
Though this be a promise of the law, yet it stands
good to the people of God ; for Jesus has removed
the curse, but he has established the blessing.

It is for saints to lead the way among men by holy
influence : they are not to be the tail, to be dragged
hither and thither by others. We must not yield
to the spirit of the age, but compel the age to do
homage to Christ. If the Lord be with us, we
shall not crave toleration for religion, but we shall
seek to seat it on the throne of society. Has not
the Lord Jesus made his people priests? Surely
they are to teach, and must not be learners from
the philosophies of unbelievers. Are we not in
Christ made kings to reign upon the earth? How,
then, can we be the servants of custom, the slaves
of human opinion?

Have you, dear friend, taken up your true
position for Jesus? Too many are silent because
diffident, if not cowardly. Should we allow the
name of the Lord Jesus to be kept in the back-
ground? Should our religion drag along as a tail?
Should it not rather lead the way and be the ruling
force with ourselves and others?

"I am with thee, and no man shall set on thee to hurt thee."—Acts xviii. 10.

SO long as the Lord had work for Paul to do in Corinth, the fury of the mob was restrained. The Jews opposed themselves and blasphemed; but they could neither stop the preaching of the gospel, nor the conversion of the hearers. God has power over the most violent minds. He makes the wrath of man to praise him when it breaks forth, but he still more displays his goodness when he restrains it; and he can restrain it. "By the greatness of thine arm they shall be as still as a stone; till thy people pass over, O Lord."

Do not, therefore, feel any fear of man when you know that you are doing your duty. Go straight on, as Jesus would have done, and those who oppose shall be as a bruised reed and as smoking flax. Many a time men have had cause to fear because they were themselves afraid; but a dauntless faith in God brushes fear aside like the cobwebs in a giant's path. No man can harm us unless the Lord permits. He who makes the devil himself to flee at a word, can certainly control the devil's agents. May be they are already more afraid of you than you are of them. Therefore, go forward, and where you looked to meet with foes you will find friends.

"Be careful for nothing; but in everything by prayer and supplication with thanksgiving let your requests be made known unto God. And the peace of God, which passeth all understanding, shall keep your hearts and minds through Christ Jesus."—Phil. iv. 6, 7.

NO care, but all prayer. No anxiety, but much joyful communion with God. Carry your desires to the Lord of your life, the guardian of your soul. Go to him with two portions of prayer, and one of fragrant praise. Do not pray doubtfully, but thankfully. Consider that you have your petitions, and therefore thank God for his grace. He is giving you grace, give him thanks. Hide nothing. Allow no want to lie rankling in your bosom; "make known your requests." Run not to man. Go only to your God, the Father of Jesus, who loves you in him.

This shall bring you God's own peace. You shall not be able to understand the peace which you shall enjoy. It will enfold you in its infinite embrace. Heart and mind through Christ Jesus shall be steeped in a sea of rest. Come life or death, poverty, pain, slander, you shall dwell in Jesus above every ruffling wind or darkening cloud. Will you not obey this dear command?

Yes, Lord, I do believe thee; but, I beseech thee, help mine unbelief.

"Be not afraid of sudden fear, neither of the desolation of the wicked, when it cometh. For the Lord shall be thy confidence, and shall keep thy foot from being taken."
Prov. iii. 25, 26.

WHEN God is abroad in judgments, he would not have his people alarmed. He has not come forth to harm, but to defend the righteous.

He would have them manifest *courage*. We who enjoy the presence of God ought to display presence of mind. Since the Lord himself may suddenly come, we ought not to be surprised at anything sudden. Serenity under the rush and roar of unexpected evils is a precious gift of divine love.

The Lord would have his chosen display *discrimination*, so that they may see that the desolation of the wicked is not a real calamity to the universe. Sin alone is evil; the punishment which follows thereupon is as a preserving salt to keep society from putrefying. We should be far more shocked at the sin which deserves hell, than at the hell which comes out of sin.

So, too, should the Lord's people exhibit great *quietness* of spirit. Satan and his serpent seed are full of all subtilty; but those who walk with God shall not be taken in their deceitful snares. Go on, believer in Jesus, and let the Lord be thy confidence.

"The wayfaring men, though fools, shall not err therein."
Isa. xxxv. 8.

THE way of holiness is so straight and plain
that the simplest minds cannot go astray if
they constantly follow it. The worldly wise have
many twists and turns, and yet they make terrible
blunders, and generally miss their end. Worldly
policy is a poor short-sighted thing, and when men
choose it as their road, it leads them over dark
mountains. Gracious minds know no better than
to do as the Lord bids them; but this keeps them
in the king's highway, and under royal protection.

Let the reader never for a moment attempt to
help himself out of a difficulty by a falsehood, or
by a questionable act; but let him keep in the
middle of the high road of truth and integrity, and
he will be following the best possible course. In
our lives we must never practise circular sailing,
nor dream of shuffling. Be just and fear not.
Follow Jesus and heed no evil consequences. If
the worst of ills could be avoided by wrong-doing,
we should, in the very attempt, have fallen into an
evil worse than any other ill could be. God's way
must be the best way. Follow it though men
think you a fool, and you will be truly wise.

Lord, lead thy servants in a plain path because
of their enemies.

> *"Meditate upon these things; give thyself wholly to them; that thy profiting may appear to all."*—1 Tim. iv. 15.

THIS is, practically, a promise that, by diligent meditation and the giving up of our whole mind to our work for the Lord, we shall make a progress which all can see. Not by hasty reading, but by deep meditation, we profit by the Word of God. Not by doing a great deal of work in a slovenly manner, but by giving our best thought to what we attempt, we shall get real profit. "In all *labour* there is profit," but not in fuss and hurry without true heart-energy.

If we divide ourselves between God and mammon, or Christ and self, we shall make no progress. We must give ourselves wholly to holy things, or else we shall be poor traders in heavenly business, and at our stock-taking no profit will be shown.

Am I a minister? Let me be a minister wholly, and not spend my energies upon secondary concerns. What have I to do with party politics, or vain amusements? Am I a Christian? Let me make my service of Jesus my occupation, my life-work, my one pursuit. We must be in-and-in with Jesus, and then out-and-out for Jesus, or else we shall make neither progress nor profit, and neither the church nor the world will feel that forceful influence which the Lord would have us exercise.

"Because thine heart was tender, and thou hast humbled thyself before the Lord, when thou heardest what I spake against this place, and against the inhabitants thereof, that they should become a desolation and a curse, and hast rent thy clothes, and wept before me; I also have heard thee, saith the Lord.—2 Kings xxii. 19.

MANY despise warning, and perish. Happy is he who trembles at the word of the Lord. Josiah did so, and he was spared the sight of the evil which the Lord determined to send upon Judah because of her great sins. Have you this tenderness? Do you practise this self-humiliation? Then you also shall be spared in the evil day. God sets a mark upon the men that sigh and cry because of the sin of the times. The destroying angel is commanded to keep his sword in its sheath till the elect of God are sheltered : these are best known by their godly fear, and their trembling at the word of the Lord. Are the times threatening? Do Popery and Infidelity advance with great strides, and do you dread national chastisement upon this polluted nation? Well you may. Yet rest in this promise, " Thou shalt be gathered into thy grave in peace ; and thine eyes shall not see all the evil which I will bring upon this place." Better still, the Lord himself may come, and then the days of our mourning shall be ended.

"And I will send hornets before thee, which shall drive out the Hivite, the Canaanite, and the Hittite, from before thee."—Ex. xxiii. 28.

WHAT the hornets were we need not consider. They were God's own army, which he sent before his people to sting their enemies, and render Israel's conquest easy. Our God by his own chosen means will fight for his people, and gall their foes, before they come into the actual battle. Often he confounds the adversaries of truth by methods in which reformers themselves have no hand. The air is full of mysterious influences which harass Israel's foes. We read in the Apocalypse that "the earth helped the woman."

Let us never fear. The stars in their courses fight against the enemies of our souls. Oftentimes when we march to the conflict we find no host to contend with. "The Lord shall fight for you, and ye shall hold your peace." God's hornets can do more than our weapons. We could never dream of the victory being won by such means as Jehovah will use. We must obey our marching orders and go forth to the conquest of the nations for Jesus, and we shall find that the Lord has gone before us, and prepared the way; so that in the end we shall joyfully confess, "His own right hand, and his holy arm, have gotten him the victory."

"Thou art my servant: O Israel, thou shalt not be forgotten of me."—Isa. xliv. 21.

OUR Jehovah cannot so forget his servants as to cease to love them. He chose them not for a time, but for ever. He knew what they would be when he called them into the divine family. He blots out their sins like a cloud; and we may be sure that he will not turn them out of doors for iniquities which he has blotted out. It would be blasphemy to imagine such a thing.

He will not forget them so as to cease to think of them. One forgetful moment on the part of our God would be our ruin. Therefore he says: "Thou shalt not be forgotten of me." Men forget us: those whom we have benefited turn against us: we have no abiding place in the fickle hearts of men; but God will never forget one of his true servants. He binds himself to us not by what we do for him, but by what he has done for us. We have been loved too long, and bought at too great a price to be now forgotten. Jesus sees in us his soul's travail, and that he never can forget. The Father sees in us the spouse of his Son, and the Spirit sees in us his own effectual work. The Lord thinketh upon us. This day we shall be succoured and sustained. Oh, that the Lord may never be forgotten of us!

"And the Lord shall be king over all the earth: in that day shall there be one Lord, and his name one."
Zech. xiv. 9.

BLESSED prospect! This is no dream of an enthusiast, but the declaration of the infallible Word. Jehovah shall be known among all people, and his gracious sway shall be acknowledged by every tribe of man. To-day, it is far from being so. Where do any bow before the Great King? How much there is of rebellion! What lords many, and gods many, there are on the earth! Even among professed Christians what diversities of ideas there are about him and his gospel! One day there shall be one King, one Jehovah, and one name for the living God. O Lord, hasten it! We daily cry, Thy kingdom come.

We will not discuss the question as to *when* this shall be, lest we lose the comfort of the certainty that it shall be. So surely as the Holy Ghost spake by his prophets, so surely shall the whole earth be filled with the glory of the Lord. Jesus did not die in vain. The Spirit of God worketh not in vain. The Father's eternal purposes shall not be frustrated. Here, where Satan triumphed, Jesus shall be crowned, and the Lord God Omnipotent shall reign. Let us go our way to our daily work and warfare made strong in faith.

"And all people of the earth shall see that thou art called by the name of the Lord ; and they shall be afraid of thee."
Deut. xxviii. 10.

THEN we can have no reason to be afraid of *them*. This would show a mean spirit, and be a token of unbelief rather than of faith. God can make us so like himself, that men shall be forced to see that we rightly bear his name, and truly belong to the Holy Jehovah. Oh, that we may obtain this grace, which the Lord waits to bestow!

Be assured that ungodly men have a fear of true saints. They hate them, but they also fear them. Haman trembled because of Mordecai, even when he sought the good man's destruction. In fact, their hate often arises out of a dread which they are too proud to confess. Let us pursue the path of truth and uprightness without the slightest tremor. Fear is not for us, but for those who do ill and fight against the Lord of hosts. If indeed the name of the Eternal God is named upon us, we are secure ; for, as of old, a Roman had but to say *Romanus sum*, I am a Roman, and he could claim the protection of all the legions of the vast empire, so every one who is a man of God has omnipotence as his guardian, and God will sooner empty heaven of angels than leave a saint without defence. Be braver than lions for the right, for God is with you.

"The Lord stood by him, and said, Be of good cheer, Paul: for as thou hast testified of me in Jerusalem, so must thou bear witness also at Rome."—Acts xxiii. 11.

ARE you a witness for the Lord, and are you just now in danger ? Then remember that you are immortal till your work is done. If the Lord has more witness for you to bear, you will live to bear it. Who is he that can break the vessel which the Lord intends again to use ?

If there is no more work for you to do for your Master, it cannot distress you that he is about to take you home, and put you where you will be beyond the reach of adversaries. Your witness-bearing for Jesus is your chief concern, and you cannot be stopped in it till it is finished : therefore be at peace. Cruel slander, wicked misrepresentation, desertion of friends, betrayal by the most trusted one, and whatever else may come, cannot hinder the Lord's purpose concerning you. The Lord stands by you in the night of your sorrow, and he says, " Thou must yet bear witness for me." Be calm, be filled with joy in the Lord.

If you do not need this promise just now, you may very soon. Treasure it up. Remember also to pray for missionaries, and all persecuted ones, that the Lord would preserve them even to the completion of their life work.

"Great peace have they which love thy law: and nothing shall offend them."—Ps. cxix. 165.

YES, a true love for the great Book will bring us great peace from the great God, and be a great protection to us. Let us live constantly in the society of the law of the Lord, and it will breed in our hearts a restfulness such as nothing else can. The Holy Spirit acts as a Comforter through the Word, and sheds abroad those benign influences which calm the tempests of the soul.

Nothing is a stumbling-block to the man who has the Word of God dwelling in him richly. He takes up his daily cross and it becomes a delight. For the fiery trial he is prepared, and counts it not strange, so as to be utterly cast down by it. He is neither stumbled by prosperity, as so many are, nor crushed by adversity, as others have been; for he lives beyond the changing circumstances of external life. When his Lord puts before him some great mystery of the faith which makes others cry, " This is an hard saying; who can hear it?" the believer accepts it without question; for his intellectual difficulties are overcome by his reverent awe of the law of the Lord, which is to him the supreme authority to which he joyfully bows. Lord, work in us this love, this peace, this rest, this day.

> "*And the Lord said unto Moses, Make thee a fiery serpent, and set it upon a pole: and it shall come to pass, that everyone that is bitten, when he looketh upon it, shall live.*"
> Num. xxi. 8.

THIS is a glorious gospel type. Jesus, numbered with the transgressors, hangs before us on the cross. A look to him will heal us of the serpent-bite of sin; will heal us at once—"When he looketh upon it, he shall live." Let the reader who is mourning his sinfulness note the words—"Everyone that looketh upon it shall live." Every looker will find this true. I have found it so. I looked to Jesus and lived at once. I know I did. Reader, if you look to Jesus you will live too. True, you are swelling with the venom, and you see no hope. True, also, *there is no hope but this one.* But this is no doubtful cure—"Everyone that is bitten, when he looketh upon it, shall live."

The brazen serpent was not lifted up as a curiosity to be gazed upon by the healthy; but its special purpose was for those who were "bitten." Jesus died as a real Saviour for real sinners. Whether the bite has made you a drunkard, or a thief, or an unchaste or a profane person, a look at the Great Saviour will heal you of these diseases, and make you live in holiness and communion with God. Look and live.

"And they shall teach no more every man his neighbour, and every man his brother, saying, Know the Lord: for they shall all know me, from the least of them unto the greatest of them, saith the Lord."—Jer. xxxi. 34.

TRULY, whatever else we do not know, we know the Lord. This day is this promise true in our experience, and it is not a little one. The least believer among us knows God in Christ Jesus. Not as fully as we desire; but yet truly and really we know the Lord. We not only know doctrines about him, but we know HIM. He is our Father and our Friend. We are acquainted with him personally. We can say, "My Lord, and my God." We are on terms of close fellowship with God, and many a happy season do we spend in his holy company. We are no more strangers to our God, but the secret of the Lord is with us.

This is more than nature could have taught us. Flesh and blood has not revealed God to us. Christ Jesus has made known the Father to our hearts. If, then, the Lord has made us know himself, is not this the fountain of all saving knowledge? To know God is eternal life. So soon as we come to acquaintance with God we have the evidence of being quickened into newness of life. O my soul, rejoice in this knowledge, and bless thy God all this day!

"For I will forgive their iniquity, and I will remember their sin no more."—Jer. xxxi. 34.

WHEN we know the Lord, we receive the forgiveness of sins. We know him as the God of Grace, passing by our transgressions. What a joyful discovery is this!

But how divinely is this promise worded: the Lord promises no more to remember our sins! Can God forget? He says he will, and he means what he says. He will regard us as though we had never sinned. The great atonement so effectually removed all sin, that it is to the mind of God no more in existence. The believer is now in Christ Jesus, as accepted as Adam in his innocence; yea, more so, for he wears a divine righteousness, and that of Adam was but human.

The Great Lord will not remember our sins so as to punish them, or so as to love us one atom the less because of them. As a debt when paid ceases to be a debt, even so doth the Lord make a complete obliteration of the iniquity of his people.

When we are mourning over our transgressions and shortcomings, and this is our duty as long as we live, let us at the same time rejoice that they will never be mentioned against us. This makes us hate sin. God's free pardon makes us anxious never again to grieve him by disobedience.

"Who shall change our vile body, that it may be fashioned like unto his glorious body."—Phil. iii. 21.

OFTEN when we are racked with pain, and unable to think or worship, we feel that this indeed is "the body of our humiliation"; and when we are tempted by the passions which rise from the flesh we do not think the word "vile" at all too vigorous a translation. Our bodies humble us; and that is about the best thing they do for us. Oh, that we were duly lowly, because our bodies ally us with animals, and even link us with the dust!

But our Saviour, the Lord Jesus, shall change all this. We shall be fashioned like his own body of glory. This will take place in all who believe in Jesus. By faith their souls have been transformed, and their bodies will undergo such a renewal as shall fit them for their regenerated spirits. How soon this grand transformation will happen we cannot tell; but the thought of it should help us to bear the trials of to-day, and all the woes of the flesh. In a little while we shall be as Jesus now is. No more aching brows, no more swollen limbs, no more dim eyes, no more fainting hearts. The old man shall be no more a bundle of infirmities, nor the sick man a mass of agony. "Like unto his glorious body." What an expression! Even our flesh shall rest in hope of such a resurrection!

"He shall choose our inheritance for us."—Ps. xlvii 4.

OUR enemies would allot us a very dreary portion, but we are not left in their hands. The Lord will cause us to stand in our lot, and our place is appointed by his infinite wisdom. A wiser mind than our own arranges our destiny. The ordaining of all things is with God, and we are glad to have it so ; we choose that God should choose for us. If we might have our own way we would wish to let all things go in God's way.

Being conscious of our own folly, we would not desire to rule our own destinies. We feel safer and more at ease when the Lord steers our vessel than we could possibly be if we could direct it according to our own judgment. Joyfully we leave the painful present and the unknown future with our Father, our Saviour, our Comforter.

O my soul, this day lay down thy wishes at Jesus' feet ! If thou hast of late been somewhat wayward and wilful, eager to be and to do after thine own mind, now dismiss thy foolish self, and place the reins in the Lord's hands. Say, "He shall choose." If others dispute the sovereignty of the Lord, and glory in the freewill of man, do thou answer them, "He shall choose for me." It is my freest choice to let him choose. As a free agent, I elect that he should have absolute sway.

"The desire of the righteous shall be granted."—Prov. x. 24.

BECAUSE it is a righteous desire it is safe for God to grant it. It would be neither good for the man himself, nor for society at large, that such a promise should be made to the unrighteous. Let us keep the Lord's commands, and he will rightfully have respect to our desires.

When righteous men are left to desire unrighteous desires, they will not be granted to them. But then these are not their real desires; they are their wanderings or blunders; and it is well that they should be refused. Their gracious desires shall come before the Lord, and he will not say them nay.

Does the Lord deny us our requests for a time? Let the promise for to-day encourage us to ask again. Has he denied us altogether? We will thank him still, for it always was our desire that he should deny us if he judged a denial to be best.

As to some things, we ask very boldly. Our chief desires are for holiness, usefulness, likeness to Christ, preparedness for heaven. These are the desires of grace rather than of nature—the desires of the righteous man rather than of the mere man. God will not stint us in these things, but will do for us exceeding abundantly. "Delight thyself also in the Lord, and he shall give thee the desires of thine heart." This day, my soul, ask largely!

"In that day shall there be upon the bells of the horses, Holiness unto the Lord"—Zech. xiv. 20.

HAPPY day when all things shall be consecrated, and the horses' bells shall ring
out holiness to the Lord! That day has come to
me. Do I not make all things holy to God?
These garments, when I put them on or take them
off, shall they not remind me of the righteousness
of Christ Jesus, my Lord? Shall not my work be
done as unto the Lord? Oh, that to-day my
clothes may be vestments, my meals sacraments,
my house a temple, my table an altar, my speech
incense, and myself a priest! Lord, fulfil thy promise, and let nothing be to me common or unclean.

Let me in faith expect this. Believing it to be
so, I shall be helped to make it so. As I myself am
the property of Jesus, my Lord may take an
inventory of all I have, for it is altogether his
own; and I resolve to prove it to be so by the use
to which I put it this day. From morning till
evening I would order all things by a happy and
holy rule. My bells shall ring—why should they
not? Even my horses shall have bells—who has
such a right to music as the saints have? But all
my bells, my music, my mirth, shall be turned to
holiness, and shall ring out the name of "The
Happy God."

"When a man's ways please the Lord, he maketh even his enemies to be at peace with him."—Prov. xvi. 7.

I MUST see that my ways please the Lord. Even then I shall have enemies; and, perhaps, all the more certainly because I endeavour to do that which is right. But what a promise this is! The Lord will make the wrath of man to praise him, and abate it so that it shall not distress me.

He can constrain an enemy to desist from harming me, even though he has a mind to do so. This he did with Laban, who pursued Jacob, but did not dare to touch him. Or he can subdue the wrath of the enemy, and make him friendly, as he did with Esau, who met Jacob in a brotherly manner, though Jacob had dreaded that he would smite him and his family with the sword. The Lord can also convert a furious adversary into a brother in Christ, and a fellow-worker, as he did with Saul of Tarsus. Oh, that he would do this in every case where a persecuting spirit appears!

Happy is the man whose enemies are made to be to him what the lions were to Daniel in the den quiet and companionable! When I meet death, who is called the last enemy, I pray that I may be at peace. Only let my great care be to please the Lord in all things. Oh, for faith and holiness; for these are a pleasure unto the Most High!

"I will be with thee: I will not fail thee, nor forsake thee."—Josh. i. 5.

THIS word to Joshua is often quoted; it is the basis of that New Testament word, "He hath said, I will never leave thee, nor forsake thee."

Beloved, a life of warfare is before us, but the Lord of Hosts is with us. Are we called to lead a great but fickle people? This promise guarantees us all the wisdom and prudence that we shall need. Have we to contend with cunning and powerful enemies? Here is strength and valour, prowess and victory. Have we a vast heritage to win? By this sign we shall achieve our purpose; the Lord himself is with us.

It would be woe to us indeed if Jehovah could fail us; but, as this can never be, the winds of disquietude are laid to sleep in the caverns of divine faithfulness. On no one occasion will the Lord desert us. Happen what may, he will be at our side. Friends drop from us, their help is but an April shower; but God is faithful, Jesus is the same for ever, and the Holy Spirit abideth in us.

Come, my heart, be calm and hopeful to-day. Clouds may gather, but the Lord can blow them away. Since God will not fail me, my faith shall not fail; and, as he will not forsake me, neither will I forsake him. Oh for a restful faith!

"For thus saith the Lord God ; Behold, I, even I, will both search my sheep, and seek them out."—Ez. xxxiv. 11.

THIS he does at the first when his elect are like wandering sheep that know not the shepherd or the fold. How wonderfully doth the Lord find out his chosen! Jesus is great as a seeking shepherd as well as a saving shepherd. Though many of those his Father gave him have gone as near to hell-gate as they well can, yet the Lord by searching and seeking discovers them, and draws nigh to them in grace. He has sought out us : let us have good hope for those who are laid upon our hearts in prayer, for he will find them out also.

The Lord repeats this process when any of his flock stray from the pastures of truth and holiness. They may fall into gross error, sad sin, and grievous hardness; but yet the Lord, who has become a surety for them to his Father, will not suffer one of them to go so far as to perish. He will by providence and grace pursue them into foreign lands, into abodes of poverty, into dens of obscurity, into deeps of despair ; he will not lose one of all that the Father has given him. It is a point of honour with Jesus to seek and to save all the flock, without a single exception. What a promise to plead, if at this hour I am compelled to cry, "I have gone astray like a lost sheep"!

"The just shall live by faith."—Rom. i. 17.

I SHALL not die. I can, I do believe in the Lord my God, and this faith will keep me alive. I would be numbered among those who in their lives are just; but even if I were perfect I would not try to live by my righteousness; I would cling to the work of the Lord Jesus, and still live by faith in him and by nothing else. If I were able to give my body to be burned for my Lord Jesus, yet I would not trust in my own courage and constancy, but still would live by faith.

> "Were I a martyr at the stake
> I'd plead my Saviour's name;
> Intreat a pardon for his sake,
> And urge no other claim."

To live by faith is a far surer and happier thing than to live by feelings or by works. The branch, by living in the vine, lives a better life than it would live by itself, even if it were possible for it to live at all apart from the stem. To live by clinging to Jesus, by deriving all from him, is a sweet and sacred thing. If even the most just must live in this fashion, how much more must I who am a poor sinner! Lord, I believe. I must trust thee wholly. What else can I do? Trusting thee is my life. I feel it to be so. I will abide by this even to the end.

---

*"He that hath pity upon the poor lendeth unto the Lord;
and that which he hath given will he pay him again."*
Prov. xix. 17.

WE are to give to the poor out of pity. Not
to be seen and applauded, much less to
get influence over them ; but out of pure sympathy
and compassion we must give them help.

We must not expect to get anything back from
the poor, not even gratitude ; but we should regard
what we have done as a loan to the Lord.   He
undertakes the obligation, and, if we look to him
in the matter, we must not look to the second
party.   What an honour the Lord bestows upon
us when he condescends to borrow of us ! That
merchant is greatly favoured who has the Lord on
his books.   It would seem a pity to have such a
name down for a paltry pittance ; let us make it
a heavy amount.   The next needy man that comes
this way, let us help him.

As for re-payment, we can hardly think of it,
and yet here is the Lord's note of hand. Blessed
be his name, his promise to pay is better than gold
and silver. Are we running a little short through
the depression of the times ? We may venture
humbly to present this bill at the Bank of Faith.
Has any one of our readers been a bit of a screw to
the poor ? Poor soul. May the Lord forgive him.

"The Lord openeth the eyes of the blind: the Lord raiseth them that are bowed down."—Ps. cxlvi. 8.

AM I bowed down? Then let me urge this word of grace before the Lord. It is his way, his custom, his promise, his delight, to raise up them that are bowed down. Is it a sense of sin, and a consequent depression of spirit, which now distresses me? Then the work of Jesus is, in this case, made and provided to raise me up into rest. O Lord, raise me, for thy mercy sake!

Is it a sad bereavement, or a great fall in circumstances? Here again the Comforter has undertaken to console. What a mercy for us that one person of the Sacred Trinity should become the Comforter! This work will be well done, since such a glorious One has made it his peculiar care.

Some are so bowed down that only Jesus can loose them from their infirmity, but he can, and he will, do it. He can raise us up to health, to hope, to happiness. He has often done so under former trials, and he is the same Saviour, and will repeat his deeds of loving-kindness. We who are to-day bowed down and sorrowful, shall yet be set on high, and those who now mock at us shall be greatly ashamed. What an honour to be raised up by the Lord! It is worth while to be bowed down that we may experience his upraising power.

"He that hath an ear, let him hear what the Spirit saith unto the churches; He that overcometh shall not be hurt of the second death."—Rev. ii. 11.

THE first death we must endure unless the Lord should suddenly come to his temple. For this let us abide in readiness, awaiting it without fear, since Jesus has transformed death from a dreary cavern into a passage leading to glory.

The thing to be feared is not the first, but the second death; not the parting of the soul from the body, but the final separation of the entire man from God. This is death indeed. This death kills all peace, joy, happiness, hope. When God is gone all is gone. Such a death is far worse than ceasing to be: it is existence without the life which makes existence worth the having.

Now, if by God's grace we fight on to the end, and conquer in the glorious war, no second death can lay its chill finger upon us. We shall have no fear of death and hell, for we shall receive a crown of life which fadeth not away. How this nerves us for the fight! Eternal life is worth a life's battle. To escape the hurt of the second death is a thing worth struggling for throughout a lifetime.

Lord, give us faith, so that we may overcome, and then grant us grace to remain unharmed though sin and Satan dog our heels!

"Bring ye all the tithes into the storehouse, that there may be meat in mine house, and prove me now herewith, saith the Lord of hosts, if I will not open you the windows of heaven, and pour you out a blessing, that there shall not be room enough to receive it."—Mal. iii. 10.

MANY read and plead this promise without noticing the condition upon which the blessing is promised. We cannot expect heaven to be opened or blessing poured out unless we pay our dues unto the Lord our God and to his cause. There would be no lack of funds for holy purposes if all professing Christians paid their fair share.

Many are poor because they rob God. Many churches, also, miss the visitations of the Spirit because they starve their ministers. If there is no temporal meat for God's servants, we need not wonder if their ministry has but little food in it for our souls. When missions pine for means, and the work of the Lord is hindered by an empty treasury, how can we look for a large amount of soul-prosperity?

Come, come! What have I given of late? Have I been mean to my God? Have I stinted my Saviour? This will never do. Let me give my Lord Jesus his tithe by helping the poor, and aiding his work, and then I shall prove his power to bless me on a large scale.

"The just man walketh in his integrity : his children are blessed after him."—Prov. xx. 7.

ANXIETY about our family is natural, but we shall be wise if we turn it into care about our own character. If we walk before the Lord in integrity, we shall do more to bless our descendants than if we bequeathed them large estates. A father's holy life is a rich legacy for his sons.

The upright man leaves his heirs his example, and this in itself will be a mine of true wealth. How many men may trace their success in life to the example of their parents !

He leaves them also his repute. Men think all the better of us as the sons of a man who could be trusted, the successors of a tradesman of excellent repute. Oh, that all young men were anxious to keep up the family name !

Above all, he leaves his children his prayers and the blessing of a prayer-hearing God, and these make our offspring to be favoured among the sons of men. God will save them even after we are dead. Oh, that they might be saved at once!

Our integrity may be God's means of saving our sons and daughters. If they see the truth of our religion proved by our lives, it may be that they will believe in Jesus for themselves. Lord, fulfil this word to my household !

"And the Lord thy God shall bless thee in all that thou doest."—Deut. xv. 18.

AN Israelitish master was to give his bond-servant liberty in due time, and when he left his service he was to start him in life with a liberal portion. This was to be done heartily and cheerfully, and then the Lord promised to bless the generous act. The spirit of this precept, and, indeed, the whole law of Christ, binds us to treat work-people well. We ought to remember how the Lord has dealt with us, and that this renders it absolutely needful that we should deal graciously with others. It becomes those to be generous who are the children of a gracious God. How can we expect our great Master to bless us in our business if we oppress those who serve us?

What a benediction is here set before the liberal mind! To be blessed in all that we do is to be blessed indeed. The Lord will send us this partly in prosperity, partly in content of mind, and partly in a sense of his favour, which is the best of all blessings. He can make us feel that we are under his special care, and are surrounded by his peculiar love. This makes this earthly life a joyous prelude to the life to come. God's blessing is more than a fortune. It maketh rich, and addeth no sorrow therewith.

"The Lord will perfect that which concerneth me."
Ps. cxxxviii. 8.

HE who has begun will carry on the work which is being wrought within my soul. The Lord is concerned about everything that concerns me. All that is now good, but not perfect, the Lord will watch over, and preserve, and carry out to completion. This is a great comfort. I could not perfect the work of grace myself. Of that I am quite sure, for I fail every day, and have only held on so long as I have because the Lord has helped me. If the Lord were to leave me, all my past experience would go for nothing, and I should perish from the way. But the Lord will continue to bless me. He will perfect my faith, my love, my character, my life-work. He will do this because he has begun a work in me. He gave me the concern I feel, and, in a measure, he has fulfilled my gracious aspirations. He never leaves a work unfinished ; this would not be for his glory, nor would it be like him. He knows how to accomplish his gracious design, and though my own evil nature, and the world, and the devil, all conspire to hinder him, I do not doubt his promise. He will perfect that which concerneth me, and I will praise him for ever. Lord, let thy gracious work make some advance this day !

"I will dwell in them, and walk in them; and I will be their God, and they shall be my people."—2 Cor. vi. 16.

HERE is a *mutual interest*. Each belongs to each. God is the portion of his people, and the chosen people are the portion of their God. The saints find in God their chief possession, and he reckons them to be his peculiar treasure. What a mine of comfort lies in this fact for each believer!

This happy condition of mutual interest leads to *mutual consideration*. God will always think of his own people, and they will always think of him. This day my God will perform all things for me; what can I do for him? My thoughts ought to run towards him, for he thinketh upon me. Let me make sure that it is so, and not be content with merely admitting that so it ought to be.

This, again, leads to *mutual fellowship*. God dwells in us, and we dwell in him; he walks with us, and we walk with God. Happy communion this!

Oh, for grace to treat the Lord as my God: to trust him, and to serve him, as his Godhead deserves! Oh, that I could love, worship, adore, and obey Jehovah in spirit and in truth! this is my heart's desire. When I shall attain to it, I shall have found my heaven. Lord, help me! Be my God in helping me to know thee as my God, for Jesus' sake.

"Say not thou, I will recompense evil; but wait on the Lord, and he shall save thee."—Prov. xx. 22.

BE not in haste. Let anger cool down. Say nothing and do nothing to avenge yourself. You will be sure to act unwisely if you take up the cudgels and fight your own battles; and, certainly, you will not show the spirit of the Lord Jesus. It is nobler to forgive, and let the offence pass. To let an injury rankle in your bosom, and to meditate revenge, is to keep old wounds open, and to make new ones. Better forget and forgive.

Peradventure, you say that you must do something or be a great loser; then do what this morning's promise advises: "Wait on the Lord, and he shall save thee." This advice will not cost you six-and-eight pence, but it is worth far more. Be calm and quiet. Wait upon the Lord: tell him your grievance: spread Rab-shakeh's letter before the Lord, and this of itself will be an ease to your burdened mind. Besides, there is the promise, "He shall save thee." God will find a way of deliverance for you. How he will do it neither you nor I can guess, but do it he will. If the Lord save you, this will be a deal better than getting into petty quarrels, and covering yourself with filth by wrestling with the unclean. Be no more angry. Leave your suit with the Judge of all.

"To him that overcometh will I give to eat of the hidden manna, and will give him a white stone, and in the stone a new name written, which no man knoweth saving he that receiveth it."—Rev. ii. 17.

MY heart, be thou stirred up to persevere in the holy war, for the reward of victory is great. To day we eat of heavenly food which falls about our camps; the food of the wilderness, the food which comes from heaven, the food which never fails the pilgrims to Canaan. But there is reserved for us in Christ Jesus a still higher degree of spiritual life, and a food for it which, as yet, is hidden from our experience. In the golden pot which was laid up in the ark there was a portion of manna hidden away, which though kept for ages never grew stale. No one ever saw it; it was hid with the ark of the covenant, in the Holy of holies. Even so, the highest life of the believer is hid with Christ, in God. We shall come to it soon. Being made victorious through the grace of our Lord Jesus, we shall eat of the King's meat, and feed upon royal dainties. We shall feed upon Jesus. He is our "hidden manna" as well as the manna of the wilderness. He is all in all to us in our highest, as well as in our lowest estate. He helps us to fight, gives us the victory, and then is himself our reward. Lord, help me to overcome.

E

"The mountains and the hills shall break forth before you into singing, and all the trees of the field shall clap their hands."—Is. lv. 12.

WHEN sin is pardoned, our greatest sorrow is ended, and our truest pleasure begins. Such is the joy which the Lord bestows upon his reconciled ones, that it overflows and fills all nature with delight. The material world has latent music in it, and a renewed heart knows how to bring it out and make it vocal. Creation is the organ, and a gracious man finds out its keys, lays his hand thereon, and wakes the whole system of the universe to the harmony of praise. Mountains and hills, and other great objects, are, as it were, the bass of the chorus; while the trees of the wood, and all things that have life, take up the air of the melodious song.

When God's word is made to prosper among us, and souls are saved, then everything seems full of song. When we hear the confessions of young believers, and the testimonies of well-instructed saints, we are made so happy that we must praise the Lord, and then it seems as if rocks and hills, and woods and fields, echoed our joy-notes, and turned the world into an orchestra. Lord, on this happy May-day, lead me out into thy tuneful world as rich in praise as a lark in full song.

"He that soweth to the Spirit shall of the Spirit reap life everlasting."—Gal. vi. 8.

SOWING looks like a losing business, for we put good corn into the ground never to see it any more. Sowing to the Spirit seems a very fanciful, dreamy business; for we deny ourselves, and apparently get nothing for it. Yet if we sow to the Spirit by studying to live unto God, seeking to obey the will of God, and laying ourselves out to promote his honour, we shall not sow in vain. Life shall be our reward, even everlasting life. This we enjoy here as we enter into the knowledge of God, communion with God, and enjoyment of God. This life flows on like an ever-deepening, ever-widening river, till it bears us to the ocean of infinite felicity, where the life of God is ours for ever and ever.

Let us not this day sow to our flesh, for the harvest will be corruption, since flesh always tends that way; but with holy self-conquest let us live for the highest, purest, and most spiritual ends, seeking to honour our most holy Lord by obeying his most gracious Spirit. What a harvest will that be when we reap life everlasting! What sheaves of endless bliss will be reaped! What a festival will that harvest be! Lord, make us such reapers, for thy Son's sake.

"And let it be, when thou hearest the sound of a going in the tops of the mulberry trees, that then thou shalt bestir thyself: for then shall the Lord go out before thee, to smite the host of the Philistines."—2 Sam. v. 24.

THERE are signs of the Lord's moving which should move us. The Spirit of God blows where he listeth, and we hear the sound thereof. Then is the time for us to be more than ever astir. We must seize the golden opportunity, and make the most we can of it. It is ours to fight the Philistines at all times; but when the Lord himself goes out before us, then we should be specially valiant in the war.

The breeze stirred the tops of the trees, and David and his men took this for the signal for an onslaught, and at their advance the Lord, himself, smote the Philistines. Oh, that this day the Lord may give us an opening to speak for him with many of our friends! Let us be on the watch to avail ourselves of the hopeful opening when it comes. Who knows but this may be a day of good tidings; a season of soul-winning. Let us keep our ear open to hear the rustle of the wind, and our minds ready to obey the signal. Is not this promise, "then shall the Lord go out before thee," a sufficient encouragement to play the man? Since the Lord goes before us, we dare not hold back.

"Rejoice not against me, O mine enemy: when I fall, I shall arise; when I sit in darkness, the Lord shall be a light unto me."—Micah vii. 8.

THIS may express the feeling of a man or woman down-trodden and oppressed. Our enemy may put out our light for a season. There is sure hope for us in the Lord; and if we are trusting in him, and holding fast our integrity, our season of downcasting and darkness will soon be over. The insults of the foe are only for a moment. The Lord will soon turn their laughter into lamentation, and our sighing into singing.

What if the great enemy of souls should for a while triumph over us, as he has triumphed over better men than we are, yet let us take heart, for we shall overcome him before long. We shall rise from our fall, for our God has not fallen, and he will lift us up. We shall not abide in darkness, although for the moment we sit in it; for our Lord is the fountain of light, and he will soon bring us a joyful day. Let us not despair, or even doubt. One turn of the wheel and the lowest will be at the top. Woe unto those who laugh now, for they shall mourn and weep when their boasting is turned into everlasting contempt. But blessed are all holy mourners, for they shall be divinely comforted.

"The Lord thy God will turn thy captivity."—Deut. xxx. 3.

GOD'S own people may sell themselves into captivity by sin. A very bitter fruit is this, of an exceeding bitter root. What a bondage it is when the child of God is sold under sin, held in chains by Satan, deprived of his liberty, robbed of his power in prayer, and his delight in the Lord! Let us watch that we come not into such bondage; but if this has already happened to us, let us by no means despair.

But we cannot be held in slavery for ever. The Lord Jesus has paid too high a price for our redemption to leave us in the enemy's hand. The way to freedom is, "Return unto the Lord thy God." Where we first found salvation we shall find it again. At the foot of Christ's cross confessing sin we shall find pardon and deliverance. Moreover, the Lord will have us obey his voice according to all that he has commanded us, and we must do this with all our heart, and all our soul, and then our captivity shall end.

Often depression of spirit and great misery of soul are removed as soon as we quit our idols and bow ourselves in obedience before the living God. We need not be captives. We may return to Zion's citizenship, and that speedily. Lord, turn our captivity!

"Let not thine heart envy sinners : but be thou in the fear of the Lord all the day long.   For surely there is an end ; and thine expectation shall not be cut off."—Prov. xxiii. 17, 18.

WHEN we see the wicked prosper we are apt to envy them.   When we hear the noise of their mirth, and our own spirit is heavy, we half think that they have the best of it.   This is foolish and sinful.   If we knew them better, and specially if we remembered their end, we should pity them.

The cure for envy lies in living under a constant sense of the divine presence, worshipping God and communing with him all the day long, however long the day may seem.   True religion lifts the soul into a higher region, where the judgment becomes more clear, and the desires are more elevated.   The more of heaven there is in our lives, the less of earth we shall covet.   The fear of God casts out envy of men.

The death-blow of envy is a calm consideration of the future.   The wealth and glory of the ungodly are a vain show.   This pompous appearance flashes out for an hour, and then is extinguished.   What is the prosperous sinner the better for his prosperity when judgment overtakes him ?   As for the godly man, his end is peace and blessedness, and none can rob him of his joy ; wherefore, let him forego envy, and be filled with sweet content.

"And there shall cleave nought of the cursed thing to thine hand: that the Lord may turn from the fierceness of his anger, and show thee mercy, and have compassion upon thee, and multiply thee, as he hath sworn unto thy fathers."

Deut. xiii. 17.

ISRAEL must conquer idolatrous cities, and destroy all the spoil, regarding all that had been polluted by idolatry as an accursed thing to be burned with fire. Now, sin of all sorts must be treated by Christians in the same manner. We must not allow a single evil habit to remain. It is now war to the knife with sins of all sorts and sizes, whether of the body, the mind, or the spirit. We do not look upon this giving up of evil as deserving mercy, but we regard it as a fruit of the grace of God, which we would on no account miss.

When God causes us to have no mercy on our sins, then he has great mercy on us. When we are angry with evil, God is no more angry with us. When we multiply our efforts against iniquity, the Lord multiplies our blessings. The way of peace, of growth, of safety, of joy in Christ Jesus, will be found by following out these words: "There shall nought of the cursed thing cleave to thine hand." Lord, purify me this day. Compassion, prosperity, increase, and joy, will surely be given to those who put away sin with solemn resolution.

"Go ye also into the vineyard; and whatsoever is right, that shall ye receive."—Matt. xx. 7.

YES, there is work in Christ's vineyard for old bodies. It is the eleventh hour, and yet he will let us work. What great grace is this! Surely every old man ought to jump at this invitation! After men are advanced in years nobody wants them as servants; they go from shop to shop, and employers look at their grey hairs, and shake their heads. But Jesus will engage old people, and give them good wages too! This is mercy indeed. Lord, help the aged to enlist in thy service without an hour's delay.

But will the Lord pay wages to worn-out old men? Do not doubt it. He says, he will give you what is right if you will work in his field. He will surely give you grace here and glory hereafter. He will grant present comfort and future rest; strength equal to your day, and a vision of glory when the night of death comes on. All these the Lord Jesus will as freely give to the aged convert as to one who enters his service in his youth.

Let me tell this to some unsaved old man or old woman, and pray the Lord to bless it, for Jesus' sake. Where can I find such persons? I will be on the look-out for them, and kindly tell them the news.

"For our heart shall rejoice in him, because we have trusted in his holy name."—Ps. xxxiii. 21.

THE root of faith produces the flower of heart-joy. We may not at the first rejoice, but it comes in due time. We trust the Lord when we are sad, and in due season he so answers our confidence that our faith turns to fruition and we rejoice in the Lord. Doubt breeds distress, but trust means joy in the long run.

The assurance expressed by the Psalmist in this verse is really a promise held out in the hands of holy confidence. Oh for grace to appropriate it. If we do not rejoice at this moment, yet we shall do so, as surely as David's God is our God.

Let us meditate upon the Lord's holy name, that we may trust him the better and rejoice the more readily. He is in character holy, just, true, gracious, faithful and unchanging. Is not such a God to be trusted? He is all-wise, almighty, and everywhere present, can we not cheerfully rely upon him? Yes, we will do so at once, and do so without reserve. Jehovah-Jireh will provide, Jehovah-Shalom will send peace, Jehovah-Tsidkenu will justify, Jehovah-Shammah will be for ever near, and in Jehovah-Nissi we will conquer every foe. They that know thy name will trust thee; and they that trust thee will rejoice in thee, O Lord.

"So that we may boldly say, The Lord is my helper, and I will not fear what man shall do unto me."—Heb. xiii. 6.

BECAUSE God will never leave nor forsake us, we may well be content with such things as we have. Since the Lord is ours, we cannot be left without a friend, a treasure, and a dwelling-place. This assurance may make us feel quite independent of men. Under such high patronage we do not feel tempted to cringe before our fellow-men, and ask of them permission to call our lives our own ; but what we say we boldly say, and defy contradiction.

He who fears God has nothing else to fear. We should stand in such awe of the living Lord that all the threats that can be used by the proudest persecutor should have no more effect upon us than the whistling of the wind. Man in these days cannot do so much against us as he could when the apostle wrote the verse at the head of this page. Racks and stakes are out of fashion. Giant Pope cannot burn the pilgrims now. If the followers of false teachers try cruel mockery and scorn, we do not wonder at it, for the men of this world cannot love the heavenly seed. What then? We must bear the world's scorn. It breaks no bones. God helping us, let us be bold, and when the world rages let it rage, but let us not fear it.

"Gad, a troop shall overcome him: but he shall over-come at the last."—Gen. xlix. 19.

SOME of us have been like the tribe of Gad. Our adversaries for a while were too many for us, they came upon us like a troop. Yes, and for the moment they overcame us; and they exulted greatly because of their temporary victory. Thus they only proved the first part of the family heritage to be really ours, for Christ's people, like Dan, shall have a troop overcoming them. This being overcome is very painful, and we should have despaired if we had not by faith believed the second line of our father's benediction, "*He shall overcome at the last.*" "All's well that ends well," said the world's poet; and he spoke the truth. A war is to be judged, not by first successes or defeats, but by that which happens "at the last." The Lord will give to truth and righteousness victory "at the last"; and, as Mr. Bunyan says, that means for ever, for nothing can come after the last.

What we need is patient perseverance in well-doing, calm confidence in our glorious Captain. Christ, our Lord Jesus, would teach us his holy art of setting the face like a flint to go through with work or suffering till we can say, "It is finished." Hallelujah. Victory! Victory! We believe the promise. "He shall overcome at the last."

" Whoso keepeth the fig tree shall eat the fruit thereof:
so he that waiteth on his master shall be honoured."
Prov. xxvii. 18.

HE who tends the fig tree has figs for his pains, and he who waits on a good master has honour as his reward. Truly the Lord Jesus is the very best of masters, and it is an honour to be allowed to do the least act for his sake. To serve some lords is to watch over a crab tree and eat the crabs as one's wages; but to serve my Lord Jesus is to keep a fig tree of the sweetest figs. His service is in itself delight, continuance in it is promotion, success in it is blessedness below, and the reward for it is glory above.

Our greatest honours will be gathered in that season when the figs will be ripe, even in the next world. Angels who are now our servitors will bear us home when our day's work is done. Heaven, where Jesus is, will be our honourable mansion, eternal bliss our honourable portion, and the Lord himself our honourable companion. Who can imagine the full meaning of this promise—" He that waiteth on his master shall be honoured"?

Lord, help me to wait upon my Master. Let me leave all idea of honour to the hour when thou thyself shalt honour me. May thy Holy Spirit make me a lowly and patient worker and waiter!

"And I will give him the morning star."—Rev. ii. 28.

UNTIL the day break, and the shadows flee away, what a blessing it is to see in Jesus "the morning star"! I remember when we read in the newspapers the idle tale that the star of Bethlehem had again appeared. On enquiry we found that it was only "the morning star"; but no great mistake had been made after all.

It is best to see Jesus as the sun; but when we cannot do so, the next best thing is to see him as that star which prophesies the day, and shows that the eternal light is near at hand. If I am not to-day all that I hope to be, yet I see Jesus, and that assures me that I shall one day be like him. A sight of Jesus by faith is the pledge of beholding him in his glory and being transformed into his image. If I have not at this hour all the light and joy I could desire, yet I shall have it; for as surely as I see the morning star I shall see the day.. The morning star is never far from the sun.

Come, my soul, has the Lord given thee the morning star? Dost thou hold fast that truth, grace, hope, and love which the Lord has given thee? Then in this thou hast the dawn of coming glory. He that makes thee overcome evil, and persevere in righteousness, has therein given thee the morning star.

"Come, and let us return unto the Lord: for he hath torn, and he will heal us ; he hath smitten, and he will bind us up."—Hosea vi. 1.

IT is the Lord's way to tear before he heals. This is the honest love of his heart, and the sure surgery of his hand. He also bruises before he binds up, or else it would be uncertain work. The law comes before the gospel ; the sense of need before the supply of it. Is the reader now under the convincing, crushing hand of the Spirit ? Has he received the spirit of bondage again to fear ? This is a salutary preliminary to real gospel healing and binding up.

Do not despair, dear heart, but come to the Lord with all thy jagged wounds, black bruises, and running sores. He alone can heal, and he delights to do it. It is our Lord's office to bind up the broken-hearted, and he is gloriously at home at it. Let us not linger, but at once return unto the Lord from whom we have gone astray. Let us show him our gaping wounds, and beseech him to know his own work, and complete it. Will a surgeon make an incision, and then leave his patient to bleed to death ? Will the Lord pull down our old house, and then refuse to build us a better one ? Dost thou ever wantonly increase the misery of poor anxious souls ? That be far from thee, O Lord.

"I will set him on high, because he hath known my name."—Ps. xci. 14.

DOES the Lord say this to me? Yes, if I have known his name. Blessed be the Lord, I am no stranger to him. I have tried him, and proved him, and known him, and, therefore, do I trust him. I know his name as a sin-hating God, for by his Spirit's convincing power I have been taught that he will never wink at evil. But I also know him as the sin-pardoning God in Christ Jesus, for he has forgiven me all trespasses. His name is faithfulness, and I know it, for he has never forsaken me though my troubles have multiplied upon me.

This knowledge is a gift of grace, and the Lord makes it to be the reason why he grants another grace-gift, namely, setting on high. This is grace upon grace. Observe that if we climb on high, the position may be dangerous; but if the Lord sets us there, it is safe. He may raise us to great usefulness, to eminent experience, to success in service, to leadership among workers, to a father's place among the little ones. If he does not do this, he may set us on high by near fellowship, clear insight, holy triumph, and gracious anticipation of eternal glory. When God sets us on high, Satan himself cannot pull us down. Oh, that this may be our case all through this day!

"Blessed are the merciful: for they shall obtain mercy."
Matt. v. 7.

IT is not meet that the man who will not forgive should be forgiven, nor shall he who will not give to the poor have his own wants relieved. God will measure to us with our own bushels, and those who have been hard masters and hard creditors, will find that the Lord will deal hardly with them. "He shall have judgment without mercy, that hath shewed no mercy."

This day let us try to give and to forgive. Let us mind the two bears—bear and forbear. Let us be kind, and gentle, and tender. Let us not put harsh constructions upon men's conduct, nor drive hard bargains, nor pick foolish quarrels, nor be difficult to please. Surely we wish to be blessed, and we also want to obtain mercy: let us be merciful, that we may have mercy. Let us fulfil the condition, that we may earn the beatitude. Is it not a pleasant duty to be kind? Is there not much more sweetness in it than in being angry and ungenerous? Why, there is a blessedness in the thing itself! Moreover, the obtaining of mercy is a rich reward. What but sovereign grace could suggest such a promise as this? We are merciful to our fellow-mortal in pence, and the Lord forgives us " all that debt."

"The upright shall have good things in possession."
Prov. xxviii. 10.

THE Book of Proverbs is also a Book of
Promises. Promises ought to be proverbs
among the people of God. This is a very remarkable one. We are accustomed to think of our good
things as in reversion, but here we are told that we
shall have them in possession.

Not all the malice and cunning of our enemies
can work our destruction : they shall fall into the
pit which they have digged. Our inheritance is so
entailed upon us that we shall not be kept out of
it, nor so turned out of the way as to miss it.

But what have we now? We have a quiet conscience through the precious blood of Jesus. We
have the love of God set upon us beyond all change.
We have power with God in prayer in all time of
need. We have the providence of God to watch
over us, the angels of God to minister to us, and,
above all, the Spirit of God to dwell in us. In fact, all
things are ours. "Whether things present or things
to come: all are yours." Jesus is ours. Yea, the
divine Trinity in Unity is ours. Hallelujah. Let
us not pine and whine, and stint and slave, since
we have good things in possession. Let us live on
our God and rejoice in him all the day. Help us,
O Holy Ghost!

"And I will restore to you the years that the locust hath eaten."—Joel ii. 25.

YES, those wasted years over which we sigh shall be restored to us. God can give us such plentiful grace that we shall crowd into the remainder of our days as much of service as will be some recompense for those years of unregeneracy over which we mourn in humble penitence.

The locusts of backsliding, worldliness, lukewarmness, are now viewed by us as a terrible plague. Oh that they had never come near us! The Lord in mercy has now taken them away, and we are full of zeal to serve him. Blessed be his name, we can raise such harvests of spiritual graces as shall make our former barrenness to disappear. Through rich grace we can turn to account our bitter experience, and use it to warn others. We can become the more rooted in humility, childlike dependence, and penitent spirituality, by reason of our former shortcomings. If we are the more watchful, zealous, and tender, we shall gain by our lamentable losses. The wasted years, by a miracle of love, can be restored. Does it seem too great a boon? Let us believe for it, and live for it, and we may yet realize it, even as Peter became all the more useful a man after his presumption was cured by his discovered weakness. Lord, aid us by thy grace.

"Therefore thus saith the Lord, If thou return, then will I bring thee again, and thou shalt stand before me : and if thou take forth the precious from the vile, thou shalt be as my mouth."—Jer. xv. 19.

POOR Jeremiah! Yet why do we say so? The weeping prophet was one of the choicest servants of God, and honoured by him above many. He was hated for speaking the truth. The word which was so sweet to him was bitter to his hearers, yet he was accepted of his Lord. He was commanded to abide in his faithfulness, and then the Lord would continue to speak through him. He was to deal boldly and truthfully with men, and perform the Lord's winnowing work upon the professors of his day, and then the Lord gave him this word, " Thou shalt be as my mouth."

What an honour! Should not every preacher, yea, every believer, covet it? For God to speak by us, what a marvel! We shall speak sure, pure truth ; and we shall speak it with power. Our word shall not return void ; it shall be a blessing to those who receive it, and those who refuse it shall do so at their peril. Our lips shall feed many. We shall arouse the sleeping and call the dead to life.

O dear reader, pray that it may be so with the writer, and with all the sent servants of our Lord.

"I will go before thee, and make the crooked places straight: I will break in pieces the gates of brass, and cut in sunder the bars of iron."—Isa. xlv. 2.

THIS was for Cyrus; but it is evermore the heritage of all the Lord's own spiritual servants. Only let us go forward by faith, and our way will be cleared for us. Crooks and turns of human craft and Satanic subtlety shall be straightened for us; we shall not need to track their devious windings. The gates of brass shall be broken, and the iron bars which fastened them shall be cut asunder. We shall not need the battering ram nor the crow-bar: the Lord himself will do the impossible for us, and the unexpected shall be a fact.

Let us not sit down in coward fear. Let us press onward in the path of duty; for the Lord hath said it, "I will go before thee." Ours not to reason why; ours but to dare and dash forward. It is the Lord's work, and he will enable us to do it: all impediments must yield before him. Hath he not said, "I will break in pieces the gates of brass?" What can hinder his purpose or balk his decrees? Those who serve God have infinite resources. The way is clear to faith though barred to human strength. When Jehovah says, "I will," as he does twice in this promise, we dare not doubt.

"If the clouds be full of rain, they empty themselves upon the earth."—Eccl. xi. 3.

WHY, then, do we dread the clouds which now darken our sky? True, for a while they hide the sun, but the sun is not quenched; he will shine out again before long. Meanwhile those black clouds are filled with rain; and the blacker they are, the more likely they are to yield plentiful showers. How can we have rain without clouds?

Our troubles have always brought us blessings, and they always will. They are the dark chariots of bright grace. These clouds will empty themselves before long, and every tender herb will be the gladder for the shower. Our God may drench us with grief, but he will not drown us with wrath; nay, he will refresh us with mercy. Our Lord's love-letters often come to us in black-edged envelopes. His wagons rumble, but they are loaded with benefits. His rod blossoms with sweet flowers and nourishing fruits. Let us not worry about the clouds, but sing because May flowers are brought to us through the April clouds and showers.

O Lord, the clouds are the dust of thy feet! How near thou art in the cloudy and dark day! Love beholds thee, and is glad. Faith sees the clouds emptying themselves and making the little hills rejoice on every side.

"Though I walk in the midst of trouble, thou wilt revive me : thou shalt stretch forth thine hand against the wrath of mine enemies, and thy right hand shall save me."
Ps. cxxxviii. 7.

WRETCHED walking in the midst of trouble Nay, blessed walking, since there is a special promise for it. Give me a promise, and what is the trouble? What doth my Lord teach me here to say? Why this—" Thou wilt revive me." I shall have more life, more energy, more faith. Is it not often so, that trouble revives us, like a breath of cold air when one is ready to faint?

How angry are my enemies and especially the arch-enemy! Shall I stretch forth my hand and fight my foes? No, my hand is better employed in doing service for my Lord. Besides, there is no need, for my God will use his far-reaching arm, and he will deal with them far better than I could if I were to try. " Vengeance is mine ; I will repay, saith the Lord." He will with his own right hand of power and wisdom save me, and what more can I desire?

Come, my heart, talk this promise over to thyself till thou canst use it as the song of thy confidence, the solace of thy loneliness. Pray to be revived thyself, and leave the rest with the Lord, who performeth all things for thee.

"For he shall deliver the needy when he crieth; the poor also, and him that hath no helper."—Ps. lxxii. 12.

THE needy cries; what else can he do? His cry is heard of God; what else need he do? Let the needy reader take to crying at once, for this will be his wisdom. Do not cry in the ears of friends, for even if they can help you it is only because the Lord enables them. The nearest way is to go straight to God, and let your cry come up before him. Straight-forward makes the best runner: run to the Lord, and not to secondary causes.

"Alas!" you cry, "I have no friend or helper." So much the better; you can rely upon God in both capacities—as without supplies and without helpers. Make your double need your double plea. Even for temporal mercies you may wait upon God, for he careth for his children in these temporary concerns. As for spiritual necessities, which are the heaviest of all, the Lord will hear your cry, and will deliver you and supply you.

O poor friend, try your rich God. O helpless one, lean on his help. He has never failed *me*, and I am sure he will never fail *you*. Come as a beggar, and God will not refuse you help. Come with no plea but his grace. Jesus is King, will he let you perish of want? What! Did you forget this?

"One man of you shall chase a thousand: for the Lord your God, he it is that fighteth for you, as he hath promised you."—Joshua xxiii. 10.

WHY count heads? One man with God is a majority though there be a thousand on the other side. Sometimes our helpers may be too many for God to work with them, as was the case with Gideon, who could do nothing till he had increased his forces by thinning out their numbers. But the Lord's host are never too few. When God would found a nation, he called Abram alone and blessed him. When he would vanquish proud Pharaoh, he used no armies, but only Moses and Aaron. The "one man ministry," as certain wise men call it, has been far more used of the Lord than trained bands with their officers. Did all the Israelites together slay so many as Samson alone? Saul and his hosts slew their thousands, but David his ten thousands.

The Lord can give the enemy long odds and yet vanquish him. If we have faith, we have God with us, and what are multitudes of men? One shepherd's dog can drive before him a great flock of sheep. If the Lord sent thee, O my brother, his strength will accomplish his divine purpose. Wherefore, rely on the promise, and be very courageous.

"The Lord shall open unto thee his good treasure."
Deut. xxviii. 12.

THIS refers first to the rain. The Lord will give this in its season. Rain is the emblem of all those celestial refreshings which the Lord is ready to bestow upon his people. Oh for a copious shower to refresh the Lord's heritage!

We seem to think that God's treasury can only be opened by a great prophet like Elijah, but it is not so, for this promise is to all the faithful in Israel, and, indeed, to each one of them. O believing friend, "the Lord shall open unto thee his good treasure." Thou, too, mayest see heaven opened, and thrust in thy hand and take out thy portion, yea, and a portion for all thy brethren round about thee. Ask what thou wilt, and thou shalt not be denied, if thou abidest in Christ, and his words abide in thee.

As yet thou hast not known all thy Lord's treasures, but he shall open them up to thine understanding. Certainly thou hast not yet enjoyed the fulness of his covenant riches, but he will direct thine heart into his love, and reveal Jesus in thee. Only the Lord himself can do this for thee; but here is his promise, and if thou wilt hearken diligently unto his voice, and obey his will, his riches in glory by Christ Jesus shall be thine.

"Ye shall serve the Lord your God, and he shall bless thy bread, and thy water."—Ex. xxiii. 25.

WHAT a promise is this! To serve God is in itself a high delight. But what an added privilege to have the blessing of the Lord resting upon us in all things! Our commonest things become blessed when we ourselves are consecrated to the Lord. Our Lord Jesus took bread and blessed it; behold, we also eat of blessed bread. Jesus blessed water and made it wine: the water which we drink is far better to us than any of the wine with which men make merry; every drop has a benediction in it. The divine blessing is on the man of God in everything, and it shall abide with him at every time.

What if we have only bread and water! Yet it is blessed bread and water. Bread and water we shall have. That is implied, for it must be there for God to bless it. "Thy bread shall be given thee, and thy waters shall be sure." With God at our table, we not only ask a blessing, but we have one. It is not only at the altar but at the table that he blesses us. He serves those well who serve him well. This table-blessing is not of debt, but of grace. Indeed, there is a treble grace; he grants us grace to serve him, by his grace feeds us with bread, and then in his grace blesses it.

*"For if these things be in you, and abound, they make
you that ye shall neither be barren nor unfruitful in the
knowledge of our Lord Jesus Christ."*—2 Pet. i. 8.

IF we desire to glorify our Lord by fruitfulness
we must have certain things within us ; for
nothing can come out of us which is not first of all
within us. We must begin with faith, which is
the groundwork of all the virtues ; and then diligently add to it virtue, knowledge, temperance,
and patience. With these we must have godliness
and brotherly love. All these put together will
most assuredly cause us to produce, as our life
fruit, the clusters of usefulness, and we shall not
be mere idle knowers, but real doers of the word.
These holy things must not only be in us, but
abound, or we shall be barren. Fruit is the overflow
of life, and we must be full before we can flow over.

We have noticed men of considerable parts and
opportunities who have never succeeded in doing
real good in the conversion of souls ; and after
close observation we have concluded that they
lacked certain graces which are absolutely essential
to fruit-bearing. For real usefulness graces are
better than gifts. As the man is, so is his work.
If we would *do* better we must *be* better. Let the
text be a gentle hint to unfruitful professors, *and
to myself also.*

"And thou saidst, I will surely do thee good."—Gen. xxxii. 12.

THIS is the sure way of prevailing with the Lord in prayer. We may humbly remind him of what he has said. Our faithful God will never run back from his word, nor will he leave it unfulfilled; yet he loves to be enquired of by his people, and put in mind of his promise. This is refreshing to their memories, reviving to their faith, and renewing to their hope. God's word is given, not for his sake, but for ours. His purposes are settled, and he needs nothing to bind him to his design of doing his people good; but he gives the promise for our strengthening and comfort. Hence he wishes us to plead it, and say to him, "Thou saidst."

"I will surely do thee good" is just the essence of all the Lord's gracious sayings. Lay a special stress on the word "surely." He will do us good, real good, lasting good, only good, every good. He will make us good, and this is to do us good in the very highest degree. He will treat us as he does his saints while we are here, and that is good. He will soon take us to be with Jesus and all his chosen, and that is supremely good. With this promise in our hearts we need not fear angry Esau, nor anyone else. If the Lord will do us good, who can do us hurt?

"And Jesus said unto them, Come ye after me, and I will make you to become fishers of men."—Mark i. 17.

ONLY by coming after Jesus can we obtain our heart's desire, and be really useful to our fellow men. Oh, how we long to be successful fishers for Jesus! We would sacrifice our lives to win souls. But we are tempted to try methods which Jesus would never have tried. Shall we yield to this suggestion of the enemy? If so, we may splash the water, but we shall never take the fish. We must follow after Jesus if we would succeed. Sensational methods, entertainments, and so forth—are these coming after Jesus? Can we imagine the Lord Jesus drawing a congregation by such means as are now commonly used? What is the result of such expedients? The result is nothing which Jesus will count up at the last great day.

We must keep to our preaching as our Master did, for by this means souls are saved. We must preach our Lord's doctrine, and proclaim a full and free gospel; for this is the net in which souls are taken. We must preach with his gentleness, boldness, and love; for this is the secret of success with human hearts. We must work under divine anointing, depending upon the sacred Spirit. Thus, coming after Jesus, and not running before him, nor aside from him, we shall be fishers of men.

"Nevertheless I say unto you, Hereafter shall ye see the Son of man sitting on the right hand of power, and coming in the clouds of heaven."—Matt. xxvi. 64.

AH, Lord, thou wast in thy lowest state when before thy persecutors thou wast made to stand like a criminal! Yet the eyes of thy faith could see beyond thy present humiliation into thy future glory. What words are these, " Nevertheless —hereafter"! I would imitate thy holy foresight, and in the midst of poverty, or sickness, or slander, I also would say, " Nevertheless—hereafter." Instead of weakness, thou hast all power ; instead of shame, all glory ; instead of derision, all worship. Thy cross has not dimmed the splendour of thy crown, neither has the spittle marred the beauty of thy face. Say, rather, thou art the more exalted and honoured because of thy sufferings.

So, Lord, I also would take courage from the " hereafter." I would forget the present tribulation in the future triumph. Help thou me by directing me into thy Father's love and into thine own patience, so that when I am derided for thy name I may not be staggered, but think more and more of the hereafter, and, therefore, all the less of to-day. I shall be with thee soon and behold thy glory. Wherefore, I am not ashamed, but say in my inmost soul, " Nevertheless—hereafter."

"In the world ye shall have tribulation: but be of good cheer; I have overcome the world."—John xvi. 33.

MY Lord's words are true as to the tribulation. I have my share of it beyond all doubt. The flail is not hung up out of the way, nor can I hope that it will be laid aside so long as I lie upon the threshing-floor. How can I look to be at home in the enemy's country, joyful while in exile, or comfortable in a wilderness? This is not my rest. This is the place of the furnace, and the forge, and the hammer. My experience tallies with my Lord's words.

I note how he bids me "be of good cheer." Alas! I am far too apt to be downcast. My spirit soon sinks when I am sorely tried. But I must not give way to this feeling. When my Lord bids me cheer up I must not dare to be cast down.

What is the argument which he uses to encourage me? Why, it is his own victory. He says, "I have overcome the world." His battle was much more severe than mine. I have not yet resisted unto blood. Why do I despair of overcoming? See, my soul, the enemy has been once overcome. I fight with a beaten foe. O world, Jesus has already vanquished thee; and in me, by his grace, he will overcome thee again. Therefore am I of good cheer, and sing unto my conquering Lord.

"Cast thy bread upon the waters: for thou shalt find it after many days."—Eccl. xi. 1.

WE must not expect to see an immediate reward for all the good we do; nor must we always confine our efforts to places and persons which seem likely to yield us a recompense for our labours. The Egyptian casts his seed upon the waters of the Nile, where it might seem a sheer waste of corn. But in due time the flood subsides, the rice or other grain sinks into the fertile mud, and rapidly a harvest is produced. Let us to-day do good to the unthankful and the evil. Let us teach the careless and the obstinate. Unlikely waters may cover hopeful soil. Nowhere shall our labour be in vain in the Lord.

It is ours to cast our bread upon the waters; it remains with God to fulfil the promise, "Thou shalt find it." He will not let his promise fail. His good word ,which we have spoken shall live, shall be found, shall be found by us. Perhaps not just yet, but some day we shall reap what we have sown. We must exercise our patience; for perhaps the Lord may exercise it. "After many days," says the Scripture, and in many instances those days run into months and years, and yet the word stands true. God's promise will keep; let us mind that we keep the precept, and keep it this day.

"For now will I break his yoke from off thee, and will burst thy bonds in sunder."—Nahum i. 13.

THE Assyrian was allowed for a season to oppress the Lord's people, but there came a time for his power to be broken. So, many a heart is held in bondage by Satan, and frets sorely under the yoke. Oh, that to such prisoners of hope the word of the Lord may come at once, according to the text,—"Now will I break his yoke from off thee, and will burst thy bonds in sunder"!

See! the Lord promises a present deliverance: *"Now"* will I break his yoke from off thee." Believe for immediate freedom, and according to thy faith so shall it be unto thee at this very hour. When God saith "now," let no man say "to-morrow."

See how complete the rescue is to be; for the yoke is not to be removed, but broken; and the bonds are not to be untied, but burst asunder. Here is a display of divine force which guarantees that the oppressor shall not return. His yoke is broken, we cannot again be bowed down by its weight. His bonds are burst asunder, they can no longer hold us. Oh, to believe in Jesus for complete and everlasting emancipation! "If the Son shall make you free, ye shall be free indeed." Come, Lord, and set free thy captives, according to thy word.

"The Lord God is my strength, and he will make my feet like hinds' feet, and he will make me to walk upon mine high places."—Hab. iii. 19.

THIS confidence of the man of God is tantamount to a promise; for that which faith is persuaded of is the purpose of God. The prophet had to traverse the deep places of poverty and famine, but he went down hill without slipping, for the Lord gave him *standing*. By-and-by he was called to the high places of the hills of conflict; and he was no more afraid to go up than to go down.

See! the Lord lent him *strength*. Nay, Jehovah himself was his strength. Think of that: the Almighty God himself becomes our strength!

Note, that the Lord also gave him *sure-footedness*. The hinds leap over rock and crag, never missing their foothold. Our Lord will give us grace to follow the most difficult paths of duty without a stumble. He can fit our foot for the crags, so that we shall be at home where apart from God we should perish.

One of these days we shall be called to higher places still. Up yonder we shall climb, even to the mount of God, the high places where the shining ones are gathered. Oh, what feet are the feet of faith, by which, following the Hind of the Morning, we shall ascend into the hill of the Lord!

"They shall be mine, saith the Lord of hosts, in that day when I make up my jewels."—Mal. iii. 17.

A DAY is coming in which the crown jewels of our great King shall be counted, that it may be seen whether they answer to the inventory which his Father gave him. My soul, wilt thou be among the precious things of Jesus? Thou art precious to him if he is precious to thee, and thou shalt be his "in that day," if he is thine in this day.

In the days of Malachi, the chosen of the Lord were accustomed so to converse with each other that their God himself listened to their talk. He liked it so well that he took notes of it; yes, and made a book of it, which he lodged in his Record Office. Pleased with their conversation, he was also pleased with them. Pause, my soul, and ask thyself: If Jesus were to listen to thy talk would he be pleased with it? Is it to his glory and to the edification of the brotherhood? Say, my soul, and be sure thou sayest the truth.

But what will the honour be for us poor creatures to be reckoned by the Lord to be his crown jewels! This honour have all the saints. Jesus not only says, "They are mine," but, "They shall be mine." He bought us, sought us, brought us in, and has so far wrought us to his image, that we shall be fought for by him with all his might.

"But against any of the children of Israel shall not a dog move his tongue, against man or beast: that ye may know how that the Lord doth put a difference between the Egyptians and Israel."—Ex. xi. 7.

WHAT! has God power over the tongues of dogs? Can he keep curs from barking? Yes, it is even so. He can even prevent an Egyptian dog from worrying one of the lambs of Israel's flock. Doth God silence dogs, and doggish ones among men, and the great dog at hell's gate? Then let us move on our way without fear.

If he lets dogs move their tongues, yet he can stop their teeth. They may make a dreadful noise, and still do us no real harm. Yet, how sweet is quiet! How delightful to move about among enemies, and perceive that God maketh them to be at peace with us! Like Daniel in the den of lions, we are unhurt amid destroyers.

Oh, that to-day, this word of the Lord to Israel might be true to me! Does the dog worry me? I will tell my Lord about him. Lord, he does not care for my pleadings; do thou speak the word of power, and he must lie down. Give me peace, O my God, and let me see thy hand so distinctly in it that I may most clearly perceive the difference which thy grace has made between me and the ungodly!

"The Lord hath heard my supplication; the Lord will receive my prayer."—Ps. vi. 9.

THE experience here recorded is mine. I can set to my seal that God is true. In very wonderful ways he has answered the prayers of his servant many and many a time. Yes, and he is hearing my present supplication, and he is not turning away his ear from me. Blessed be his holy name!

What then? Why, for certain the promise which lies sleeping in the Psalmist's believing confidence is also mine. Let me grasp it by the hand of faith: "The Lord will receive my prayer." He will accept it, think of it, and grant it in the way and time which his loving wisdom judges to be best. I bring my poor prayer in my hand to the great King, and he gives me audience, and graciously receives my petition. My enemies will not listen to me, but my Lord will. They ridicule my tearful prayers, but my Lord does not; he receives my prayer into his ear and his heart.

What a reception this is for a poor sinner! We receive Jesus, and then the Lord receives us and our prayers for his Son's sake. Blessed be that dear name which franks our prayers so that they freely pass even within the golden gates. Lord, teach me to pray, since thou hearest my prayers.

"And I give unto them eternal life; and they shall never perish, neither shall any man pluck them out of my hand."
John x. 28.

WE believe in the eternal security of the saints. First, because they are Christ's, and he will never lose the sheep which he has bought with his blood, and received of his Father.

Next, because he gives them eternal life, and if it be eternal, well then, it is eternal, and there can be no end to it, unless there can be an end to hell, and heaven, and God. If spiritual life can die out, it is manifestly not eternal life, but temporary life. But the Lord speaks of eternal life, and that effectually shuts out the possibility of an end.

Observe, further, that the Lord expressly says, "They shall never perish." As long as words have a meaning, this secures believers from perishing. The most obstinate unbelief cannot force this meaning out of this sentence.

Then, to make the matter complete, he declares that his people are in his hand, and he defies all their enemies to pluck them out of it. Surely it is a thing impossible even for the fiend of hell. We must be safe in the grasp of an Almighty Saviour.

Be it ours to dismiss carnal fear as well as carnal confidence, and rest peacefully in the hollow of the Redeemer's hand.

"If any of you lack wisdom, let him ask of God, that giveth to all men liberally, and upbraideth not; and it shall be given him."—James i. 5.

"IF any of you lack wisdom." There is no "if" in the matter, for I am sure I lack it. What do I know? How can I guide my own way? How can I direct others? Lord, I am a mass of folly, and wisdom I have none.

Thou sayest, "Let him ask of God." Lord, I now ask. Here at thy footstool I ask to be furnished with heavenly wisdom for this day's perplexities, ay, and for this day's simplicities; for I know I may do very stupid things, even in plain matters, unless thou dost keep me out of mischief.

I thank thee that all I have to do is to ask. What grace is this on thy part, that I have only to pray in faith, and thou wilt give me wisdom! Thou dost here promise me a liberal education, and that, too, without an angry tutor, or a scolding usher. This, too, thou wilt bestow without a fee— bestow it on a fool who lacks wisdom. O Lord, I thank thee for that positive and expressive word, "It shall be given him." I believe it. Thou wilt this day make thy babe to know the hidden wisdom which the carnally prudent never learn. Thou wilt guide me with thy counsel, and afterwards receive me to glory.

"I will also leave in the midst of thee an afflicted and poor people, and they shall trust in the name of the Lord."
Zeph. iii. 12

WHEN true religion is ready to die out among the wealthy it finds a home among the poor of this world, rich in faith. The Lord has even now his faithful remnant. Am I one of them?

Perhaps it is because men are afflicted and poor that they learn to trust in the name of the Lord. He that hath no money must try what he can do on trust. He whose own name is good for nothing in his own esteem, acts wisely to rest in another name, even that best of names, the name of Jehovah God will always have a trusting people, and these will be an afflicted and poor people. Little as the world thinks of them, their being left in the midst of a nation is the channel of untold blessings to it. Here we have the conserving salt which keeps in check the corruption which is in the world through lust.

Again the question comes home to each one of us, Am I one of them? Am I afflicted by the sin within me and around me? Am I poor in spirit, poor spiritually in my own judgment? Do I trust in the Lord? That is the main business. Jesus reveals the name, the character, the person of God; am I trusting in him? If so, I am left in this world for a purpose. Lord, help me to fulfil it.

"They shall feed and lie down, and none shall make them afraid."—Zeph. iii. 13.

YESTERDAY we thought of the afflicted and poor people whom the Lord left to be a living seed in a dead world. The prophet says of such that they shall not work iniquity nor speak lies. So that while they had neither rank nor riches to guard them, they were also quite unable to use those weapons in which the wicked place so much reliance : they could neither defend themselves by sin nor by subtlety.

What then? Would they be destroyed? By no means? They should both feed and rest, and be not merely free from danger, but even quiet from fear of evil. Sheep are very feeble creatures, and wolves are terrible enemies ; yet at this hour sheep are more numerous than wolves, and the cause of the sheep is always winning, while the cause of the wolves is always declining. One day flocks of sheep will cover the plains, and not a wolf will be left. The fact is that sheep have a shepherd, and this gives them provender, protection, and peace. "*None*"—which means not one, whether in human or diabolical form—"shall make them afraid." Who shall terrify the Lord's flock when he is near? We lie down in green pastures, for Jesus himself is food and rest to our souls.

"Fear not ; for thou shalt not be ashamed."—Isa. liv. 4.

WE shall not be ashamed of our *faith.* Carping critics may assail the Scriptures upon which we ground our belief, but every year the Lord will make it more and more clear that in his Book there is no error, no excess, and no omission. It is no discredit to be a simple believer ; the faith which looks alone to Jesus is a crown of honour on any man's head, and better than a star on his breast.

We shall not be ashamed of our *hope.* It shall be even as the Lord has said. We shall be fed, led, blest and rested. Our Lord will come, and then the days of our mourning shall be ended. How we shall glory in the Lord who first gave us lively hope, and then gave us that which we hoped for !

We shall not be ashamed of our *love.* Jesus is to us the altogether lovely, and never, never, shall we have to blush because we have yielded our hearts to him. The sight of our glorious Wellbeloved will justify the most enthusiastic attachment to him. None will blame the martyrs for dying for him. When the enemies of Christ are clothed with everlasting contempt, the lovers of Jesus shall find themselves honoured by all holy beings, because they chose the reproach of Christ rather than the treasures of Egypt.

"Israel then shall dwell in safety alone: the fountain of Jacob shall be upon a land of corn and wine; also his heavens shall drop down dew."—Deut. xxxiii. 28.

THE more we dwell alone, the more safe shall we be. God would have his people separate from sinners. His call to them is, "Come ye out from among them." A Christian world is such a monstrosity as the Scriptures never contemplate. A worldly Christian is spiritually diseased. Those who compromise with Christ's enemies may be reckoned with them.

Our safety lies, not in making terms with the enemy, but in dwelling alone with our best Friend. If we do this, we shall dwell in safety, despite the sarcasms, the slanders, and the sneers of the world. We shall be safe from the baleful influence of its unbelief, its pride, its vanity, its filthiness.

God also will make us dwell in safety alone in that day when sin shall be visited on the nations by wars and famines.

The Lord brought Abram from Ur of the Chaldees, but he stopped half-way. He had no blessing till, having set out to go to the land of Canaan, to the land of Canaan he came. He was safe alone even in the midst of foes. Lot was not safe in Sodom though in a circle of friends. Our safety is in dwelling apart with God.

"I the Lord do keep it ; I will water it every moment : lest any hurt it, I will keep it night and day."—Isa. xxvii. 3.

WHEN the Lord himself speaks in his own proper person rather than through a prophet, the word has a peculiar weight to believing minds. It is Jehovah himself who is the keeper of his own vineyard ; he does not trust it to any other, but he makes it his own personal care. Are they not well kept whom God himself keeps ?

We are to receive gracious watering, not only every day and every hour, "but every moment." How we ought to grow ! How fresh and fruitful every plant should be ! What rich clusters the vines should bear !

But disturbers come ; little foxes and the boar. Therefore, the Lord himself is our guardian, and that at all hours, both "night and day." What, then, can harm us ? Why are we afraid ? He tends, he waters, he guards ; what more do we need ?

Twice in this verse the Lord says, "I will." What truth, what power, what love, what immutability we find in the great "I will" of Jehovah ! Who can resist his will ? If he says "I will," what room is there for doubt ? With an "I will" of God we can face all the hosts of sin, death, and hell. O Lord, since thou sayest, "I will keep thee," I reply, "I will praise thee !"

"For the Lord will not forsake his people for his great name's sake; because it hath pleased the Lord to make you his people."—1 Sam. xii. 22.

GOD'S choice of his people is the reason for his abiding by them, and not forsaking them. He chose them for his love, and he loves them for his choice. His own good pleasure is the source of their election, and his election is the reason for the continuance of his pleasure in them. It would dishonour his great name for him to forsake them, since it would either show that he made an error in his choice, or that he was fickle in his love. God's love has this glory, that it never changes, and this glory he will never tarnish.

By all the memories of the Lord's former lovingkindnesses let us rest assured that he will not forsake us. He who has gone so far as to make us his people, will not undo the creation of his grace. He has not wrought such wonders for us that he might leave us after all. His Son Jesus has died for us, and we may be sure that he has not died in vain. Can he forsake those for whom he shed his blood? Because he has hitherto taken pleasure in choosing and in saving us, it will be his pleasure still to bless us. Our Lord Jesus is no changeable Lover. Having loved his own, he loves them to the end.

"The Lord shall bless thee out of Zion: and thou shalt see the good of Jerusalem all the days of thy life."—Ps. cxxviii. 5.

THIS is a promise to the God-fearing man who walks in the ways of holiness with earnest heed. He shall have domestic blessedness; his wife and children shall be a source of great home happiness. But then as a member of the church he desires to see the cause prosper, for he is as much concerned for the Lord's house as for his own. When the Lord builds our house, it is but fitting that we should desire to see the Lord's house builded. Our goods are not truly good unless we promote by them the good of the Lord's chosen church.

Yes, you shall get a blessing when you go up to the assemblies of Zion; you shall be instructed, enlivened, and comforted, where prayer and praise ascend, and testimony is borne to the Great Sacrifice. "The Lord shall bless thee out of Zion."

Nor shall you alone be profited; the church itself shall prosper; believers shall be multiplied, and their holy work shall be crowned with success. Certain gracious men have this promise fulfilled to them as long as they live. Alas! when they die the cause often flags. Let us be among those who bring good things to Jerusalem all their days. Lord, of thy mercy make us such! Amen.

"For whosoever hath, to him shall be given, and he shall have more abundance."—Matt. xiii. 12.

WHEN the Lord has given to a man much grace he will give him more. A little faith is a nest egg; more faith will come to it. But then it must not be seeming faith, but real and true. What a necessity is laid upon us to make sure work in religion, and not to profess much, and possess nothing! for one of these days the very profession will be taken from us, if that be all we have. The threatening is as true as the promise.

Blessed be the Lord, it is his way when he has once made a beginning to go on bestowing the graces of his Spirit, till he who had but little, and yet truly had that little, is made to have abundance. Oh, for that abundance! Abundance of grace is a thing to be coveted. It would be well to *know* much, but better to *love* much. It would be delightful to have abundance of skill to serve God, but better still to have abundance of faith to trust in the Lord for skill and everything.

Lord, since thou hast given me a sense of sin, deepen my hatred of evil. Since thou hast caused me to trust Jesus, raise my faith to full assurance. Since thou hast made me to love thee, cause me to be carried away with vehement affection for thee!

"For the Lord your God is he that goeth with you, to fight for you against your enemies, to save you."—Deut. xx. 4.

WE have no enemies but the enemies of God. Our fights are not against men, but against spiritual wickednesses. We war with the devil, and the blasphemy, and error, and despair, which he brings into the field of battle. We fight with all the armies of sin—impurity, drunkenness, oppression, infidelity, and ungodliness. With these we contend earnestly, but not with sword or spear; the weapons of our warfare are not carnal.

Jehovah, our God, abhors everything which is evil, and, therefore, he goeth with us to fight for us in this crusade. He will save us, and he will give us grace to war a good warfare, and win the victory. We may depend upon it that if we are on God's side God is on our side. With such an august ally the conflict is never in the least degree doubtful. It is not that truth is mighty and must prevail, but that might lies with the Father who is Almighty, with Jesus who has all power in heaven and in earth, and with the Holy Spirit who worketh his will among men.

Soldiers of Christ, gird on your armour. Strike home in the name of the God of holiness, and by faith grasp his salvation. Let not this day pass without striking a blow for Jesus and holiness.

"Now will I rise, saith the Lord; now will I be exalted; now will I lift up myself." —Isa. xxxiii. 10.

WHEN the spoilers had made the land as waste as if devoured by locusts, and the warriors who had defended the country sat down and wept like women, then the Lord came to the rescue. When travellers ceased from the roads to Zion, and Bashan and Carmel were as vineyards from which the fruit has failed, then the Lord arose. God is exalted in the midst of an afflicted people, for they seek his face and trust him. He is still more exalted when in answer to their cries he lifts up himself to deliver them and overthrow their enemies.

Is it a day of sorrow with us? Let us now expect to see the Lord glorified in our deliverance. Are we drawn out in fervent prayer? Do we cry day and night unto him? Then the set time for his grace is near. God will lift up himself at the right season. He will arise when it will be most for the display of his glory. We wish for his glory more than we long for our own deliverance. Let the Lord be exalted, and our chief desire is obtained.

Lord, help us in such a way that we may see that thou thyself art working. May we magnify thee in our inmost souls. Make all around us to see how good and great a God thou art.

"Let my heart be sound in thy statutes: that I be not ashamed."—Ps. cxix. 80.

WE may regard this inspired prayer as containing within itself the assurance that those who keep close to the Word of God shall never have cause to be ashamed of doing so.

See, the prayer is for soundness of heart. A sound creed is good, a sound judgment concerning it is better, but a sound heart towards the truth is best of all. We must love the truth, feel the truth, and obey the truth, otherwise we are not truly sound in God's statutes. Are there many in these evil days who are sound ? Oh, that the writer and the reader may be two of this sort !

Many will be ashamed in the last great day, when all disputes will be decided. Then they will see the folly of their inventions, and be filled with remorse because of their proud infidelity and wilful defiance of the Lord ; but he who believed what the Lord taught, and did what the Lord commanded, will stand forth justified in what he did. Then shall the righteous shine forth as the sun. Men much slandered and abused shall find their shame turned into glory in that day.

Let us pray the prayer of our text, and we may be sure that its promise will be fulfilled to us. If the Lord makes us sound, he will keep us safe.

"Yea, though I walk through the valley of the shadow of death, I will fear no evil: for thou art with me; thy rod and thy staff they comfort me."—Ps. xxiii. 4.

SWEET are these words in describing a deathbed assurance. How many have repeated them in their last hours with intense delight!

But the verse is equally applicable to agonies of spirit in the midst of life. Some of us, like Paul, die daily through a tendency to gloom of soul. Bunyan puts the Valley of the Shadow of Death far earlier in the pilgrimage than the river which rolls at the foot of the celestial hills. We have some of us traversed the dark and dreadful defile of "the shadow of death" several times, and we can bear witness that the Lord alone enabled us to bear up amid its wild thoughts, its mysterious horrors, its terrible depressions. The Lord has sustained us, and kept us above all real fear of evil, even when our spirit has been overwhelmed. We have been pressed and oppressed, but yet we have lived, for we have felt the presence of the Great Shepherd, and have been confident that his crook would prevent the foe from giving us any deadly wound.

Should the present time be one darkened by the raven wings of a great sorrow, let us glorify God by a peaceful trust in him.

"The Lord shall sell Sisera into the hand of a woman."
Judges iv. 9.

RATHER an unusual text, but there may be souls in the world that may have faith enough to grasp it. Barak, the man, though called to the war, had little stomach for the fight unless Deborah would go with him, and so the Lord determined to make it a woman's war. By this means he rebuked the slackness of the man, and gained for himself the more renown, and cast the more shame upon the enemies of his people.

The Lord can still use feeble instrumentalities. Why not me? He may use persons who are not commonly called to great public engagements. Why not you? The woman who slew the enemy of Israel was no Amazon, but a wife who tarried in her tent. She was no orator, but a woman who milked the cows and made butter. May not the Lord use any one of us to accomplish his purpose? Somebody may come to the house to-day, even as Sisera came to Jael's tent. Be it ours, not to slay him, but to save him. Let us receive him with great kindness, and then bring forth the blessed truth of salvation by the Lord Jesus, our great Substitute, and press home the command, "Believe and live." Who knoweth but some stout-hearted sinner may be slain by the gospel to-day?

"The fear of the Lord prolongeth days: but the years of the wicked shall be shortened."—Prov. x. 27.

THERE is no doubt about it. The fear of the Lord leads to virtuous habits, and these prevent that waste of life which comes of sin and vice. The holy rest which springs out of faith in the Lord Jesus also greatly helps a man when he is ill. Every physician rejoices to have a patient whose mind is fully at ease. Worry kills, but confidence in God is like healing medicine.

We have therefore all the arrangements for long life, and if it be really for our good, we shall see a good old age, and come to our graves as shocks of corn in their season. Let us not be overcome with sudden expectation of death the moment we have a finger-ache, but let us rather expect that we may have to work on through a considerable length of days.

And what if we should soon be called to the higher sphere? Certainly there would be nothing to deplore in such a summons, but everything to rejoice in. Living or dying we are the Lord's. If we live, Jesus will be with us; if we die, we shall be with Jesus.

The truest lengthening of life is to live while we live, wasting no time, but using every hour for the highest ends. So be it this day.

"Therefore thus saith the Lord concerning the king of Assyria, He shall not come into this city, nor shoot an arrow there, nor come before it with shield, nor cast a bank against it."—2 Kings xix. 32.

NEITHER did Sennacherib molest the city. He had boasted loudly, but he could not carry out his threats. The Lord is able to stop the enemies of his people in the very act. When the lion has the lamb between his jaws, the great Shepherd of the sheep can rob him of his prey. Our extremity only provides an opportunity for a grander display of divine power and wisdom.

In the case before us, the terrible foe did not put in an appearance before the city which he thirsted to destroy. No annoying arrow could he shoot over the walls, and no besieging engines could he put to work to batter down the castles, and no banks could he cast up to shut in the inhabitants. Perhaps in our case also the Lord will prevent our adversaries from doing us the least harm. Certainly he can alter their intentions, or render their designs so abortive that they will gladly forego them. Let us trust in the Lord and keep his way, and he will take care of us. Yea, he will fill us with wondering praise as we see the perfection of his deliverance.

Let us not fear the enemy till he actually comes, and then let us trust in the Lord.

"And Amaziah said to the man of God, But what shall we do for the hundred talents which I have given to the army of Israel? And the man of God answered, The Lord is able to give thee much more than this."
2 Chron. xxv. 9.

IF you have made a mistake, bear the loss of it; but do not act contrary to the will of the Lord. The Lord can give you much more than you are likely to lose; and if he does not, will you begin bargaining and chaffering with God? The king of Judah had hired an army from idolatrous Israel, and he was commanded to send home the fighting men because the Lord was not with them. He was willing to send away the host, only he grudged paying the hundred talents for nothing. Oh for shame! If the Lord will give the victory without the hirelings, surely it was a good bargain to pay their wages and to be rid of them.

Be willing to lose money for conscience sake, for peace sake, for Christ's sake. Rest assured that losses for the Lord are not losses. Even in this life they are more than recompensed: in some cases the Lord prevents any loss from happening. As to our immortal life, what we lose for Jesus is invested in heaven. Fret not at apparent disaster, but listen to the whisper, "The Lord is able to give thee much more than this."

"And he saith unto him, Verily, verily, I say unto you, Hereafter ye shall see heaven open, and the angels of God ascending and descending upon the Son of man."—John i. 51.

YES, to our faith this sight is plain even at this day. We do see heaven opened. Jesus himself has opened that kingdom to all believers. We gaze into the place of mystery and glory, for he has revealed it to us. We shall enter it soon, for he is the way.

Now we see the explanation of Jacob's ladder. Between earth and heaven there is a holy commerce; prayer ascends, and answers come down, by the way of Jesus, the Mediator. We see this ladder when we see our Lord. In him a stair-way of light now furnishes a clear passage to the throne of the Most High. Let us use it, and send up by it the messengers of our prayers. We shall live the angelic life ourselves if we run up to heaven in intercession, and lay hold upon the blessings of the covenant, and then descend again to scatter those gifts among the sons of men.

This choice sight which Jacob only saw in a dream we will turn into a bright reality. This very day we will be up and down the ladder each hour; climbing in communion, and coming down in labour to save our fellow-men. This is thy promise, O Lord Jesus, let us joyfully see it fulfilled.

"Be ye also patient; stablish your hearts: for the coming of the Lord draweth nigh."—James v. 8.

THE last word in the Canticle of love is, " Make haste, my beloved," and among the last words of the Apocalypse we read, " The Spirit and the Bride say, Come "; to which the heavenly Bridegroom answers, " Surely I come quickly." Love longs for the glorious appearing of the Lord, and enjoys this sweet promise—" The coming of the Lord draweth nigh." This stays our minds as to the future. We look out with hope through this window.

This sacred " window of agate " lets in a flood of light upon the present, and puts us into fine condition for immediate work or suffering. Are we tried? Then the nearness of our joy whispers patience. Are we growing weary because we do not see the harvest of our seed-sowing? Again this glorious truth cries to us, " Be patient." Do our multiplied temptations cause us in the least to waver? Then the assurance, that before long the Lord will be here, preaches to us from this text, " Stablish your hearts." Be firm, be stable, be constant, "stedfast, unmoveable, always abounding in the work of the Lord." Soon will you hear the silver trumpets which announce the coming of your King. Be not in the least afraid. Hold the fort, for he is coming; yea, he may appear this very day.

"Surely the righteous shall give thanks unto thy name: the upright shall dwell in thy presence."—Ps. cxl. 13.

OH that my heart may be upright, that I may always be able to bless the name of the Lord! He is so good to those that be good, that I would fain be among them, and feel myself full of thankfulness every day. Perhaps, for a moment, the righteous are staggered when their integrity results in severe trial; but assuredly the day shall come when they shall bless their God that they did not yield to evil suggestions and adopt a shifty policy. In the long run true men will thank the God of the right for leading them by a right way. Oh that I may be among them!

What a promise is implied in this second clause, "The upright shall dwell in thy presence"! They shall stand accepted where others appear only to be condemned. They shall be the courtiers of the Great King, indulged with audience whensoever they desire it. They shall be favoured ones upon whom Jehovah smiles, and with whom he graciously communes. Lord, I covet this high honour, this precious privilege: it will be heaven on earth to me to enjoy it. Make me in all things upright, that I may to-day, and to-morrow, and every day stand in thy heavenly presence. Then will I give thanks unto thy name evermore. Amen.

"And the Lord looked upon him, and said, Go in this thy might, and thou shalt save Israel from the hand of the Midianites: have not I sent thee?"—Judges vi. 14.

WHAT a look was that which the Lord gave to Gideon! He looked him out of his discouragements into a holy bravery. If our look to the Lord saves us, what will not his look at us do? Lord, look on me this day, and nerve me for its duties and conflicts.

What a word was this which Jehovah spake to Gideon! "Go." He must not hesitate. He might have answered, "What, go in all this weakness!" But the Lord put that word out of court by saying, "Go in this thy might." The Lord had looked might into him, and he had now nothing to do but to use it, and save Israel by smiting the Midianites. It may be that the Lord has more to do by me than I ever dreamed of. If he has looked upon me he has made me strong. Let me by faith exercise the power with which he has entrusted me. He never bids me "idle away my time in this my might." Far from it. I must "go," because he strengthens me.

What a question is that which the Lord puts to me even as he put it to Gideon! "Have not I sent thee?" Yes, Lord, thou hast sent me, and I will go in thy strength. At thy command I go, and, going, I am assured that thou wilt conquer by me.

"Call unto me, and I will answer thee, and shew thee great and mighty things, which thou knowest not."
Jer. xxxiii. 3.

GOD encourages us to pray. They tell us that prayer is a pious exercise which has no influence except upon the mind engaged in it. We know better. Our experience gives the lie a thousand times over to this infidel assertion. Here Jehovah, the living God, distinctly promises to answer the prayer of his servant. Let us call upon him again, and admit no doubt upon the question of his hearing us and answering us. He that made the ear, shall he not hear? He that gave parents a love to their children, will he not listen to the cries of his own sons and daughters?

God will answer his pleading people in their anguish. He has wonders in store for them. What they have never seen, heard of, or dreamed of, he will do for them. He will invent new blessings if needful. He will ransack sea and land to feed them: he will send every angel out of heaven to succour them, if their distress requires it. He will astound us with his grace, and make us feel that it was never before done in this fashion. All he asks of us is that we will call upon him. He cannot ask less of us. Let us cheerfully render him our prayers at once.

> *"Nevertheless I will remember my covenant with thee in the days of thy youth, and I will establish unto thee an everlasting covenant."*—Ez. xvi. 60.

NOTWITHSTANDING our sins the Lord is still faithful in his love to us.

He looks back. See how he remembers those early days of ours when he took us into covenant with himself, and we gave ourselves over to him. Happy days those! The Lord does not twit us with them, and charge us with being insincere. No, he looks rather to his covenant with us than to our covenant with him. There was no hypocrisy in that sacred compact, on his part, at any rate. How gracious is the Lord thus to look back in love!

He looks forward also. He is resolved that the covenant shall not fail. If *we* do not stand to it, *he* does. He solemnly declares, "I will establish unto thee an everlasting covenant." He has no mind to draw back from his promises. Blessed be his name, he sees the sacred seal, "the blood of the everlasting covenant," and he remembers our Surety, in whom he ratified that covenant, even his own dear Son; and therefore he rests in his covenant engagements. "He abideth faithful; he cannot deny himself."

O Lord, lay this precious word upon my heart, and help me to feed upon it all this day!

"*God shall be with you.*"—Gen. xlviii. 21.

GOOD old Jacob could no more be with Joseph, for his hour had come to die: but he left his son without anxiety, for he said with confidence, "God shall be with you." When our dearest relations, or our most helpful friends, are called home by death, we must console ourselves with the reflection that the Lord is not departed from us, but lives for us, and abides with us for ever.

If God be with us, we are in ennobling company, even though we are poor and despised. If God be with us, we have all-sufficient strength, for nothing can be too hard for the Lord. If God be with us, we are always safe, for none can harm those who walk under his shadow. Oh, what a joy we have here! Not only *is* God with us, but he *will be* with us. With us as individuals; with us as families; with us as churches. Is not the very name of Jesus, Immanuel—God with us? Is not this the best of all, that God is with us? Let us be bravely diligent, and joyously hopeful. Our cause must prosper, the truth must win, for the Lord is with those who are with him.

All this day may this sweet word be enjoyed by every believer who turns to "Faith's Cheque Book" No greater happiness is possible.

"So he giveth his beloved sleep."—Ps. cxxvii. 2.

OURS is not a life of anxious care, but of happy faith. Our heavenly Father will supply the wants of his own children, and he knoweth what we have need of before we ask him. We may therefore go to our beds at the proper hour, and not wear ourselves out by sitting up late to plot, and plan, and contrive. If we have learned to rely upon our God we shall not lie awake with fear gnawing at our hearts ; but we shall leave our care with the Lord, our meditation of him shall be sweet, and he will give us refreshing sleep.

To be the Lord's beloved is the highest possible honour, and he who has it may feel that ambition itself could desire no more, and therefore every selfish wish may go to sleep. What more is there even in heaven than the love of God ? Rest, then, O soul, for thou hast all things.

Yet we toss to and fro unless the Lord himself gives us not only the reasons for rest, but rest itself. Yea, he doth this. Jesus himself is our peace, our rest, our all. On his bosom we sleep in perfect security, both in life and in death.

> " Sprinkled afresh with pardoning blood,
>   I lay me down to rest,
>   As in the embraces of my God,
>   Or on my Saviour's breast."

"He will be our guide even unto death."—Ps. xlviii. 14.

WE need a guide. Sometimes we would give all that we have to be told exactly what to do, and where to turn. We are willing to do right, but we do not know which out of two roads we are to follow. Oh, for a guide!

The Lord our God condescends to serve us as guide. He knows the way, and will pilot us along it till we reach our journey's end in peace. Surely we do not desire more infallible direction. Let us place ourselves absolutely under his guidance, and we shall never miss our way. Let us make him our God, and we shall find him our guide. If we follow his law we shall not miss the right road of life, provided we first learn to lean upon him in every step that we take.

Our comfort is, that as he is our God for ever and ever, he will never cease to be with us as our guide. "Even unto death" will he lead us, and then we shall dwell with him eternally, and go no more out for ever. This promise of divine guidance involves life-long security: salvation at once, guidance unto our last hour, and then endless blessedness. Should not each one seek this in youth, rejoice in it in middle life, and repose in it in old age? This day let us look up for guidance before we trust ourselves out of doors.

"Man shall not live by bread alone, but by every word that proceedeth out of the mouth of God."—Matt. iv. 4.

IF God so willed it we could live without bread, even as Jesus did for forty days; but we could not live without his Word. By that Word we were created, and by it alone can we be kept in being, for he sustaineth all things by the Word of his power. Bread is a second cause; the Lord himself is the first source of our sustenance. He can work without the second cause as well as with it; and we must not tie him down to one mode of operation. Let us not be too eager after the visible, but let us look to the invisible God. We have heard believers say that in deep poverty, when bread ran short, their appetites became short too; and to others, when common supplies failed, the Lord has sent in unexpected help.

But we must have the Word of the Lord. With this alone we can withstand the devil. Take this from us, and our enemy will have us in his power, for we shall soon faint. Our souls need food, and there is none for them outside of the Word of the Lord. All the books and all the preachers in the world cannot furnish us a single meal: it is only the Word from the mouth of God that can fill the mouth of a believer. Lord, evermore give us this bread. We prize it above royal dainties.

"But I will deliver thee in that day, saith the Lord: and thou shalt not be given into the hand of the men of whom thou art afraid."—Jer. xxxix. 17.

WHEN the Lord's faithful ones are suffering for him, they shall have sweet messages of love from himself, and sometimes they shall have glad tidings for those who sympathize with them and help them. Ebed-melech was only a despised Ethiopian, but he was kind to Jeremiah, and so the Lord sent him this special promise by the mouth of his prophet. Let us be ever mindful of God's persecuted servants, and he will reward us.

Ebed-melech was to be delivered from the men whose vengeance he feared. He was only a poor black man, but Jehovah would take care of him. Thousands were slain by the Chaldeans, but this lowly negro could not be hurt. We, too, may be fearful of some great ones who are bitter against us; but if we have been faithful to the Lord's cause in the hour of persecution, he will be faithful to us. After all, what can man do without the Lord's permission? He puts a bit into the mouth of rage, and a bridle upon the head of power. Let us fear the Lord, and we shall have no one else to fear. No cup of cold water given to a despised prophet of God shall be without its reward; and if we stand up for Jesus, Jesus will stand up for us.

"For God so loved the world, that he gave his only-begotten Son, that whosoever believeth in him should not perish, but have everlasting life."—John iii. 16.

OF all the stars in the sky the pole-star is the most useful to the mariner. This text is a pole-star, for it has guided more souls to salvation than any other Scripture. It is among promises what the Great Bear is among constellations.

Several words in it shine with peculiar brilliance. Here we have *God's love*, with a SO to it, which marks its measureless greatness. Then we have *God's gift* in all its freeness and greatness. This also is *God's Son*, that unique and priceless gift of a love which could never fully show itself till heaven's Only-begotten had been sent to live and die for men. These three points are full of light.

Then there is *the simple requirement* of believing, which graciously points to a way of salvation suitable for guilty men. This is backed by *a wide description*—"whosoever believeth in him." Many have found room in "whosoever" who would have felt themselves shut out by a narrower word. Then comes *the great promise*, that believers in Jesus shall not perish, but have everlasting life. This is cheering to every man who feels that he is ready to perish, and that he cannot save himself. We believe in the Lord Jesus, and we have eternal life.

"*Sing, O heavens; and be joyful, O earth; and break forth into singing, O mountains: for the Lord hath comforted his people, and will have mercy upon his afflicted.*"
Isa. xlix. 13.

SO sweet are the comforts of the Lord, that not only the saints themselves may sing of them, but even the heavens and the earth may take up the song. It takes something to make a mountain sing; and yet the prophet summons quite a choir of them. Lebanon, and Sirion, and the high hills of Bashan and Moab, he would set them all singing because of Jehovah's grace to his own Zion. May we not also make mountains of difficulty, and trial, and mystery, and labour become occasions for praise unto our God? "Break forth into singing, O mountains!"

This word of promise, that our God will have mercy upon his afflicted, has a whole peal of bells connected with it. Hear their music—"Sing!" "Be joyful!" "Break forth into singing." The Lord would have his people happy because of his unfailing love. He would not have us sad and doubtful; he claims from us the worship of believing hearts. He cannot fail us: why should we sigh or sulk as if he would do so? Oh for a well-tuned harp! Oh for voices like those of the cherubim before the throne!

"The angel of the Lord encampeth round about them that fear him, and delivereth them." —Ps. xxxiv. 7.

WE cannot see the angels, but it is enough that they can see us. There is one great Angel of the Covenant, whom not having seen we love, and his eye is always upon us both day and night. He has a host of holy ones under him, and he causes these to be watchers over his saints and to guard them from all ill. If devils do us mischief, shining ones do us service.

Note that the Lord of angels does not come and go, and pay us transient visits, but he and his armies encamp around us. The head-quarters of the army of salvation are where those live whose trust is in the living God. This camp surrounds the faithful, so that they cannot be attacked from any quarter unless the adversary can break through the entrenchments of the Lord of angels. We have a fixed protection, a permanent watch. Sentinelled by the messengers of God, we shall not be surprised by sudden assaults, nor swallowed up by overwhelming forces. Deliverance is promised in this verse—deliverance by the great Captain of our salvation, and that deliverance we shall obtain again and again until our warfare is accomplished and we exchange the field of conflict for the home of rest.

"Mine eyes shall be upon the faithful of the land, that they may dwell with me: he that walketh in a perfect way, he shall serve me."—Ps. ci. 6.

IF David spoke thus, we may be sure that the Son of David will be of the same mind. Jesus looks out for faithful men, and he fixes his eyes upon them, to observe them, to bring them forward, to encourage them, and to reward them. Let no true-hearted man think that he is overlooked; the King himself has his eye upon him.

There are two results of this royal notice. First we read, "that they may dwell with me." Jesus brings the faithful into his house, he sets them in his palace, he makes them his companions, he delights in their society. We must be true to our Lord, and he will then manifest himself to us. When our faithfulness costs us most it will be best rewarded; the more furiously men reject the more joyfully will our Lord receive us.

Next, he says of the sincere man, " he shall serve me." Jesus will use for his own glory those who scorn the tricks of policy, and are faithful to himself, his Word, and his Cross. These shall be in his royal retinue, the honoured servants of his Majesty. Communion and usefulness are the wages of faithfulness. Lord make me faithful, that I may dwell with thee, and serve thee.

"Thou shalt arise, and have mercy upon Zion: for the time to favour her, yea, the set time, is come. For thy servants take pleasure in her stones, and favour the dust thereof."—Ps. cii. 13, 14.

YES, our prayers for the church will be heard. The set time is come. We love the prayer meeting, and the Sunday-school, and all the services of the Lord's house. We are bound in heart to all the people of God, and can truly say,

> "There's not a lamb in all thy flock
>   I would disdain to feed;
> There's not a foe before whose face
>   I'd fear thy cause to plead."

If this is the general feeling, we shall soon enjoy times of refreshing from the presence of the Lord. Our assemblies will be filled, saints will be revived, and sinners will be converted. This can only come of the Lord's mercy; but it will come, and we are called upon to expect it. The time, the set time, is come. Let us bestir ourselves. Let us love every stone of our Zion, even though it may be fallen down. Let us treasure up the least truth, the least ordinance, the least believer, even though some may despise them as only so much dust. When we favour Zion, God is about to favour her. When we take pleasure in the Lord's work, the Lord himself will take pleasure in it.

"And whosoever liveth and believeth in me shall never die. Believest thou this?"—John xi. 26.

YES, Lord, we believe it; we shall never die. Our soul may be separated from our body, and this is death of a kind; but our soul shall never be separated from God, which is the true death—the death which was threatened to sin—the death penalty which is the worst that can happen. We believe this most assuredly, for who shall separate us from the love of God which is in Christ Jesus our Lord? We are members of the body of Christ; will Christ lose parts of his body? We are married to Jesus; will he be bereaved and widowed? It is not possible. There is a life within us which is not capable of being divided from God: yea, and the Holy Spirit dwells within us, and how then can we die? Jesus, himself, is our life, and therefore there is no dying for us, for he cannot die again. In him we died unto sin once, and the capital sentence cannot a second time be executed. Now we live, and live for ever. The reward of righteousness is life everlasting, and we have nothing less than the righteousness of God, and therefore can claim the very highest reward.

Living and believing, we believe that we shall live and enjoy. Wherefore we press forward with full assurance that our life is secure in our living Head.

"The Lord knoweth how to deliver the godly out of temptations, and to reserve the unjust unto the day of judgment to be punished."—2 Peter ii. 9.

THE godly are tempted and tried. That is not true faith which is never put to the test. But the godly are delivered out of their trials, and that not by chance, nor by secondary agencies, but by the Lord himself. He personally undertakes the office of delivering those who trust him. God loves the godly or godlike, and he makes a point of knowing where they are, and how they fare.

Sometimes their way seems to be a labyrinth, and they cannot imagine how they are to escape from threatening danger. What they do not know their Lord knows. He knows whom to deliver, and when to deliver, and how to deliver. He delivers in the way which is most beneficial to the godly, most crushing to the tempter, and most glorifying to himself. We may leave the " how " with the Lord, and be content to rejoice in the fact that he will, in some way or other, bring his own people through all the dangers, trials, and temptations of this mortal life, to his own right hand in glory.

This day it is not for me to pry into my Lord's secrets, but patiently to wait his time, knowing this, that though I know nothing, my heavenly Father knows.

"For I will surely deliver thee, and thou shalt not fall by the sword, but thy life shall be for a prey unto thee: because thou hast put thy trust in me, saith the Lord."
Jer. xxxix. 18.

BEHOLD the protecting power of trust in God. The great men of Jerusalem fell by the sword, but poor Ebed-melech was secure, for his confidence was in Jehovah. Where else should a man trust but in his Maker? We are foolish when we prefer the creature to the Creator. Oh, that we could in all things live by faith, then should we be delivered in all time of danger! No one ever did trust in the Lord in vain, and no one ever shall.

The Lord saith, "I will surely deliver thee." Mark the divine "surely." Whatever else may be uncertain, God's care of believers is sure. God himself is the guardian of the gracious. Under his sacred wing there is safety even when every danger is abroad. Can we accept this promise as sure? Then in our present emergency we shall find that it stands fast. We hope to be delivered because we have friends, or because we are prudent, or because we can see hopeful signs; but none of these things are one half so good as God's simple "because thou hast put thy trust in me." Dear reader, try this way, and, trying it, you will keep to it all your life. It is as sweet as it is sure.

"Cast thy burden upon the Lord, and he shall sustain thee: he shall never suffer the righteous to be moved."
Ps. lv. 22.

IT is a heavy burden, roll it on Omnipotence. It is thy burden now, and it crushes thee; but when the Lord takes it, he will make nothing of it. If thou art called still to bear it, "he will sustain thee." It will be on thee, and not on thee. Thou wilt be so upheld under it that the burden will be a blessing. Bring the Lord into the matter and thou wilt stand upright under that which in itself would bow thee down.

Our worst fear is lest our trial should drive us from the path of duty; but this the Lord will never suffer. If we are righteous before him he will not endure that our affliction should move us from our standing. In Jesus he accepts us as righteous, and in Jesus he will keep us so.

What about the present moment? Art thou going forth to this day's trial alone? Are thy poor shoulders again to be galled with the oppressive load? Be not so foolish. Tell the Lord all about thy grief, and leave it with him. Don't cast your burden down, and then take it up again; but roll it on the Lord, and leave it there. Then shalt thou walk at large, a joyful and unburdened believer, singing the praises of thy great Burden-bearer.

"Blessed are they that mourn: for they shall be comforted."—Matt. v. 4.

BY the valley of weeping we come to Zion. One would have thought mourning and being blessed were in opposition, but the infinitely wise Saviour puts them together, in this beatitude. What he has joined together let no man put asunder. Mourning for sin—our own sins, and the sins of others—is the Lord's seal set upon his faithful ones. When the Spirit of grace is poured upon the house of David, or any other house, they shall mourn. By holy mourning we receive the best of our blessings, even as the rarest commodities come to us by water. Not only shall the mourner be blessed at some future day, but Christ pronounces him blessed even now.

The Holy Spirit will surely comfort those hearts which mourn for sin. They shall be comforted by the application of the blood of Jesus, and by the cleansing power of the Holy Ghost. They shall be comforted as to the abounding sin of their city and of their age by the assurance that God will glorify himself, however much men may rebel against him. They shall be comforted with the expectation that they shall be wholly freed from sin before long, and shall soon be taken up to dwell for ever in the glorious presence of their Lord.

"I will save her that halteth."—Zeph. iii. 19.

THERE are plenty of these lame ones, both male and female. You may meet "her that halteth" twenty times in an hour. They are in the right road, and exceedingly anxious to run in it with diligence, but they are lame, and make a sorry walk of it. On the heavenly road there are many cripples. It may be that they say in their hearts—What will become of us? Sin will overtake us, Satan will throw us down. Ready-to-halt is our name and our nature; the Lord can never make good soldiers of us, nor even nimble messengers to go on his errands. Well, well! he will save us, and that is no small thing. He says, "I will save her that halteth." In saving us he will greatly glorify himself. Everybody will ask—How came this lame woman to run the race and win the crown? And then the praise will all be given to almighty grace.

Lord, though I halt in faith, in prayer, in praise, in service, and in patience, save me, I beseech thee! Only thou canst save such a cripple as I am. Lord, let me not perish because I am among the hindmost, but gather up by thy grace the slowest of thy pilgrims—even me. Behold he hath said it shall be so, and therefore, like Jacob, prevailing in prayer, I go forward though my sinew be shrunk.

"The people that do know their God shall be strong, and do exploits."—Dan. xi. 32.

"THE Lord is a man of war, Jehovah is his name." Those who enlist under his banner shall have a commander who will train them for the conflict, and give them both vigour and valour. The times of which Daniel wrote were of the very worst kind, and then it was promised that the people of God would come out in their best colours: they would be strong and stout to confront the powerful adversary.

Oh, that we may know our God; his power, his faithfulness, his immutable love, and so may be ready to risk everything in his behalf. He is one whose character excites our enthusiasm, and makes us willing to live and to die for him. Oh, that we may know our God by familiar fellowship with him; for then we shall become like him, and shall be prepared to stand up for truth and righteousness. He who comes forth fresh from beholding the face of God will never fear the face of man. If we dwell with him, we shall catch the heroic spirit, and to us a world of enemies will be but as the drop of a bucket. A countless array of men, or even of devils, will seem as little to us as the nations are to God, and he counts them only as grasshoppers. Oh, to be valiant for truth in this day of falsehood.

"I will allure her, and bring her into the wilderness, and speak comfortably unto her."—Hosea ii. 14.

THE goodness of God sees us allured by sin, and it resolves to try upon us the more powerful allurements of love. Do we not remember when the Lover of our souls first cast a spell upon us and charmed us away from the fascinations of the world? He will do this again and again whenever he sees us likely to be ensnared by evil.

He promises to draw us apart, for there he can best deal with us, and this separated place is not to be a Paradise, but a wilderness, since in such a place there will be nothing to take off our attention from our God. In the deserts of affliction the presence of the Lord becomes everything to us, and we prize his company beyond any value which we set upon it when we sat under our own vine and fig-tree in the society of our fellows. Solitude and affliction bring more to themselves and to their heavenly Father than any other means.

When thus allured and secluded the Lord has choice things to say to us for our comfort. He "speaks to our heart," as the original has it. Oh that at this time we may have this promise explained in our experience! Allured by love, separated by trial, and comforted by the Spirit of truth, may we know the Lord and sing for joy!

"Thy shoes shall be iron and brass; and as thy days, so shall thy strength be."—Deut. xxxiii. 25.

HERE are two things provided for the pilgrim: shoes and strength.

As for the shoes: they are very needful for travelling along rough ways, and for trampling upon deadly foes. We shall not go barefoot—this would not be suitable for princes of the blood royal. Our shoes shall not be at all of the common sort, for they shall have soles of durable metal, which will not wear out even if the journey be long and difficult. We shall have protection proportionate to the necessities of the road and the battle. Wherefore let us march boldly on, fearing no harm even though we tread on serpents, or set our foot upon the dragon himself.

As for the strength : it shall be continued as long as our days shall continue, and it shall be proportioned to the stress and burden of those days. The words are few, "as thy days thy strength," but the meaning is full. This day we may look for trial, and for work which will require energy, but we may just as confidently look for equal strength. This word given to Asher is given to us also who have faith wherewith to appropriate it. Let us rise to the holy boldness which it is calculated to create within the believing heart.

"Unto them that look for him shall he appear the second time without sin unto salvation."—Heb. ix. 28.

THIS is our hope. He to whom we have already looked as coming once to bear the sins of many will have another manifestation to the sons of men ; this is a happy prospect in itself. But that second appearing has certain peculiar marks which glorify it exceedingly.

Our Lord will have ended the business of sin. He has so taken it away from his people, and so effectually borne its penalty, that he will have nothing to do with it at his second coming. He will present no sin-offering, for he will have utterly put sin away.

Our Lord will then complete the salvation of his people. They will be finally and perfectly saved, and will in every respect enjoy the fulness of that salvation. He comes not to bear the result of our transgressions, but to bring the result of his obedience ; not to remove our condemnation, but to perfect our salvation.

Our Lord thus appears only to those who look for him. He will not be seen in this character by men whose eyes are blinded with self and sin. To them he will be a terrible Judge, and nothing more. We must first look *to* him, and then look *for* him ; and in both cases our look shall be life.

"*And they that be wise shall shine as the brightness of the firmament; and they that turn many to righteousness as the stars for ever and ever.*"—Dan. xii. 3.

HERE is something to wake me up. This is worth living for. *To be wise* is a noble thing in itself: in this place it refers to a divine wisdom which only the Lord himself can bestow. Oh to know myself, my God, my Saviour! May I be so divinely taught that I may carry into practice heavenly truth, and live in the light of it! Is my life a wise one? Am I seeking that which I ought to seek? Am I living as I shall wish I had lived when I come to die? Only such wisdom can secure for me eternal brightness as of yonder sunlit skies.

To be a winner of souls is a glorious attainment. I had need be wise if I am to turn even one to righteousness; much more if I am to turn many. Oh for the knowledge of God, of men, of the Word, and of Christ, which will enable me to convert my fellow-men, and to convert large numbers of them! I would give myself to this, and never rest till I accomplish it. This will be better than winning stars at court. This will make me a star, a shining star, a star shining for ever and ever; yea more, it will make me shine as many stars. My soul, arouse thyself! Lord, quicken me!

"And I will betroth thee unto me for ever ; yea, I will betroth thee unto me in righteousness, and in judgment, and in lovingkindness, and in mercies. I will even betroth thee unto me in faithfulness ; and thou shalt know the Lord."
Hosea ii. 19, 20.

BETROTHMENT unto the Lord! What an honour and a joy! My soul, is Jesus indeed thine by his own condescending betrothal? Then, mark, it is for ever. He will never break his engagement, much less sue out a divorce against a soul joined to himself in marriage bonds.

Three times the Lord says, "I will betroth thee." What words he heaps together to set forth the betrothal! Righteousness comes in to make the covenant legal ; none can forbid these lawful banns. Judgment sanctions the alliance with its decree : none can see folly or error in the match. Lovingkindness warrants that this is a love union, for without love betrothal is bondage, and not blessedness. Meanwhile, mercy smiles, and even sings ; yea, she multiplies herself into "mercies," because of the abounding grace of this holy union.

Faithfulness is the registrar, and records the marriage, and the Holy Spirit says "Amen" to it, as he promises to teach the betrothed heart all the sacred knowledge needful for its high destiny. What a promise!

"And their sins and iniquities will I remember no more."
Heb. x. 17.

ACCORDING to this gracious covenant the Lord treats his people as if they had never sinned. Practically, he forgets all their trespasses. Sins of all kinds he treats as if they had never been; as if they were quite erased from his memory. O miracle of grace! God here doth that which in certain aspects is impossible to him. His mercy worketh miracles which far transcend all other miracles.

Our God ignores our sin now that the sacrifice of Jesus has ratified the covenant. We may rejoice in him without fear that he will be provoked to anger against us because of our iniquities. See! he puts us among the children; he accepts us as righteous; he takes delight in us as if we were perfectly holy. He even puts us into places of trust; makes us guardians of his honour, trustees of the crown jewels, stewards of the gospel. He counts us worthy, and gives us a ministry; this is the highest and most special proof that he does not remember our sins. Even when we forgive an enemy, we are very slow to trust him; we judge it to be imprudent so to do. But the Lord forgets our sins, and treats us as if we had never erred. O my soul, what a promise is this! Believe it and be happy.

"He that overcometh, the same shall be clothed in white raiment."—Rev. iii. 5.

WARRIOR of the cross, fight on! Never rest till thy victory is complete, for thine eternal reward will prove worthy of a life of warfare.

See, here is perfect purity for thee! A few in Sardis kept their garments undefiled, and their recompense is to be spotless. Perfect holiness is the prize of our high calling, let us not miss it.

See, here is joy! Thou shalt wear holiday robes, such as men put on at wedding feasts; thou shalt be clothed with gladness, and be made bright with rejoicing. Painful struggles shall end in peace of conscience, and joy in the Lord.

See, here is victory! Thou shalt have thy triumph. Palm, and crown, and white robe shall be thy guerdon; thou shalt be treated as a conqueror, and owned as such by the Lord himself.

See, here is priestly array! Thou shalt stand before the Lord in such raiment as the sons of Aaron wore; thou shalt offer the sacrifices of thanksgiving, and draw near unto the Lord with the incense of praise.

Who would not fight for a Lord who gives such large honours to the very least of his faithful servants? Who would not be clothed in a fool's coat for Christ's sake, seeing he will robe us with glory?

"But go thou thy way till the end be: for thou shalt rest, and stand in thy lot at the end of the days."
Dan. xii. 13.

WE cannot understand all the prophecies, but yet we regard them with pleasure, and not with dismay. There can be nothing in the Father's decree which should justly alarm his child. Though the abomination of desolation be set up, yet the true believer shall not be defiled; rather shall he be purified, and made white, and tried. Though the earth be burned up no smell of fire shall come upon the chosen. Amid the crash of matter, and the wreck of worlds, the Lord Jehovah will preserve his own.

Calmly resolute in duty, brave in conflict, patient in suffering, let us go our way, keeping to our road, and neither swerving from it nor loitering in it. The end will come; let us go our way till it does.

Rest will be ours. All other things swing to and fro, but our foundation standeth sure. God rests in his love, and, therefore, we rest in it. Our peace is, and ever shall be, like a river. A lot in the heavenly Canaan is ours, and we shall stand in it, come what may. The God of Daniel will give a worthy portion to all who dare to be decided for truth and holiness as Daniel was. No den of lions shall deprive us of our sure inheritance.

"And it shall be at that day, saith the Lord, that thou shalt call me Ishi; and shalt call me no more Baali; for I will take away the names of Baalim out of her mouth, and they shall no more be remembered by their name."
Hosea ii. 16, 17.

THAT day has come. We view our God no more as Baal, our tyrant lord and mighty master, for we are not under law, but under grace. We now think of Jehovah, our God, as our Ishi, our beloved husband, our lord in love, our next-of-kin in bonds of sacred relationship. We do not reverence him less, but we love him more. We do not serve him less obediently, but we serve him for a higher and more endearing reason. We no longer tremble under his lash, but rejoice in his love. The slave is changed into a child, and the task into a pleasure.

Is it so with thee, dear reader? Has grace cast out slavish fear and implanted filial love? How happy are we in such an experience! Now we call the Sabbath a delight, and worship is never a weariness. Prayer is now a privilege, and praise is a holiday. To obey is heaven; to give to the cause of God is a banquet. Thus have all things become new. Our mouth is filled with singing, and our heart with music. Blessed be our heavenly Ishi for ever and for ever.

"I will give you the sure mercies of David."—Acts xiii. 34.

NOTHING of man is sure ; but everything of God is so: Especially are covenant mercies sure mercies, even as David said "an everlasting covenant, ordered in all things and sure."

We are sure that the Lord meant his mercy. He did not speak mere words : there is substance and truth in every one of his promises. His mercies are mercies indeed. Even if a promise seems as if it must drop through by reason of death, yet it never shall, for the good Lord will make good his word.

We are sure that the Lord will bestow promised mercies on all his covenanted ones. They shall come in due course to all the chosen of the Lord. They are sure to all the seed, from the least of them unto the greatest of them.

We are sure that the Lord will continue his mercies to his own people. He does not give and take. What he has granted us is the token of much more. That which we have not yet received is as sure as that which has already come ; therefore, let us wait before the Lord and be still. There is no justifiable reason for the least doubt. God's love, and word, and faithfulness are sure. Many things are questionable, but of the Lord we sing—

> " For his mercies shall endure
> Ever faithful, ever sure."

"*Humble yourselves therefore under the mighty hand of
God, that he may exalt you in due time.*"—1 Peter v. 6.

THIS is tantamount to a promise: if we will
bow down, the Lord will lift us up. Humility
leads to honour: submission is the way to exaltation. That same hand of God which presses us
down is waiting to raise us up when we are prepared to bear the blessing. We stoop to conquer.
Many cringe before men, and yet miss the patronage they crave ; but he that humbles himself under
the hand of God shall not fail to be enriched,
uplifted, sustained, and comforted by the ever-
gracious One. It is a habit of Jehovah to cast
down the proud, and lift up the lowly.

Yet there is a time for the Lord's working. We
ought now to humble ourselves, even at this present
moment ; and we are bound to keep on doing so
whether the Lord lays his afflicting hand upon us
or not. When the Lord smites, it is our special
duty to accept the chastisement with profound submission. But as for the Lord's exaltation of us,
that can only come "in due time," and God is the
best judge of that day and hour. Do we cry out
impatiently for the blessing ? Would we wish for
untimely honour ? What are we at ? Surely we
are not truly humbled, or we should wait with quiet
submission. So let us do.

" He hath cast out thine enemy."—Zeph. iii. 15.

WHAT a casting out was that! Satan has lost his throne in our nature even as he lost his seat in heaven. Our Lord Jesus has destroyed the enemy's reigning power over us. He may worry us, but he cannot claim us as his own. His bonds are no longer upon our spirits: the Son has made us free, and we are free indeed.

Still is the arch-enemy the accuser of the brethren; but even from this position our Lord has driven him. Our advocate silences our accuser. The Lord rebukes our enemies, and pleads the causes of our soul, so that no harm comes of all the devil's revilings.

As a tempter, the evil spirit still assails us, and insinuates himself into our minds; but thence also is he cast out as to his former pre-eminence. He wriggles about like a serpent, but he cannot rule like a sovereign. He hurls in blasphemous thoughts when he has opportunity; but what a relief it is when he is told to be quiet, and is made to slink off like a whipped cur! Lord, do this for any who are at this time worried and wearied by his barkings. Cast out their enemy, and be thou glorious in their eyes. Thou hast cast him down, Lord cast him out. Oh that thou wouldst banish him from the world!

"I will see you again, and your heart shall rejoice."
John xvi. 22.

SURELY he will come a second time, and then, when he sees us, and we see him, there will be rejoicings indeed. Oh for that joyous return!

But this promise is being daily fulfilled in another sense. Our gracious Lord has many "agains" in his dealings with us. He gave us pardon, and he sees us again, and repeats the absolving word as fresh sins cause us grief. He has revealed to us our acceptance before God, and when our faith in that blessing grows a little dim, he comes to us again and again, and says, "Peace be unto you"; and our hearts are glad.

Beloved, all our past mercies are tokens of future mercies. If Jesus has been with us, he will see us again. Look upon no former favour as a dead and buried thing, to be mourned over; but regard it as a seed sown, which will grow, and push its head up from the dust, and cry, "I will see you again." Are the times dark because Jesus is not with us as he used to be? Let us pluck up courage; for he will not be long away. His feet are as those of a roe or young hart, and they will soon bring him to us. Wherefore let us begin to be joyous, since he saith to us even now, "I will see you again."

"And call upon me in the day of trouble: I will deliver thee, and thou shalt glorify me."—Ps. l. 15.

THIS is a promise indeed!

Here is an urgent occasion—"the day of trouble." It is dark at noon on such a day, and every hour seems blacker than the one which came before it. Then is this promise in season: it is written for the cloudy day.

Here is condescending advice, "call upon me." We ought not to need the exhortation: it should be our constant habit all the day and every day. What a mercy to have liberty to call upon God! What wisdom to make good use of it! How foolish to go running about to men! The Lord invites us to lay our case before him, and surely we will not hesitate to do so.

Here is reassuring encouragement: "I will deliver thee." Whatever the trouble may be, the Lord makes no exceptions, but promises full, sure, happy deliverance. He will himself work out our deliverance by his own hand. We believe it, and the Lord honours faith.

Here is an ultimate result: "Thou shalt glorify me." Ah! that we will do most abundantly. When he has delivered us we will loudly praise him; and as he is sure to do it, let us begin to glorify him at once

"And I will establish my covenant between me and thee and thy seed after thee in their generations for an everlasting covenant, to be a God unto thee, and to thy seed after thee."—Gen. xvii. 7.

O LORD, thou hast made a covenant with me, thy servant, in Christ Jesus my Lord; and now, I beseech thee, let my children be included in its gracious provisions. Permit me to believe this promise as made to me as well as to Abraham. I know that my children are born in sin, and shapen in iniquity, even as those of other men; therefore, I ask nothing on the ground of their birth, for well I know that "that which is born of the flesh is flesh," and nothing more. Lord, make them to be born under thy covenant of grace by thy Holy Spirit!

I pray for my descendants throughout all generations. Be thou their God as thou art mine. My highest honour is that thou hast permitted me to serve thee; may my offspring serve thee in all years to come. O God of Abraham, be the God of his Isaac! O God of Hannah, accept her Samuel!

If, Lord, thou hast favoured me in my family, I pray thee remember other households of thy people which remain unblest. Be the God of all the families of Israel. Let not one of those who fear thy name be tried with a godless and wicked household, for thy Son Jesus Christ's sake. Amen.

"Now therefore go, and I will be with thy mouth, and teach thee what thou shalt say."—Ex. iv. 12.

MANY a true servant of the Lord is slow of speech, and when called upon to plead for his Lord, he is in great confusion lest he should spoil a good cause by his bad advocacy. In such a case it is well to remember that the Lord made the tongue which is so slow, and we must take care that we do not blame our Maker. It may be that a slow tongue is not so great an evil as a fast one, and fewness of words may be more of a blessing than floods of verbiage. It is also quite certain that real saving power does not lie in human rhetoric, with its tropes, and pretty phrases, and grand displays. Lack of fluency is not so great a lack as it looks.

If God be with our mouth, and with our mind, we shall have something better than the sounding brass of eloquence, or the tinkling cymbal of persuasion. God's teaching is wisdom; his presence is power. Pharaoh had more reason to be afraid of stammering Moses than of the most fluent talker in Egypt; for what he said had power in it; he spoke plagues and deaths. If the Lord be with us in our natural weakness we shall be girt with supernatural power. Therefore, let us speak for Jesus boldly, as we ought to speak.

"But if the priest buy any soul with his money, he shall eat of it, and he that is born in his house : they shall eat of his meat."—Lev. xxii. 11.

STRANGERS, sojourners, and servants upon hire were not to eat of holy things. It is so in spiritual matters still. But two classes were free at the sacred table, those who were *bought* with the priest's money, and those who were *born* into the priest's house. Bought and born, these were the two indisputable proofs of a right to holy things.

Bought. Our great High Priest has bought with a price all those who put their trust in him. They are his absolute property—altogether the Lord's. Not for what they are in themselves, but for their owner's sake they are admitted into the same privileges which he himself enjoys, and " they shall eat of his meat." He has meat to eat which worldlings know not of. " Because ye belong to Christ," therefore shall ye share with your Lord.

Born. This is an equally sure way to privilege ; if born in the priest's house we take our place with the rest of the family. Regeneration makes us fellow-heirs, and of the same body ; and, therefore, the peace, the joy, the glory, which the Father has given to Christ, Christ has given to us. Redemption and regeneration have given us a double claim to the divine permit of this promise.

"The Lord bless thee, and keep thee."—Num. vi. 24.

THIS first clause of the high-priest's benediction is substantially a promise. That blessing which our great High Priest pronounces upon us is sure to come, for he speaks the mind of God.

What a joy to abide under the divine blessing! This puts a gracious flavour into all things. If we are blessed, then all our possessions and enjoyments are blessed; yea, our losses and crosses, and even our disappointments are blessed. God's blessing is deep, emphatic, effectual. A man's blessing may begin and end in words; but the blessing of the Lord makes rich and sanctifies. The best wish we can have for our dearest friend is not "May prosperity attend thee," but "The Lord bless thee."

It is equally a delightful thing to be kept of God; kept by him, kept near him, kept in him. They are kept indeed whom God keeps; they are preserved from evil, they are reserved unto boundless happiness. God's keeping goes with his blessing, to establish it and cause it to endure.

The author of this little book desires that the rich blessing and sure keeping here pronounced may come upon every reader who may at this moment be looking at these lines. Should the author be living, please breathe the text to God as a prayer for his servant.

"The law of his God is in his heart; none of his steps shall slide."—Ps. xxxvii. 31.

PUT the law into the heart, and the whole man is right. This is where the law should be; for then it lies, like the tables of stone in the ark, in the place appointed for it. In the head it puzzles, on the back it burdens, in the heart it upholds.

What a choice word is here used, "the law of his God"! When we know the Lord as our own God his law becomes liberty to us. God with us in covenant makes us eager to obey his will and walk in his commands. Is the precept my Father's precept? Then I delight in it.

We are here guaranteed that the obedient-hearted man shall be sustained in every step that he takes. He will do that which is right, and he shall therefore do that which is wise. Holy action is always the most prudent, though it may not at the time seem to be so. We are moving along the great high road of God's providence and grace when we keep to the way of his law. The Word of God has never misled a single soul yet; its plain directions to walk humbly, justly, lovingly, and in the fear of the Lord, are as much words of wisdom to make our way prosperous as rules of holiness to keep our garments clean. He walks surely who walks righteously.

"Behold, the Lord thy God hath set the land before thee : go up and possess it, as the Lord God of thy fathers hath said unto thee ; fear not, neither be discouraged."
Deut. i. 21.

THERE is a heritage of grace which we ought to be bold enough to win for our own possession. All that one believer has gained is free to another. We may be strong in faith, fervent in love, and abundant in labour ; there is nothing to prevent it ; let us go up and take possession. The sweetest experience and the brightest grace are as much for us as for any of our brethren. Jehovah has set it before us ; no one can deny our right ; let us go up and possess it in his name.

The world also lies before us to be conquered for the Lord Jesus. We are not to leave any country or corner of it unsubdued. That slum near our house is before us, not to baffle our endeavours, but to yield to them. We have only to summon courage enough to go forward, and we shall win dark homes and hard hearts for Jesus. Let us never leave the people in a lane or alley to die because we have not enough faith in Jesus and his gospel to go up and possess the land. No spot is too benighted, no person is so profane as to be beyond the power of grace. Cowardice, begone! Faith marches to the conquest.

"Only be thou strong and very courageous, that thou mayest observe to do according to all the law, which Moses my servant commanded thee: turn not from it to the right hand or to the left, that thou mayest prosper whithersoever thou goest."—Josh. i. 7.

YES, the Lord will be with us in our holy war, but he demands of us that we strictly follow his rules. Our victories will very much depend upon our obeying him *with all our heart*, throwing strength and courage into the actions of our faith. If we are half-hearted we cannot expect more than half a blessing.

We must obey the Lord *with care and thoughtfulness.* "Observe to do" is the phrase used, and it is full of meaning. This is referred to every part of the divine will; we must obey *with universal readiness.* Our rule of conduct is "according to all the law." We may not pick and choose, but we must take the Lord's commands as they come, one and all. In all this we must go on *with exactness and constancy.* Ours is to be a straightforward course, which bends neither to the right nor to the left. We are not to err by being more rigid than the law, nor turn out of levity to a more free and easy way. With such obedience there will come spiritual prosperity. O Lord, help us to see if it be not even so! We shall not test thy promise in vain.

"The Lord God will help me."—Isa. l. 7.

THESE are in prophecy the words of Messiah in the day of his obedience unto death, when he gave his back to the smiters, and his cheeks to them that plucked off the hair. He was confident in divine support, and trusted in Jehovah.

O my soul, thy sorrows are as the small dust of the balance compared with thy Lord's! Canst thou not believe that the Lord God will help thee? Thy Lord was in a peculiar position; for as the representative of sinful men—their substitute and sacrifice—it was needful that the Father should leave him, and cause him to come under desertion of soul. No such necessity is laid upon thee: thou art not bound to cry, "Why hast thou forsaken me?" Did thy Saviour even in such a case still rely upon God, and canst not thou? He died for thee, and thus made it impossible that thou shouldst be left alone; wherefore, be of good cheer.

In this day's labours or trials say, "The Lord God will help me." Go forth boldly. Set your face like a flint, and resolve that no faintness or shamefacedness shall come near you. If God helps, who can hinder? If you are sure of omnipotent aid, what can be too heavy for you? Begin the day joyously, and let no shade of doubt come between thee and the eternal sunshine.

"Every branch in me that beareth not fruit he taketh away: and every branch that beareth fruit, he purgeth it, that it may bring forth more fruit."—John xv. 2.

THIS is a precious promise to one who lives for fruitfulness. At first it seems to wear a sharp aspect. Must the fruitful bough be pruned? Must the knife cut even the best and most useful? No doubt it is so, for very much of our Lord's purging work is done by means of afflictions of one kind or another. It is not the evil but the good who have the promise of tribulation in this life. But, then, the end makes more than full amends for the painful nature of the means. If we may bring forth more fruit for our Lord, we will not mind the pruning and the loss of leafage.

Still, purging is sometimes wrought by the Word apart from trial, and this takes away whatever appeared rough in the flavour of the promise. We shall by the Word be made more gracious and more useful. The Lord, who has made us, in a measure, fruit-bearing, will operate upon us till we reach a far higher degree of fertility. Is not this a great joy? Truly there is more comfort in a promise of fruitfulness than if we had been warranted riches, or health, or honour.

Lord Jesus, speedily fulfil thy gracious word to me, and cause me to abound in fruit to thy praise!

"The Lord maketh poor, and maketh rich: he bringeth low, and lifteth up."—1 Sam. ii. 7.

ALL my changes come from him who never changes. If I had grown rich, I should have seen his hand in it, and I should have praised him; let me equally see his hand if I am made poor, and let me as heartily praise him. When we go down in the world, it is of the Lord, and so we may take it patiently: when we rise in the world, it is of the Lord, and we may accept it thankfully. In any case, the Lord hath done it, and it is well.

It seems that Jehovah's way is to lower those whom he means to raise, and to strip those whom he intends to clothe. If it is his way, it is the wisest and best way. If I am now enduring the bringing low I may well rejoice, because I see in it the preface to the lifting up. The more we are humbled by grace, the more we shall be exalted in glory. That impoverishment which will be over-ruled for our enrichment is to be welcomed.

O Lord, thou hast taken me down of late, and made me feel my insignificance and sin. It is not a pleasant experience, but I pray thee make it a profitable one to me. Oh, that thou wouldst thus fit me to bear a greater weight of delight and of usefulness; and when I am ready for it, then grant it to me, for Christ's sake! Amen.

"Truly my soul waiteth upon God: from him cometh my salvation."—Ps. lxii. 1.

BLESSED posture!—waiting truly and only upon the Lord. Be this our condition all this day, and every day. Waiting his leisure, waiting in his service, waiting in joyful expectation, waiting in prayer, and content. When the very soul thus waits, it is in the best and truest condition of a creature before his Creator, a servant before his Master, a child before his Father. We allow no dictation to God, nor complaining of him; we will permit no petulance, and no distrust. At the same time, we practise no running before the cloud, and no seeking to others for aid: neither of these would be waiting upon God. God, and God alone, is the expectation of our hearts.

Blessed assurance!—from him salvation is coming; it is on the road. It will come from him, and from no one else. He shall have all the glory of it, for he alone can and will perform it. And he will perform it most surely in his own time and manner. He will save from doubt, and suffering, and slander, and distress. Though we see no sign of it as yet, we are satisfied to bide the Lord's will, for we have no suspicion of his love and faithfulness. He will make sure work of it before long, and we will praise him at once for the coming mercy.

"For thou art my lamp, O Lord: and the Lord will lighten my darkness."—2 Sam. xxii. 29.

AM I in the light? Then thou, O Lord, art my lamp. Take thee away, and my joy would be gone; but as long as thou art with me, I can do without the torches of time and the candles of created comfort. What a light the presence of God casts on all things! We heard of a lighthouse which could be seen for twenty miles, but our Jehovah is not only a God at hand, but far off is he seen, even in the enemy's country. O Lord, I am as happy as an angel when thy love fills my heart. Thou art all my desire.

Am I in the dark? Then thou, O Lord, wilt lighten my darkness. Before long things will change. Affairs may grow more and more dreary, and cloud may be piled upon cloud; but if it grows so dark that I cannot see my own hand, still I shall see the hand of the Lord. When I cannot find a light within me, or among my friends, or in the whole world, the Lord, who said "Let there be light," and there was light, can say the same again. He will speak me into the sunshine yet. I shall not die, but live. The day is already breaking. This sweet text shines like a morning star. I shall clap my hands for joy ere many hours are passed.

"It shall come to pass, that before they call, I will answer; and while they are yet speaking, I will hear."
Isa. lxv. 24.

QUICK work this! The Lord hears us before we call; and often answers us in the same speedy manner. Foreseeing our needs, and our prayers, he so arranges providence that before the need actually arises he has supplied it, before the trial assails us he has armed us against it. This is the promptitude of omniscience, and we have often seen it exercised. Before we dreamed of the affliction which was coming, the strong consolation which was to sustain us under it had arrived. What a prayer-answering God we have!

The second clause suggests the telephone. Though God be in heaven and we upon earth, yet he makes our word, like his own word, to travel very swiftly. When we pray aright we speak into the ear of God. Our gracious Mediator presents our petitions at once, and the great Father hears them and smiles upon them. Grand praying this! Who would not be much in prayer when he knows that he has the ear of the King of kings? This day I will pray in faith, not only believing that I shall be heard, but that I am heard; not only that I shall be answered, but that I have the answer already. Holy Spirit, help me in this!

"And I will for this afflict the seed of David, but not for ever."—1 Kings xi. 39.

IN the family of grace there is discipline, and that discipline is severe enough to make it an evil and a bitter thing to sin. Solomon, turned aside by his foreign wives, had set up other gods, and grievously provoked the God of his father; therefore, ten parts out of twelve of the kingdom were rent away, and set up as a rival state. This was a sore affliction to the house of David, and it came upon that dynasty distinctly from the hand of God, as the result of unholy conduct. The Lord will chasten his best beloved servants if they cease from full obedience to his laws : perhaps at this very hour such chastening is upon us. Let us humbly cry, " O Lord, show me wherefore thou contendest with me."

What a sweet saving clause is that—" but not for ever " ! The punishment of sin is everlasting, but the fatherly chastisement of it in a child of God is but for a season. The sickness, the poverty, the depression of spirit, will pass away when they have had their intended effect. Remember, we are not under law, but under grace. The rod may make us smart, but the sword shall not make us die. Our present grief is meant to bring us to repentance. that we may not be destroyed with the wicked.

"And whatsoever ye shall ask in my name, that will I do, that the Father may be glorified in the Son."
John xiv. 13.

IT is not every believer who has yet learned to pray in Christ's name. To ask not only for his sake, but in his name, as authorized by him, is a high order of prayer. We would not dare to ask for some things in that blessed name, for it would be a wretched profanation of it , but when the petition is so clearly right that we dare set the name of Jesus to it, then it must be granted.

Prayer is all the more sure to succeed because it is for the Father's glory through the Son. It glorifies his truth, his faithfulness, his power, his grace. The granting of prayer, when offered in the name of Jesus, reveals the Father's love to him, and the honour which he has put upon him. The glory of Jesus and of the Father are so wrapped up together, that the grace which magnifies the one magnifies the other. The channel is made famous through the fulness of the fountain, and the fountain is honoured through the channel by which it flows If the answering of our prayers would dishonour our Lord, we would not pray ; but since in this thing he is glorified, we will pray without ceasing in that dear name in which God and his people have a fellowship of delight.

"He that covereth his sins shall not prosper: but whoso confesseth and forsaketh them shall have mercy."
Prov. xxviii. 13.

HERE is the way of mercy for a guilty and repenting sinner. He must cease from the habit of covering sin. This is attempted by falsehood, which denies sin; by hypocrisy, which conceals it; by boasting, which justifies it; and by loud profession, which tries to make amends for it.

The sinner's business is to confess and forsake. The two must go together. Confession must be honestly made to the Lord himself; and it must include within itself acknowledgment of the wrong, sense of its evil, and abhorrence of it. We must not throw the fault upon others, nor blame circumstances, nor plead natural weakness. We must make a clean breast of it, and plead guilty to the indictment. There can be no mercy till this is done.

Furthermore, we must forsake the evil: having owned our fault, we must disown all present and future intent to abide in it. We cannot remain in rebellion and yet dwell with the King's Majesty. The habit of evil must be quitted, together with all places, companions, pursuits, and books, which might lead us astray. Not *for* confession, nor *for* reformation, but in connection with them we find pardon by faith in the blood of Jesus.

"And he answered, Fear not: for they that be with us are more than they that be with them."—2 Kings vi. 16.

HORSES and chariots, and a great host, shut up the prophet in Dothan. His young servant was alarmed. How could they escape from such a body of armed men? But the prophet had eyes which his servant had not, and he could see a greater host with far superior weapons guarding him from all harm. Horses of fire are mightier than horses of flesh, and chariots of fire are far preferable to chariots of iron.

Even so is it at this hour. The adversaries of truth are many, influential, learned, and crafty; and truth fares ill at their hands; and yet the man of God has no cause for trepidation. Agencies, seen and unseen, of the most potent kind, are on the side of righteousness. God has armies in ambush which will reveal themselves in the hour of need. The forces which are on the side of the good and the true far outweigh the powers of evil. Therefore, let us keep our spirits up, and walk with the gait of men who possess a cheering secret, which has lifted them above all fear. We are on the winning side. The battle may be sharp, but we know how it will end. Faith, having God with her, is in a clear majority: "They that be with us are more than they that be with them."

"If thou seek him, he will be found of thee."—1 Chron. xxviii. 9.

WE need our God; he is to be had for the seeking; and he will not deny himself to any one of us if we personally seek his face. It is not, if thou deserve him, or purchase his favour, but merely if thou "seek" him. Those who already know the Lord must go on seeking his face by prayer, by diligent service, and by holy gratitude: to such he will not refuse his favour and fellowship. Those who, as yet, have not known him to their souls' rest should at once commence seeking, and never cease till they find him as their Saviour, their Friend, their Father, and their God.

What strong assurance this promise gives to the seeker! "He that seeketh findeth." You, yes *you*, if you seek your God shall find him. When you find him you have found life, pardon, sanctification, preservation, and glory. Will you not seek, and seek on, since you shall not seek in vain? Dear friend, seek the Lord at once. Here is the place, and now is the time. Bend that stiff knee; yes, bend that stiffer neck, and cry out for God, for the living God. In the name of Jesus seek cleansing and justification. You shall not be refused. Here is David's testimony to his son Solomon, and it is the writer's personal witness to the reader. Believe it and act upon it, for Christ's sake.

"So that a man shall say, Verily there is a reward for the righteous: verily he is a God that judgeth in the earth."
Ps. lviii. 11.

GOD'S judgments in this life are not always clearly to be seen, for in many cases one event happeneth alike to all. This is the state of probation, not of punishment or reward. Yet at times God works terrible things in righteousness, and even the careless are compelled to own his hand.

Even in this life righteousness has that kind of reward which it prefers above all others, namely, the smile of God, which creates a quiet conscience. Sometimes other recompenses follow, for God will be in no man's debt. But, at the same time, the chief reward of the righteous lies in the hereafter.

Meanwhile, on a large scale, we mark the presence of the great Ruler among the nations. He breaks in pieces oppressive thrones, and punishes guilty peoples. No one can study the history of the rise and fall of empires without perceiving that there is a power which makes for righteousness, and, in the end, brings iniquity before its bar, and condemns it with unsparing justice. Sin shall not go unpunished, and goodness shall not remain unrewarded. The Judge of all the earth must do right. Therefore, let us fear before him, and no more dread the power of the wicked.

"He shall deliver thee in six troubles : yea, in seven there shall no evil touch thee."—Job v. 19.

ELIPHAZ in this spoke the truth of God. We may have as many troubles as the work-days of the week, but the God who worked on those *six* days will work for us till our deliverance is complete. We shall rest with him, and in him on our Sabbath. The rapid succession of trials is one of the sorest tests of faith. Before we have recovered from one blow, it is followed by another and another till we are staggered. Still, the equally quick succession of deliverances is exceedingly cheering. New songs are rung out upon the anvil by the hammer of affliction, till we see in the spiritual world the antitype of "the Harmonious Blacksmith." Our confidence is, that when the Lord makes our trials six, six they will be, and no more.

It may be that we have no rest-day, for *seven* troubles come upon us. What then ? " In seven there shall no evil touch thee." Evil may roar at us, but it shall be kept at more than arm's length, and shall not even touch us. Its hot breath may distress us, but its little finger cannot be laid upon us.

With our loins girt about us we will meet the six or the seven troubles, and leave fear to those who have no Father, no Saviour, and no Sanctifier.

"For his anger endureth but a moment; in his favour is life: weeping may endure for a night, but joy cometh in the morning."—Ps. xxx. 5.

A MOMENT under our Father's anger seems very long, and yet it is but a moment after all. If we grieve his Spirit we cannot look for his smile; but he is a God ready to pardon, and he soon puts aside all remembrance of our faults. When we faint and are ready to die because of his frown, his favour puts new life into us.

This verse has another note of the semi-quaver kind. Our weeping night soon turns into joyous day. Brevity is the mark of mercy in the hour of the chastisement of believers. The Lord loves not to use the rod on his chosen; he gives a blow or two, and all is over; yea, and the life and the joy, which follow the anger and the weeping, more than make amends for the salutary sorrow.

Come, my heart, begin thy hallelujahs! Weep not all through the night, but wipe thine eyes in anticipation of the morning. These tears are dews which mean us as much good as the sunbeams of the morrow. Tears clear the eyes for the sight of God in his grace; and make the vision of his favour more precious. A night of sorrow supplies those shades of the picture by which the high lights are brought out with distinctness. All is well.

"Surely the wrath of man shall praise thee: the remainder of wrath shalt thou restrain."—Ps. lxxvi. 10.

WICKED men will be wrathful. Their anger we must endure as the badge of our calling, the token of our separation from them: if we were of the world the world would love its own. Our comfort is that the wrath of man shall be made to redound to the glory of God. When in their wrath the wicked crucified the Son of God they were unwittingly fulfilling the divine purpose, and in a thousand cases the wilfulness of the ungodly is doing the same. They think themselves free, but like convicts in chains they are unconsciously working out the decrees of the Almighty.

The devices of the wicked are overruled for their defeat. They act in a suicidal way, and baffle their own plottings. Nothing will come of their wrath which can do us real harm. When they burned the martyrs the smoke which blew from the stake sickened men of Popery more than anything else.

Meanwhile, the Lord has a muzzle and a chain for bears. He restrains the more furious wrath of the enemy. He is like a miller who holds back the mass of the water in the stream, and what he does allow to flow he uses for the turning of his wheel. Let us not sigh, but sing. All is well, however hard the wind blows.

"I love them that love me ; and those that seek me early shall find me."—Prov. viii. 17.

WISDOM loves her lovers, and seeks her seekers. He is already wise who seeks to be wise, and he has almost found wisdom who diligently seeks her. What is true of wisdom in general is specially true of wisdom embodied in our Lord Jesus. Him we are to love and to seek, and in return we shall enjoy his love, and find himself.

Our business is to seek Jesus *early in life*. Happy are the young whose morning is spent with Jesus! It is never too soon to seek the Lord Jesus. Early seekers make certain finders. We should seek him *early by diligence*. Thriving tradesmen are early risers, and thriving saints seek Jesus eagerly. Those who find Jesus to their enrichment give their hearts to seeking him. We must seek him *first, and thus earliest*. Above all things Jesus. Jesus first, and nothing else even as a bad second.

The blessing is that he will be found. He reveals himself more and more clearly to our search. He gives himself up more fully to our fellowship. Happy men who seek one who, when he is found, remains with them for ever, a treasure growingly precious to their hearts and understandings.

Lord Jesus, I have found thee ; be found of me to an unutterable degree of joyous satisfaction.

"For it is written, I will destroy the wisdom of the wise, and will bring to nothing the understanding of the prudent."—1 Cor. i. 19.

THIS verse is a threatening so far as the worldly-wise are concerned, but to the simple believer it is a promise. The professedly learned are for ever trying to bring to nothing the faith of the humble believer, but they fail in their attempts. Their arguments break down, their theories fall under their own weight, their deep-laid plots discover themselves before their purpose is accomplished. The old gospel is not extinct yet, nor will it be while the Lord liveth. If it could have been exterminated it would have perished from off the earth long ago.

We cannot destroy the wisdom of the wise, nor need we attempt it, for the work is in far better hands. The Lord himself says, "I will," and he never resolves in vain. Twice does he in this verse declare his purpose, and we may rest assured that he will not turn aside from it.

What clean work the Lord makes of philosophy and "modern thought" when he puts his hand to it! He brings the fine appearance down to nothing; he utterly destroys the wood, hay, and stubble. It is written that so it shall be, and so shall it be. Lord, make short work of it. Amen, and Amen.

"I will feed my flock, and I will cause them to lie down, saith the Lord God."—Ezek. xxxiv. 15.

UNDER the divine shepherdry saints are fed to the full. Theirs is not a windy, unsatisfying mess of mere human "thought"; but the Lord feeds them upon the solid, substantial truth of divine revelation. There is real nutriment for the soul in Scripture brought home to the heart by the Holy Spirit. Jesus, himself, is the true life-sustaining food of believers. Here our Great Shepherd promises that such sacred nourishment shall be given us by his own self. If, on the Sabbath, our earthly shepherd is empty-handed, the Lord is not.

When filled with holy truth the mind rests. Those whom Jehovah feeds are at peace. No dog shall worry them, no wolf shall devour them, no restless propensities shall disturb them. They shall lie down and digest the food which they have enjoyed. The doctrines of grace are not only sustaining, but consoling: in them we have the means for building up and lying down. If preachers do not give us rest, let us look to the Lord for it.

This day may the Lord cause us to feed in the pastures of the Word, and make us to lie down in them. May no folly, and no worry, but Meditation and Peace mark this day.

"I will judge between cattle and cattle."—Ezek. xxxiv. 22.

SOME are fat and flourishing, and therefore they are unkind to the feeble. This is a grievous sin, and causes much sorrow. Those thrustings with side and with shoulder, those pushings of the diseased with the horn, are a sad means of offence in the assemblies of professing believers. The Lord takes note of these proud and unkind deeds, and he is greatly angered by them, for he loves the weak.

Is the reader one of the despised? Is he a mourner in Zion, and a marked man because of his tender conscience? Do his brethren judge him harshly? Let him not resent their conduct; above all, let him not push and thrust in return. Let him leave the matter in the Lord's hands. He is the Judge. Why should we wish to intrude upon his office? He will decide much more righteously than we can. His time for judgment is the best, and we need not be in a hurry to hasten it on.

Let the hard-hearted oppressor tremble. Even though he may ride rough-shod over others with impunity for the present, all his proud speeches are noted, and for every one of them account must be given before the bar of the Great Judge.

Patience, my soul! Patience! the Lord knoweth thy grief. Thy Jesus hath pity upon thee!

"I have chosen thee in the furnace of affliction."
Isa. xlviii. 10.

THIS has long been the motto fixed before our eye upon the wall of our bed-chamber, and in many ways it has also been written on our heart. It is no mean thing to be chosen of God. God's choice makes chosen men choice men. Better to be the elect of God than the elect of a whole nation. So eminent is this privilege, that whatever drawback may be joined to it we very joyfully accept it, even as the Jew ate the bitter herbs for the sake of the Paschal Lamb. We choose the furnace, since God chooses us in it.

We are chosen as an afflicted people, and not as a prosperous people, chosen not in the palace, but in the furnace. In the furnace beauty is marred, fashion is destroyed, strength is melted, glory is consumed, and yet here eternal love reveals its secrets, and declares its choice. So has it been in our case. In times of severest trial God has made to us our calling and election plain, and we have made it sure: then have we chosen the Lord to be our God, and he has shown that we are assuredly his chosen. Therefore, if to-day the furnace be heated seven times hotter, we will not dread it, for the glorious Son of God will walk with us amid the glowing coals.

"As for me, I will call upon God; and the Lord shall save me."—Ps. lv. 16.

YES, I must and will pray. What else can I do? What better can I do? Betrayed, forsaken, grieved, baffled, O my Lord, I will call upon thee. My Ziklag is in ashes, and men speak of stoning me; but I encourage my heart in the Lord, who will bear me through this trial as he has borne me through so many others. Jehovah shall save me; I am sure he will, and I declare my faith.

The Lord and no one else shall save me. I desire no other helper, and would not trust in an arm of flesh even if I could. I will cry to him evening, and morning, and noon, and I will cry to no one else, for he is All-sufficient.

How he will save me I cannot guess; but he will do it, I know. He will do it in the best and surest way, and he will do it in the largest, truest, and fullest sense. Out of this trouble and all future troubles the great I AM will bring me as surely as he lives; and when death comes, and all the mysteries of eternity follow thereon, still will this be true: "*the Lord shall save me.*" This shall be my song all through this autumn day. Is it not as a ripe apple from the tree of life? I will feed upon it. How sweet it is to my taste!

"Their soul shall be as a watered garden."—Jer. xxxi. 12.

OH, to have one's soul under heavenly cultiva-
tion ; no longer a wilderness, but a garden of
the Lord!   Enclosed from the waste, walled around
by grace, planted by instruction, visited by love,
weeded by heavenly discipline, and guarded by
divine power, one's favoured soul is prepared to
yield fruit unto the Lord.

But a garden may become parched for want of
water, and then all its herbs decline, and are ready
to die.   O my soul, how soon would this be the
case were the Lord to leave thee !   In the East, a
garden without water soon ceases to be a garden
at all : nothing can come to perfection, grow, or
even live.   When irrigation is kept up, the result
is charming.   Oh, to have one's soul watered by
the Holy Spirit uniformly—every part of the garden
having its own stream ; plentifully—a sufficient
refreshment coming to every tree and herb, however thirsty by nature it may be ; continually—
each hour bringing not only its heat, but its
refreshment ; wisely—each plant receiving just
what it needs.   In a garden you can see by the
verdure where the water flows, and you can soon
perceive when the Spirit of God comes.

O Lord, water me this day, and cause me to
yield thee a full reward, for Jesus' sake.   Amen.

"Although my house be not so with God; yet he hath made with me an everlasting covenant, ordered in all things, and sure: for this is all my salvation, and all my desire, although he make it not to grow."—2 Sam. xxiii. 5.

THIS is not so much one promise as an aggregate of promises—a box of pearls. The covenant is the ark which contains all things.

These are the last words of David, but they may be mine to-day. Here is *a sigh:* things are not with me and mine as I could wish; there are trials, cares, and sins. These make the pillow hard.

Here is *a solace*—" He hath made with me an everlasting covenant." Jehovah has pledged himself to me, and sealed the compact with the blood of Jesus. I am bound to my God, and my God to me.

This brings into prominence *a security*, since this covenant is everlasting, well ordered and sure. There is nothing to fear from the lapse of time, the failure of some forgotten point, or the natural uncertainty of things. The covenant is a rocky foundation to build on for life or for death.

David feels *satisfaction:* he wants no more for salvation or delectation. He is delivered, and he is delighted. The covenant is all a man can desire.

O my soul, turn thou this day to thy Lord Jesus, whom the great Lord has given to be a covenant to the people. Take him to be thine all in all.

"But the word of the Lord endureth for ever. And this is the word which by the gospel is preached unto you." 1 Pet. i. 25.

ALL human teaching and, indeed, all human beings, shall pass away as the grass of the meadow; but we are here assured that the word of the Lord is of a very different character, for it shall endure for ever.

We have here *a divine gospel;* for what word can endure for ever but that which is spoken by the eternal God?

We have here *an ever-living gospel,* as full of vitality as when it first came from the lip of God; as strong to convince and convert, to regenerate and console, to sustain and sanctify, as ever it was in its first days of wonder-working.

We have *an unchanging gospel,* which is not to-day green grass, and to-morrow dry hay; but always the abiding truth of the immutable Jehovah. Opinions alter, but truth certified by God can no more change than the God who uttered it.

Here, then, we have *a gospel to rejoice in,* a word of the Lord upon which we may lean all our weight. "For ever" includes life, death, judgment, and eternity. Glory be to God in Christ Jesus for everlasting consolation. Feed on the word to-day, and all the days of thy life.

"If ye keep my commandments, ye shall abide in my love."—John xv. 10.

THESE things cannot be parted—abiding in obedience, and abiding in the love of Jesus. A life under the rule of Christ can alone prove that we are the objects of our Lord's delight. We must keep our Lord's command if we would bask in his love. If we live in sin we cannot live in the love of Christ. Without the holiness which pleases God, we cannot please Jesus. He who cares nothing for holiness knows nothing of the love of Jesus.

Conscious enjoyment of our Lord's love is a delicate thing. It is far more sensitive to sin and holiness than mercury is to cold and heat. When we are tender of heart, and careful in thought, lip, and life to honour our Lord Jesus, then we receive tokens of his love without number. If we desire to perpetuate such bliss we must perpetuate holiness. The Lord Jesus will not hide his face from us unless we hide our face from him. Sin makes the cloud which darkens our Sun: if we will be watchfully obedient and completely consecrated, we may walk in the light, as God is in the light, and have as sure an abiding in the love of Jesus as Jesus has in the love of the Father. Here is a sweet promise with a solemn "if." Lord, let me have this "if" in my hand; for as a key it opens this casket.

"Then shall we know, if we follow on to know the Lord."—Hos. vi. 3.

NOT all at once, but by degrees shall we attain to holy knowledge, and our business is to persevere and learn by little and little. We need not despair, though our progress may be slow, for we shall yet know. The Lord, who has become our teacher, will not give us up, however slow of understanding we may be; for it is not for his honour that any degree of human folly should baffle his skill. The Lord delights to make the simple wise.

Our duty is to keep to our main topic, and follow on to know, not this peculiar doctrine nor that, but Jehovah himself. To know Father, Son, and Spirit, the Triune God, this is life eternal: let us keep to this, for in this way we shall gain complete instruction. By following on to know the Lord, we learn healing after being torn, binding up after smiting, and life after death. Experience has its perfect work when the heart follows the trackway of the Almighty Lord.

My soul, keep thou close to Jesus, follow on to know God in Jesus, and so shalt thou come to the knowledge of Christ, which is the most excellent of all the sciences. The Holy Ghost will lead thee into all truth. Is not this his gracious office? Rely upon him to fulfil it.

"And ye shall know that I am the Lord, when I have opened your graves, O my people, and brought you up out of your graves."—Ezek. xxxvii. 13.

INDEED it must be so: those who receive life from the dead are sure to recognize the hand of the Lord in such a resurrection. This is the greatest and most remarkable of all changes that a man can undergo—to be brought out of the grave of spiritual death, and made to rejoice in the light and liberty of spiritual life. None could work this but the living God, the Lord and giver of life.

Ah me! how well do I remember when I was lying in the valley full of dry bones, as dry as any of them! Blessed was the day when free and sovereign grace sent the man of God to prophesy upon me! Glory be to God for the stirring which that word of faith caused among the dry bones. More blessed still was that heavenly breath from the four winds which made me live! Now know I the quickening Spirit of the ever-living Jehovah. Truly Jehovah is the living God, for he made me live. My new life even in its pinings and sorrowings is clear proof to me that the Lord can kill and make alive. He is the only God. He is all that is great, gracious, and glorious, and my quickened soul adores him as the great I AM. All glory be unto his sacred name! As long as I live I will praise him.

"But I will have mercy upon the house of Judah, and will save them by the Lord their God, and will not save them by bow, nor by sword, nor by battle, by horses, nor by horsemen."—Hosea i. 7.

PRECIOUS word! Jehovah himself will deliver his people in the greatness of his mercy, but he will not do it by the ordinary means. Men are slow to render to God the glory due unto his name. If they go to battle with sword and bow, and win the victory, they ought to praise their God; yet they do not, but begin to magnify their own right arm, and glory in their horses and horsemen. For this reason our Jehovah often determines to save his people without second means, that all the honour may be to himself alone.

Look, then, my heart, to the Lord alone, and not to man. Expect to see God all the more clearly when there is no one else to look to. If I have no friend, no adviser, no one at my back, let me be none the less confident if I can feel that the Lord himself is on my side; yea, let me be glad if he gives victory without battle, as the text seems to imply. Why do I ask for horses and horsemen if Jehovah himself has mercy upon me, and lifts up his arm for my defence? Why need I bow or sword if God will save? Let me trust, and not be afraid, from this day forth and for evermore. Amen.

"The Lord will be with you."—2 Chron. xx. 17.

THIS was a great mercy for Jehoshaphat, for a great multitude had come out against him ; and it will be a great mercy for me, for I have great need, and I have no might or wisdom. If the Lord be with me, it matters little who may desert me. If the Lord be with me, I shall conquer in the battle of life, and the greater my trials the more glorious will be my victory. How can I be sure that the Lord is with me?

For certain he is with me if I am with him. If I trust in his faithfulness, believe his words, and obey his commands, he is assuredly with me. If I am on Satan's side God is against me, and cannot be otherwise ; but if I live to honour God I may be sure that he will honour me.

I am quite sure that God is with me if Jesus is my sole and only Saviour. If I have placed my soul in the hands of God's Only-begotten Son, then I may be sure that the Father will put forth all his power to preserve me, that his Son may not be dishonoured.

Oh for faith to take hold upon the short but sweet text for to-day! O Lord, fulfil this word to thy servant! Be with me in the house, in the street, in the field, in the shop, in company, and alone. Be thou also with all thy people.

"Wait on the Lord: be of good courage, and he shall strengthen thine heart: wait, I say, on the Lord."
Ps. xxvii. 14.

WAIT! Wait! Let your waiting be on the Lord! He is worth waiting for. He never disappoints the waiting soul.

While waiting keep up your spirits. Expect a great deliverance, and be ready to praise God for it.

The promise which should cheer you is in the middle of the verse—" He shall strengthen thine heart." This goes at once to the place where you need help. If the heart be sound, all the rest of the system will work well. The heart wants calming and cheering ; and both of these will come if it be strengthened. A forceful heart rests and rejoices, and throbs force into the whole man.

No one else can get at that secret urn of life, the heart, so as to pour strength into it. He alone who made it can make it strong. God is full of strength, and, therefore, he can impart it to those who need it. Oh, be brave ; for the Lord will impart his strength to you, and you shall be calm in tempest, and glad in sorrow.

He who penned these lines can write as David did—" Wait, *I say*, on the Lord." I do, indeed, say it. I know by long and deep experience that it is good for me to wait upon the Lord.

"It shall come to pass, that in the place where it was said unto them, Ye are not my people, there it shall be said unto them, Ye are the sons of the living God."—Hosea i. 10.

SOVEREIGN grace can make strangers into sons, and the Lord here declares his purpose to deal thus with rebels, and make them know what he has done. Beloved reader, the Lord has done this in my case; has he done the like for you? Then let us join hands and hearts in praising his adorable name.

Some of us were so decidedly ungodly that the Lord's Word most truly said to our conscience and heart, "Ye are not my people." In the house of God, and in our own homes, when we read the Bible, this was the voice of God's Spirit in our soul, "Ye are not my people." Truly a sad condemning voice it was. But now, in the same places, from the same ministry and Scripture, we hear a voice, which saith, "Ye are the sons of the living God." Can we be grateful enough for this? Is it not wonderful? Does it not give us hope for others? Who is beyond the reach of almighty grace? How can we despair of any, since the Lord has wrought so marvellous a change in us?

He who has kept this one great promise will keep every other; wherefore, let us go forward with songs of adoration and confidence.

"A bruised reed shall he not break, and the smoking flax shall he not quench."—Is. xlii. 3.

THEN I may reckon upon tender treatment from my Lord. Indeed, I feel myself to be at best as weak, as pliant, as worthless as a reed. Someone said, "I don't care a rush for you"; and the speech, though unkind, was not untrue. Alas! I am worse than a reed when it grows by the river, for that at least can hold up its head. I am bruised, sorely, sadly bruised. There is no music in me now; there is a rift which lets out all the melody. Ah, me! Yet Jesus will not break me; and if *he* will not, then I mind little what others try to do. O sweet and compassionate Lord, I nestle down beneath thy protection, and forget my bruises!

Truly I am also fit to be likened to "the smoking flax," whose light is gone, and only its smoke remains. I fear I am rather a nuisance than a benefit. My fears tell me that the devil has blown out my light, and left me an obnoxious smoke, and that my Lord will soon put an extinguisher upon me. Yet I perceive that though there were snuffers under the law, there were no extinguishers; and Jesus will not quench me; therefore, I am hopeful. Lord, kindle me anew, and cause me to shine forth to thy glory, and to the extolling of thy tenderness.

"Happy is the man that feareth alway."—Prov. xxviii. 14.

THE fear of the Lord is the beginning and the foundation of all true religion. Without a solemn awe and reverence of God there is no foothold for the more brilliant virtues. He whose soul does not worship will never live in holiness.

He is happy who feels a jealous fear of doing wrong. Holy fear looks not only before it leaps, but even before it moves. It is afraid of error, afraid of neglecting duty, afraid of committing sin. It fears ill company, loose talk, and questionable policy. This does not make a man wretched, but it brings him happiness. The watchful sentinel is happier than the soldier who sleeps at his post. He who foreseeth evil and escapes it is happier than he who walks carelessly on and is destroyed.

Fear of God is a quiet grace which leads a man along a choice road, of which it is written, "No lion shall be there, neither shall any ravenous beast go up thereon." Fear of the very appearance of evil is a purifying principle, which enables a man, through the power of the Holy Spirit, to keep his garments unspotted from the world. In both senses he that "feareth alway" is made happy. Solomon had tried both worldliness and holy fear: in the one he found vanity, in the other happiness. Let us not repeat his trial, but abide by his verdict.

"Blessed shalt thou be when thou comest in, and blessed shalt thou be when thou goest out."—Deut. xxviii. 6.

THE blessings of the law are not cancelled. Jesus confirmed the promise when he bore the penalty. If I keep the commands of my Lord, I may appropriate this promise without question.

This day I will *come in* to my house without fear of evil tidings, and I will come into my closet expecting to hear good news from my Lord. I will not be afraid to come in unto myself by self-examination, nor to come in to my affairs by a diligent inspection of my business. I have a good deal of work to do indoors, within my own soul; oh for a blessing upon it all, the blessing of the Lord Jesus, who has promised to abide with me.

I must also *go out*. Timidity makes me wish that I could stay within doors, and never go into the sinful world again. But I must go out in my calling, and I must go out that I may be helpful to my brethren, and useful to the ungodly. I must be a defender of the faith and an assailant of evil. Oh for a blessing upon my going out this day! Lord, let me go where thou leadest, on thy errands, under thy command, and in the power of thy Spirit.

Lord Jesus, turn in with me and be my guest; and then walk out with me, and cause my heart to burn whilst thou speakest with me by the way.

"It is good for a man that he bear the yoke in his youth."
Lam. iii. 27.

THIS is as good as a promise. It has been good, it is good, and it will be good for me to bear the yoke.

Early in life I had to feel the weight of conviction, and ever since it has proved a soul-enriching burden. Should I have loved the gospel so well had I not learned by deep experience the need of salvation by grace? Jabez was more honourable than his brethren because his mother bare him with sorrow, and those who suffer much in being born unto God make strong believers in sovereign grace.

The yoke of censure is an irksome one, but it prepares a man for future honour. He is not fit to be a leader who has not run the gauntlet of contempt. Praise intoxicates if it be not preceded by abuse. Men who rise to eminence without a struggle usually fall into dishonour.

The yoke of affliction, disappointment, and excessive labour is by no means to be sought for; but when the Lord lays it on us in our youth it frequently develops a character which glorifies God and blesses the church.

Come, my soul, bow thy neck; take up thy cross. It was good for thee when young, it will not harm thee now. For Jesus' sake, shoulder it cheerfully.

"Believe on the Lord Jesus Christ, and thou shalt be saved, and thy house."—Acts xvi. 31.

THIS gospel for a man with a sword at his throat, is the gospel for me. This would suit me if I were dying, and it is all that I need while I am living. I look away from self, and sin, and all idea of personal merit, and I trust the Lord Jesus as the Saviour whom God has given. I believe in him, I rest on him, I accept him to be my all in all. Lord, I am saved, and I shall be saved to all eternity, for I believe in Jesus. Blessed be thy name for this. May I daily prove by my life that I am saved from selfishness, and worldliness, and every form of evil.

But those last words about my "house": Lord, I would not run away with half a promise when thou dost give a whole one. I beseech thee, save all my family. Save the nearest and dearest. Convert the children, and the grandchildren, if I have any. Be gracious to my servants, and all who dwell under my roof, or work for me. Thou makest this promise to me personally if I believe in the Lord Jesus; I beseech thee to do as thou hast said.

I would go over in my prayer every day the names of all my brothers and sisters, parents, children, friends, relatives, servants, and give thee no rest till that word is fulfilled, "and thy house."

"His heavens shall drop down dew."—Deut. xxxiii. 28.

WHAT the dew in the East is to the world of nature, that is the influence of the Spirit in the realm of grace. How greatly do I need it! Without the Spirit of God I am a dry and withered thing. I droop, I fade, I die. How sweetly does this dew refresh me! When once favoured with it I feel happy, lively, vigorous, elevated. I want nothing more. The Holy Spirit brings me life, and all that life requires. All else without the dew of the Spirit is less than nothing to me: I hear, I read, I pray, I sing, I go to the table of communion, and I find no blessing there until the Holy Ghost visits me. But when he bedews me, every means of grace is sweet and profitable.

What a promise is this for me! "His heavens shall drop down dew." I shall be visited with grace. I shall not be left to my natural drought, or to the world's burning heat, or to the sirocco of Satanic temptation. Oh, that I may at this very hour feel the gentle, silent, saturating dew of the Lord! Why should I not? He who has made me to live as the grass lives in the meadow, will treat me as he treats the grass: he will refresh me from above. Grass cannot call for dew as I do. Surely, the Lord who visits the unpraying plant will answer to his pleading child.

"Blessed is the man that endureth temptation: for when he is tried, he shall receive the crown of life, which the Lord hath promised to them that love him."—James i. 12.

YES, he is blessed while he is enduring the trial. No eye can see this till it has been anointed with heavenly eye-salve. But he must endure it, and neither rebel against God, nor turn aside from his integrity. He is blessed who has gone through the fire, and has not been consumed as a counterfeit.

When the test is over, then comes the hall-mark of divine approval—"the crown of life." As if the Lord said, "Let him live; he has been weighed in the balances, and he is not found wanting." *Life* is the reward: not mere being; but holy, happy, true existence, the realization of the divine purpose concerning us. Already a higher form of spiritual life and enjoyment crowns those who have safely passed through fiercest trials of faith and love.

The Lord hath promised the crown of life to those who love him. Only lovers of the Lord will hold out in the hour of trial; the rest will either sink, or sulk, or slink back to the world. Come, my heart, dost thou love thy Lord? Truly? Deeply? Wholly? Then that love will be tried; but many waters will not quench it, neither will the floods drown it. Lord, let thy love nourish mine to the end.

"And a man shall be as an hiding-place from the wind, and a covert from the tempest."—Isa. xxxii. 2.

WHO this MAN is we all know. Who could he be but the Second Man, the Lord from heaven, the Man of sorrows, the Son of man? What a hiding-place he has been to his people! He bears the full force of the wind himself, and so he shelters those who hide themselves in him. We *have* thus escaped the wrath of God, and we shall thus escape the anger of men, the cares of this life, and the dread of death. Why do we stand in the wind when we may so readily and so surely get out of it by hiding behind our Lord? Let us this day run to him, and be at peace.

Often the common wind of trouble rises in its force and becomes a tempest, sweeping everything before it. Things which looked firm and stable rock in the blast, and many and great are the falls among our carnal confidences. Our Lord Jesus, the glorious Man, is a covert which is never blown down. In him we mark the tempest sweeping by, but we ourselves rest in delightful serenity.

This day let us just stow ourselves away in our hiding-place, and sit and sing under the protection of our covert. Blessed Jesus! Blessed Jesus! How we love thee! Well we may, for thou art to us a shelter in the time of storm.

"And whosoever shall give to drink unto one of these little ones a cup of cold water only in the name of a disciple, verily I say unto you, he shall in no wise lose his reward."
Matt. x. 42.

WELL, I can do as much as *that*. I can do a kind act towards the Lord's servant. The Lord knows I love them all, and would count it an honour to wash their feet. For the sake of their Master I love the disciples.

How gracious of the Lord to mention so insignificant an action—"to give to drink a cup of cold water only"! This I can do, however poor : this I may do, however lowly : this I will do right cheerfully. This, which seems so little, the Lord notices —notices when done to the least of his followers. Evidently it is not the cost, nor the skill, nor the quantity, that he looks at, but the motive: that which we do to a disciple, because he is a disciple, his Lord observes, and recompenses. He does not reward us for the merit of what we do, but according to the riches of his grace.

I give a cup of cold water, and he makes me to drink of living water. I give to one of his little ones, and he treats me as one of them. Jesus finds an apology for his liberality in that which his grace has led me to do, and he says, "He shall in no wise lose his reward."

"The righteous shall flourish like the palm tree: he shall grow like a cedar in Lebanon."—Ps. xcii. 12.

THESE trees are not trained and pruned by man: palms and cedars are "trees of the Lord," and it is by his care that they flourish; even so it is with the saints of the Lord, they are his own care. These trees are evergreen and are beautiful objects at all seasons of the year. Believers are not sometimes holy and sometimes ungodly: they stand in the beauty of the Lord under all weathers. Everywhere these trees are noteworthy: no one can gaze upon a landscape in which there are either palms or cedars without his attention being fixed upon these royal growths. The followers of Jesus are the observed of all observers: like a city set on a hill they cannot be hid.

The child of God flourishes like a palm tree, which pushes all its strength upward in one erect column without a single branch. It is a pillar with a glorious capital. It has no growth to the right or to the left, but sends all its force heavenward, and bears its fruit as near the sky as possible. Lord, fulfil this type in me.

The cedar braves all storms, and grows near the eternal snows, the Lord himself filling it with a sap which keeps its heart warm and its boughs strong. Lord, so let it be with me, I pray thee. Amen.

"And of Benjamin he said, The beloved of the Lord shall dwell in safety by him; and the Lord shall cover him all the day long, and he shall dwell between his shoulders."—Deut. xxxiii. 12.

YES, there is no safety like that which comes of dwelling near to God. For his best beloved the Lord can find no surer or safer place. O Lord, let me always abide under thy shadow, close to thy wounded side. Nearer and nearer would I come to thee, my Lord; and when once specially near thee, I would abide there for ever.

What a covering is that which the Lord gives to his chosen! Not a fair roof shall cover him, nor a bomb-proof casement, nor even an angel's wing, but Jehovah himself. Nothing can come at us when we are thus covered. This covering the Lord will grant us all the day long, however long the day. Lord, let me abide this day consciously beneath this canopy of love, this pavilion of sovereign power.

Does the third clause mean that the Lord in his temple would dwell among the mountains of Benjamin, or that the Lord would be where Benjamin's burden should be placed, or does it mean that we are borne upon the shoulders of the Eternal? In any case, the Lord is the support and strength of his saints. Lord, let me ever enjoy thy help, and then my arms will be sufficient for me.

"The Lord thy God in the midst of thee is mighty; he will save, he will rejoice over thee with joy; he will rest in his love, he will joy over thee with singing."—Zeph. iii. 17.

WHAT a word is this! Jehovah God in the centre of his people in all the majesty of his power! This presence alone suffices to inspire us with peace and hope. Treasures of boundless might are stored in our Jehovah, and he dwells in his church, therefore may his people shout for joy.

We not only have his presence, but he is engaged upon his choice work of salvation. "He will save." He is always saving: he takes his name of Jesus from it. Let us not fear any danger, for he is mighty to save.

Nor is this all. He abides evermore the same; he loves, he finds rest in loving, he will not cease to love. His love gives him joy. He even finds a theme for song in his beloved. This is exceedingly wonderful. When God wrought creation he did not sing, but simply said, "It is very good"; but when he came to redemption, then the sacred Trinity felt a joy to be expressed in song. Think of it, and be astonished! Jehovah Jesus sings a marriage song over his chosen bride. She is to him his love, his joy, his rest, his song. O Lord Jesus, by thine immeasurable love to us teach us to love thee, to rejoice in thee, and to sing unto thee our life-psalm.

"Thy people shall be willing in the day of thy power."
Ps. cx. 3.

BLESSED be the God of grace that it is so! He has a people whom he has chosen from of old to be his peculiar portion. These by nature have wills as stubborn as the rest of the froward sons of Adam; but when the day of his power comes, and grace displays its omnipotence, they become willing to repent, and to believe in Jesus. None are saved unwillingly, but the will is made sweetly to yield itself. What a wondrous power is this, which never violates the will, and yet rules it! God does not break the lock, but he opens it by a master-key which he alone can handle.

Now are we willing to be, to do, or to suffer as the Lord wills. If at any time we grow rebellious he has but to come to us with power, and straightway we run in the way of his commands with all our hearts. May this be a day of power with me as to some noble effort for the glory of God and the good of my fellow-men! Lord, I am willing; may I not hope that this is a day of thy power? I am wholly at thy disposal; willing, yea, eager, to be used of thee for thy holy purposes. O Lord, let me not have to cry, "To will is present with me, but how to perform that which I would, I find not"; but give me power as thou givest me will.

"Knowing that tribulation worketh patience."—Rom. v. 3.

THIS is a promise in essence if not in form.
We have need of patience, and here we see the
way of getting it. It is only by enduring that we
learn to endure, even as by swimming men learn
to swim. You could not learn that art on dry land,
nor learn patience without trouble. Is it not worth
while to suffer tribulation for the sake of gaining
that beautiful equanimity of mind which quietly
acquiesces in all the will of God?

Yet our text sets forth a singular fact, which is
not according to nature, but is supernatural. Tribulation in and of itself worketh petulance, unbelief,
and rebellion. It is only by the sacred alchemy
of grace that it is made to work in us patience.
We do not thresh the wheat to lay the dust: yet
the flail of tribulation does this upon God's floor.
We do not toss a man about in order to give him
rest, and yet so the Lord dealeth with his children.
Truly this is not the manner of man, but greatly
redounds to the glory of our all-wise God.

Oh, for grace to let my trials bless me! Why
should I wish to stay their gracious operation?
Lord, I ask thee to remove my affliction, but I
beseech thee ten times more to remove my im-
patience. Precious Lord Jesus, with thy cross
engrave the image of thy patience on my heart.

"But there the glorious Lord will be unto us a place of broad rivers and streams ; wherein shall go no galley with oars, neither shall gallant ship pass thereby."—Isa. xxxiii. 21.

THE Lord will be to us the greatest good without any of the drawbacks which seem necessarily to attend the best earthly things. If a city is favoured with broad rivers, it is liable to be attacked by galleys with oars, and other ships of war. But when the Lord represents the abundance of his bounty under this figure, he takes care expressly to shut out the fear which the metaphor might suggest. Blessed be his perfect love !

Lord, if thou send me wealth like broad rivers do not let the galley with oars come up in the shape of worldliness or pride. If thou grant me abundant health and happy spirits, do not let "the gallant ship" of carnal ease come sailing up the flowing flood. If I have success in holy service, broad as the German Rhine, yet let me never find the galley of self-conceit and self-confidence floating on the waves of my usefulness. Should I be so supremely happy as to enjoy the light of thy countenance year after year, yet let me never despise thy feeble saints, nor allow the vain notion of my own perfection to sail up the broad rivers of my full assurance. Lord, give me that blessing which maketh rich, and neither addeth sorrow, nor aideth sin.

"For, lo, I will command, and I will sift the house of Israel among all nations, like as corn is sifted in a sieve, yet shall not the least grain fall upon the earth."
Amos ix. 9.

THE sifting process is going on still. Wherever we go, we are still being winnowed and sifted. In all countries God's people are being tried "like as corn is sifted in a sieve." Sometimes the devil holds the sieve, and tosses us up and down at a great rate, with the earnest desire to get rid of us for ever. Unbelief is not slow to agitate our heart and mind with its restless fears. The world lends a willing hand at the same process, and shakes us to the right and to the left with great vigour. Worst of all, the church, so largely apostate as it is, comes in to give a more furious force to the sifting process.

Well, well! let it go on. Thus is the chaff severed from the wheat. Thus is the wheat delivered from dust and chaff. And how great is the mercy which comes to us in the text, "yet shall not the least grain fall upon the earth"! All shall be preserved that is good, true, gracious. Not one of the least of believers shall be lost, neither shall any believer lose anything worth calling a loss. We shall be so kept in the sifting that it shall be a real gain to us through Christ Jesus.

"And it shall come to pass, that every thing that liveth, which moveth, whithersoever the rivers shall come, shall live."—Ezek. xlvii. 9.

THE living waters, in the prophet's vision, flowed into the Dead Sea, and carried life with them, even into that stagnant lake. Where grace goes, spiritual life is the immediate and the everlasting consequence. Grace proceeds sovereignly according to the will of God, even as a river in all its windings follows its own sweet will ; and wherever it comes it does not wait for life to come to it, but it creates life by its own quickening flow. Oh that it would pour along our streets, and flood our slums! Oh that it would now come into my house, and rise till every chamber were made to swim with it! Lord, let the living water flow to my family and my friends, and let it not pass *me* by. I hope I have drunk of it already ; but I desire to bathe in it, yea, to swim in it. O my Saviour, I need life more abundantly. Come to me, I pray thee, till every part of my nature is vividly energetic and intensely active. Living God, I pray thee, fill me with thine own life.

I am a poor, dry stick ; come and make me so to live that, like Aaron's rod, I may bud and blossom and bring forth fruit unto thy glory. Quicken me, for the sake of my Lord Jesus. Amen.

"If the Lord were pleased to kill us, he would not have received a burnt offering and a meat offering at our hands, neither would he have shewed us all these things."
Judges xiii. 23.

THIS is a sort of promise deduced by logic. It is an inference fairly drawn from ascertained facts. It was not likely that the Lord had revealed to Manoah and his wife that a son would be born to them, and yet had it in his heart to destroy them. The wife reasoned well, and we shall do well if we follow her line of argument.

The Father has accepted the great sacrifice of Calvary, and has declared himself well pleased therewith; how can he now be pleased to kill us? Why a substitute if the sinner must still perish? The accepted sacrifice of Jesus puts an end to fear.

The Lord has shown us our election, our adoption, our union to Christ, our marriage to the Well-beloved: how can he now destroy us? The promises are loaded with blessings, which necessitate our being preserved unto eternal life. It is not possible for the Lord to cast us away, and yet fulfil his covenant. The past assures us, and the future re-assures us. We shall not die, but live; for we have seen Jesus, and in him we have seen the Father by the illumination of the Holy Ghost. Because of this life-giving sight we must live for ever.

"Lo, the people shall dwell alone, and shall not be reckoned among the nations."—Num. xxiii. 9.

WHO would wish to dwell among the nations, and to be numbered with them? Why, even the professing church is such that to follow the Lord fully within its bounds is very difficult. There is such a mingling and mixing that one often sighs for "a lodge in some vast wilderness."

Certain it is that the Lord would have his people follow a separated path as to the world, and come out decidedly and distinctly from it. We are set apart by the divine decree, purchase, and calling, and our inward experience has made us greatly to differ from men of the world; and therefore our place is not in their Vanity Fair, nor in their City of Destruction, but in the narrow way where all true pilgrims must follow their Lord.

This may not only reconcile us to the world's cold shoulder and sneers, but even cause us to accept them with pleasure as being a part of our covenant portion. Our names are not in the same book, we are not of the same seed, we are not bound for the same place, neither are we trusting to the same guide, therefore it is well that we are not of their number. Only let us be found in the number of the redeemed, and we are content to be odd and solitary to the end of the chapter

"For thou wilt light my candle."—Ps. xviii. 28.

IT may be that my soul sits in darkness; and if this be of a spiritual kind, no human power can bring me light. Blessed be God! he can enlighten my darkness, and at once light my candle. Even though I may be surrounded by a "darkness which might be felt," yet he can break the gloom, and immediately make it bright around me.

The mercy is, that if he lights the candle none can blow it out, neither will it go out for lack of substance, nor burn out of itself through the lapse of hours. The lights which the Lord kindled in the beginning are shining still. The Lord's lamps may need trimming, but he does not put them out.

Let me, then, like the nightingale, sing in the dark. Expectation shall furnish me with music, and hope shall pitch the tune. Soon I shall rejoice in a candle of God's lighting. I am dull and dreary just now. Perhaps it is the weather, or bodily weakness, or the surprise of a sudden trouble; but whatever has made the darkness, it is God alone who will bring the light. My eyes are unto him alone. I shall soon have the candle of the Lord shining about me; and, further on in his own good time, I shall be where they need no candle, neither light of the sun. Hallelujah!

"There remaineth therefore a rest to the people of God."
Heb. iv. 9.

GOD has provided a Sabbath, and some must enter into it. Those to whom it was first preached entered not in because of unbelief; therefore, that Sabbath remains for the people of God. David sang of it; but he had to touch the minor key, for Israel refused the rest of God. Joshua could not give it, nor Canaan yield it : it remains for believers.

Come, then, let us labour to enter into this rest. Let us quit the weary toil of sin and self. Let us cease from all confidence, even in those works of which it might be said, "They are very good." Have we any such? Still, let us cease from our own works, as God did from his. Now let us find solace in the finished work of our Lord Jesus. Everything is fully done : justice demands no more. Great peace is our portion in Christ Jesus.

As to providential matters, the work of grace in the soul, and the work of the Lord in the souls of others, let us cast these burdens upon the Lord, and rest in him. When the Lord gives us a yoke to bear, he does so that by taking it up we may find rest. By faith we labour to enter into the rest of God, and we renounce all rest in self-satisfaction or indolence. Jesus himself is perfect rest, and we are filled to the brim in him.

"He shall glorify me: for he shall receive of mine, and shall shew it unto you."—John xvi. 14.

THE Holy Ghost himself cannot better glorify the Lord Jesus than by showing to us Christ's own things. Jesus is his own best commendation. There is no adorning him except with his own gold.

The Comforter shows us that which he has received of our Lord Jesus. We never see anything aright till he reveals it. He has a way of opening our minds, and of opening the Scriptures, and by this double process he sets forth our Lord to us. There is much art in setting forth a matter, and that art belongs in the highest degree to the Spirit of truth. He shows us the things themselves. This is a great privilege, as those know who have enjoyed the hallowed vision.

Let us seek the illumination of the Spirit; not to gratify our curiosity, nor even to bring us personal comfort, so much as to glorify the Lord Jesus. Oh to have worthy ideas of him! Grovelling notions dishonour our precious Lord. Oh to have such vivid impressions of his person, and work, and glory, that we may with heart and soul cry out to his praise! Where there is a heart enriched by the Holy Ghost's teaching there will be a Saviour glorified beyond expression. Come, Holy Spirit, heavenly light, and show us Jesus our Lord.

"Open thy mouth wide, and I will fill it."—Ps. lxxxi. 10.

WHAT an encouragement to pray! Our human notions would lead us to ask small things because our deservings are so small; but the Lord would have us request great blessings. Prayer should be as simple a matter as the opening of the mouth; it should be a natural, unconstrained utterance. When a man is earnest he opens his mouth wide, and our text urges us to be fervent in our supplications.

Yet it also means that we may make bold with God, and ask many and large blessings at his hands. Read the whole verse, and see the argument: "I am Jehovah, thy God, which brought thee out of the land of Egypt: open thy mouth wide, and I will fill it." Because the Lord has given us so much he invites us to ask for more, yea, to expect more.

See how the little birds in their nests seem to be all mouth when the mother comes to feed them. Let it be the same with us. Let us take in grace at every door. Let us drink it in as a sponge sucks up the water in which it lies. God is ready to fill us if we are only ready to be filled. Let our needs make us open our mouths; let our faintness cause us to open our mouths and pant; yea, let our alarm make us open our mouths with a child's cry. The opened mouth shall be filled by the Lord himself. So be it unto us, O Lord, this day.

"He hath given meat unto them that fear him : he will ever be mindful of his covenant."—Ps. cxi. 5.

THOSE who fear God need not fear want. Through all these long years the Lord has always found meat for his own children, whether they have been in the wilderness, or by the brook Cherith, or in captivity, or in the midst of famine. Hitherto the Lord has given us day by day our daily bread, and we doubt not that he will continue to feed us till we want no more.

As to the higher and greater blessings of the covenant of grace, he will never cease to supply them as our case demands. He is mindful that he made the covenant, and never acts as if he regretted it. He is mindful of it when we provoke him to destroy us. He is mindful to love us, keep us, and comfort us, even as he engaged to do. He is mindful of every jot and tittle of his engagements, never suffering one of his words to fall to the ground.

We are sadly unmindful of our God, but he is graciously mindful of us. He cannot forget his Son who is the Surety of the Covenant, nor his Holy Spirit who actively carries out the covenant, nor his own honour, which is bound up with the covenant. Hence the foundation of God standeth sure, and no believer shall lose his divine inheritance, which is his by a covenant of salt.

"And Joseph said unto his brethren, I die: and God will surely visit you, and bring you out of this land unto the land which he sware to Abraham, to Isaac, and to Jacob."
Gen. l. 24.

JOSEPH had been an incarnate providence to his brethren. All our Josephs die, and a thousand comforts die with them. Egypt was never the same to Israel after Joseph was dead, nor can the world again be to some of us what it was when our beloved ones were alive.

But see how the pain of that sad death was alleviated! They had a promise that the living God would *visit them.* A visit from Jehovah! What a favour! What a consolation! What a heaven below! O Lord, visit us this day; though indeed we are not worthy that thou shouldest come under our roof.

But more was promised: the Lord would *bring them out.* They would find in Egypt a cold welcome when Joseph was dead; nay, it would become to them a house of bondage. But it was not to be so for ever; they would come out of it by a divine deliverance, and march to the land of promise. We shall not weep here for ever. We shall be called home to the glory-land to join our dear ones. Wherefore, "comfort one another with these words."

*"As for me, I will behold thy face in righteousness :
I shall be satisfied, when I awake, with thy likeness."*
Ps. xvii. 15.

THE portion of other men fills their bodies, and
enriches their children, but the portion of
the believer is of another sort. Men of the world
have their treasure in this world, but men of the
world to come look higher and further.

Our possession is twofold. We have God's *presence* here and his *likeness* hereafter. Here we behold the face of the Lord in righteousness, for we
are justified in Christ Jesus. Oh, the joy of beholding
the face of a reconciled God! The glory of God in
the face of Jesus Christ yields us heaven below, and
it will be to us the heaven of heaven above.

But seeing does not end it: we are to be changed
into that which we gaze upon. We shall sleep
a while and then wake up to find ourselves as
mirrors which reflect the beauties of our Lord.
Faith sees God with a transforming look. The
heart receives the image of Jesus into its own
depths, till the character of Jesus is imprinted on
the soul. This is satisfaction. To see God and
to be like him—what more can I desire? David's
assured confidence is here by the Holy Ghost
made to be the Lord's promise. I believe it.
I expect it. Lord, vouchsafe it. Amen.

"And I, if I be lifted up from the earth, will draw all men unto me."—John xii. 32.

COME, ye workers, be encouraged. You fear that you cannot draw a congregation. Try the preaching of a crucified, risen, and ascended Saviour; for this is the greatest "draw" that was ever yet manifested among men. What drew you to Christ but Christ? What draws you to him now but his own blessed self? If you have been drawn to religion by anything else, you will soon be drawn away from it; but Jesus has held you, and will hold you even to the end. Why, then, doubt his power to draw others? Go with the name of Jesus to those who have hitherto been stubborn, and see if it does not draw them.

No sort of man is beyond this drawing power. Old and young, rich and poor, ignorant and learned, depraved or amiable—all men shall feel the attractive force. Jesus is the one magnet. Let us not think of any other. Music will not draw to Jesus, neither will eloquence, logic, ceremonial, or noise. Jesus himself must draw men to himself; and Jesus is quite equal to the work in every case. Be not tempted by the quackeries of the day; but as workers for the Lord work in his own way, and draw with the Lord's own cords. Draw *to* Christ, and draw *by* Christ, for then Christ will draw by you.

"And the remnant of Jacob shall be in the midst of many people as a dew from the Lord, as the showers upon the grass, that tarrieth not for man, nor waiteth for the sons of men."—Micah v. 7.

IF this be true of the literal Israel, much more is it true of the spiritual Israel, the believing people of God. When saints are what they should be, they are an incalculable blessing to those among whom they are scattered.

They are as the dew; for in a quiet, unobtrusive manner they refresh those around them. Silently but effectually they minister to the life, growth, and joy of those who dwell with them. Coming fresh from heaven, glistening like diamonds in the sun, gracious men and women attend to the feeble and insignificant till each blade of grass has its own drop of dew. Little as individuals, they are, when united, all-sufficient for the purposes of love which the Lord fulfils through them. Dewdrops accomplish the refreshing of broad acres. Lord, make us like the dew!

Godly people are as showers which come at God's bidding without man's leave and license. They work for God whether men desire it or not; they no more ask human permission than the rain does. Lord, make us thus boldly prompt, and free in thy service wherever our lot is cast.

"Howbeit when he, the Spirit of truth, is come, he will guide you into all truth."—John xvi. 13.

TRUTH is like a vast cavern into which we desire to enter, but we are not able to traverse it alone. At the entrance it is clear and bright; but if we would go further and explore its innermost recesses, we must have a guide, or we shall lose ourselves. The Holy Spirit, who knows all truth perfectly, is the appointed guide of all true believers, and he conducts them as they are able to bear it, from one inner chamber to another, so that they behold the deep things of God, and his secret is made plain to them.

What a promise is this for the humbly enquiring mind! We desire to know the truth, and to enter into it. We are conscious of our own aptness to err, and we feel the urgent need of a guide. We rejoice that the Holy Spirit is come and abides among us. He condescends to act as a guide to us, and we gladly accept his leadership. "All truth" we wish to learn, that we may not be one-sided and out of balance. We would not be willingly ignorant of any part of revelation lest thereby we should miss blessing, or incur sin. The Spirit of God has come that he may guide us into all truth: let us with obedient hearts hearken to his words and follow his lead.

"He goeth before you into Galilee: there shall ye see him, as he said unto you."—Mark xvi. 7.

WHERE he appointed to meet his disciples, there he would be in due time. Jesus keeps his tryst. If he promises to meet us at the mercy-seat, or in public worship, or in the ordinances, we may depend upon it that he will be there. We may wickedly stay away from the appointed meeting-place, but he never does. He says, "Where two or three are met together in my name, there am I"; he says not "There will I be," but, "I am there already."

Jesus is always first in fellowship: "He goeth before you." His heart is with his people, his delight is in them, he is never slow to meet them. In all fellowship he goeth before us.

But he reveals himself to those who come after him: "There shall ye see him." Joyful sight! We care not to see the greatest of mere men, but to see HIM is to be filled with joy and peace. And we shall see him, for he promises to come to those who believe in him, and to manifest himself to them. Rest assured that it will be so, for he does everything according to his word of promise: "As he said unto you." Catch at those last words, and be assured that to the end he will do for you "as he said unto you."

"Thou shalt no more be termed Forsaken."—Isa. lxii. 4.

"FORSAKEN" is a dreary word. It sounds like a knell. It is the record of sharpest sorrows, and the prophecy of direst ills. An abyss of misery yawns in that word "Forsaken." Forsaken by one who pledged his honour! Forsaken by a friend so long tried and trusted! Forsaken by a dear relative! Forsaken by father and mother! Forsaken by all! This is woe indeed, and yet it may be patiently borne if the Lord will take us up.

But what must it be to feel forsaken of God? Think of that bitterest of cries, "My God, my God, why hast thou forsaken me?" Have we ever in any degree tasted the wormwood and the gall of "Forsaken," in that sense? If so, let us beseech our Lord to save us from any repetition of so unspeakable a sorrow. Oh that such darkness may never return! Men in malice said to a saint, "God hath forsaken him; persecute and take him." But it was always false. The Lord's loving favour shall compel our cruel foes to eat their own words, or, at least, to hold their tongues.

The reverse of all this is that superlative word, *Hephzibah*—"the Lord delighteth in thee." This turns weeping into dancing. Let those who dreamed that they were forsaken hear the Lord say, "I will never leave thee nor forsake thee."

"And the priest shall put some of the blood upon the horns of the altar of sweet incense before the Lord."
Lev. iv. 7.

THE altar of incense is the place where saints present their prayers and praises; and it is delightful to think of it as sprinkled with the blood of the great sacrifice. This it is which makes all our worship acceptable with Jehovah: he sees the blood of his own Son, and therefore accepts our homage.

It is well for us to fix our eyes upon the blood of the one offering for sin. Sin mingles even with our holy things, and our best repentance, faith, prayer, and thanksgiving could not be received of God were it not for the merit of the atoning sacrifice. Many sneer at "the blood;" but to us it is the foundation of comfort and hope. That which is on the horns of the altar is meant to be prominently before our eyes when we draw near to God. The blood gives strength to prayer, and hence it is on the altar's horns. It is "before the Lord," and therefore it ought to be before us. It is on the altar before we bring the incense; it is there to sanctify our offerings and gifts.

Come, let us pray with confidence, since the victim is offered, the merit has been pleaded, the blood is within the veil, and the prayers of believers must be sweet unto the Lord.

"I have set before thee an open door, and no man can shut it."—Rev. iii. 8.

SAINTS who remain faithful to the truth of God have an open door before them. My soul, thou hast resolved to live and die by that which the Lord has revealed in his Word, and therefore before thee stands this open door.

I will enter in by the open door of communion with God. Who shall say me nay? Jesus has removed my sin, and given me his righteousness, therefore I may freely enter. Lord, I do so by thy grace.

I have also before me an open door into the mysteries of the Word. I may enter into the deep things of God. Election, Union to Christ, the Second Advent—all these are before me, and I may enjoy them. No promise and no doctrine are now locked up against me.

An open door of access is before me in private, and an open door of usefulness in public. God will hear me; God will use me. A door is opened for my onward march to the church above, and for my daily fellowship with saints below. Some may try to shut me up or shut me out, but all in vain.

Soon shall I see an open door into heaven: the pearl gate will be my way of entrance, and then I shall go in unto my Lord and King, and be with God eternally shut in.

"And I will strengthen them in the Lord: and they shall walk up and down in his name, saith the Lord."
Zech. x. 12.

A SOLACE for sick saints. They have grown faint, and they fear that they shall never rise from the bed of doubt and fear; but the great Physician can both remove the disease, and take away the weakness which has come of it. He will strengthen the feeble. This he will do in the best possible way, for it shall be "in Jehovah." Our strength is far better in God than in self. In the Lord it causes fellowship, in ourselves it would create pride. In ourselves it would be sadly limited, but in God it knows no bound.

When strength is given, the believer uses it. He walks up and down in the name of the Lord. What an enjoyment it is to walk abroad after illness, and what a delight to be strong in the Lord after a season of prostration! The Lord gives his people liberty to walk up and down, and an inward leisure to exercise that liberty. He makes gentlemen of us: we are not slaves who know no rest, and see no sights, but we are free to travel at our ease throughout Immanuel's land.

Come, my heart, be thou no more sick and sorry. Jesus bids thee be strong, and walk with God in holy contemplation. Obey his word of love.

" And the Lord thy God will circumcise thine heart, and the heart of thy seed, to love the Lord thy God with all thine heart, and with all thy soul, that thou mayest live."—Deut. xxx. 6.

HERE we read of the true circumcision.

Note the author of it: "The Lord thy God." He alone can deal effectually with our heart, and take away its carnality and pollution. To make us love God with all our heart and soul is a miracle of grace which only the Holy Ghost can work. We must look to the Lord alone for this, and never be satisfied with anything short of it.

Note where this circumcision is wrought. It is not of the flesh, but of the spirit. It is the essential mark of the covenant of grace. Love to God is the indelible token of the chosen seed; by this secret seal the election of grace is certified to the believer. We must see to it that we trust in no outward ritual, but are sealed in heart by the operation of the Holy Ghost.

Note what the result is—"that thou mayest live." To be carnally minded is death. In the overcoming of the flesh we find life and peace. If we mind the things of the Spirit, we shall live. Oh that Jehovah, our God, may complete his gracious work upon our inner natures, that in the fullest and highest sense we may live unto the Lord.

"If my people, which are called by my name, shall humble themselves, and pray, and seek my face, and turn from their wicked ways; then will I hear from heaven, and will forgive their sin, and will heal their land."—2 Chron. vii. 14.

CALLED by the name of the Lord, we are nevertheless erring men and women. What a mercy it is that our God is ready to forgive! Whenever we sin let us hasten to the mercy-seat of our God, seeking pardon.

We are to humble ourselves. Should we not be humbled by the fact that after receiving so much love we yet transgress? O Lord, we bow before thee in the dust, and own our grievous ingratitude. Oh the infamy of sin! Oh the sevenfold infamy of it in persons so favoured as we have been!

Next, we are to pray for mercy, for cleansing, for deliverance from the power of sin. O Lord, hear us even now, and shut not out our cry.

In this prayer we are to seek the Lord's face. He has left us because of our faults, and we must entreat him to return. O Lord, look on us in thy Son Jesus, and smile upon thy servants.

With this must go our own turning from evil, God cannot turn to us unless we turn from sin.

Then comes the triple promise of hearing, pardon, and healing. Our Father, grant us these at once, for our Lord Jesus Christ's sake.

"Whosoever therefore shall confess me before men, him will I confess also before my Father which is in heaven."
Matt. x. 32.

GRACIOUS promise! It is a great joy to me to confess my Lord. Whatever my faults may be, I am not ashamed of Jesus, nor do I fear to declare the doctrines of his cross. O Lord, I have not hid thy righteousness within my heart.

Sweet is the prospect which the text sets before me! Friends forsake and enemies exult, but the Lord does not disown his servant. Doubtless my Lord will own me even here, and give me new tokens of his favourable regard. But there comes a day when I must stand before the great Father. What bliss to think that Jesus will confess me then! He will say, "This man truly trusted me, and was willing to be reproached for my name's sake; and therefore I acknowledge him as mine." The other day a great man was made a knight, and the Queen handed him a jewelled garter; but what of that? It will be an honour beyond all honours for the Lord Jesus to confess us in the presence of the divine Majesty in the heavens. Never let me be ashamed to own my Lord. Never let me indulge a cowardly silence, or allow a faint-hearted compromise. Shall I blush to own him who promises to own me?

"As the living Father hath sent me, and I live by the Father: so he that eateth me, even he shall live by me."
John vi. 57.

WE live by virtue of our union with the Son of God. As God-man Mediator, the Lord Jesus lives by the self-existent Father who has sent him, and in the same manner we live by the Saviour who has quickened us. He who is the source of our life is also the sustenance of it. Living is sustained by feeding. We must support the spiritual life by spiritual food, and that spiritual food is the Lord Jesus. Not his life, or death, or offices, or work, or word alone, but himself, as including all these. On Jesus, himself, we feed.

This is set forth to us in the Lord's Supper, but it is actually enjoyed by us when we meditate upon our Lord, believe in him with appropriating faith, take him into ourselves by love, and assimilate him by the power of the inner life. We know what it is to feed on Jesus, but we cannot speak it or write it. Our wisest course is to practise it, and to do so more and more. We are entreated to eat abundantly, and it will be to our infinite profit to do so when Jesus is our meat and our drink.

Lord, I thank thee that this, which is a necessity of my new life, is also its greatest delight. So, I do at this hour feed on thee.

"Because I live, ye shall live also."—John xiv. 19.

JESUS has made the life of believers in him *as certain* as his own. As sure as the head lives the members live also. If Jesus has not risen from the dead, then are we dead in our sins; but since he has risen, all believers are risen in him. His death has put away our transgressions, and loosed the bonds which held us under the death sentence. His resurrection proves our justification: we are absolved, and mercy saith, "The Lord hath put away thy sin, thou shalt not die."

Jesus has made the life of his people *as eternal* as his own. How can they die as long as he lives, seeing they are one with him? Because he dieth no more, and death hath no more dominion over him, so they shall no more return to the graves of their old sins, but shall live unto the Lord in newness of life. O believer, when, under great temptation, thou fearest that thou shalt one day fall by the hand of the enemy, let this re-assure thee. Thou shalt never lose thy spiritual life, for it is hid with Christ in God. Thou dost not doubt the immortality of thy Lord; therefore, do not think that he will let thee die, since thou art one with him. The argument for thy life is *his life*, and of that thou canst have no fear; wherefore rest in thy living Lord.

"He that feareth the commandment shall be rewarded."
Prov. xiii. 13.

HOLY awe of God's Word is at a great discount. Men think themselves wiser than the Word of the Lord, and sit in judgment upon it. "So did not I, because of the fear of God." We accept the inspired Book as infallible, and prove our esteem by our obedience. We have no terror of the Word, but we have a filial awe of it. We are not in fear of its penalties, because we have a fear of its commands.

This holy fear of the commandment produces the restfulness of humility, which is far sweeter than the recklessness of pride. It becomes a guide to us in our movements; a drag when we are going down-hill, and a stimulus when we are climbing it. Preserved from evil and led into righteousness by our reverence of the command, we gain a quiet conscience, which is a well of wine; a sense of freedom from responsibility, which is as life from the dead; and a confidence of pleasing God, which is heaven below. The ungodly may ridicule our deep reverence for the Word of the Lord; but what of that? The prize of our high calling is a sufficient consolation for us. The rewards of obedience make us scorn the scorning of the scorner.

"They that sow in tears shall reap in joy."—Ps. cxxvi. 5.

WEEPING times are suitable for sowing : we do not want the ground to be too dry. Seed steeped in the tears of earnest anxiety will come up all the sooner. The salt of prayerful tears will give the good seed a flavour which will preserve it from the worm : truth spoken in awful earnestness has a double life about it. Instead of stopping our sowing because of our weeping, let us redouble our efforts because the season is so propitious.

Our heavenly seed could not fitly be sown laughing. Deep sorrow and concern for the souls of others are a far more fit accompaniment of godly teaching than anything like levity. We have heard of men who went to war with a light heart, but they were beaten ; and it is mostly so with those who sow in the same style.

Come, then, my heart, sow on in thy weeping, for thou hast the promise of a joyful harvest. Thou shalt reap. Thou, thyself, shalt see some result of thy labour. This shall come to thee in so large a measure as to give thee joy, which a poor, withered, and scanty harvest would not do. When thine eyes are dim with silver tears, think of the golden corn. Bear cheerfully the present toil and disappointment ; for the harvest day will fully recompense thee.

"I will correct thee in measure."—Jer. xxx. 11.

TO be left uncorrected would be a fatal sign: it would prove that the Lord had said, " He is given unto idols, let him alone." God grant that such may never be our portion! Uninterrupted prosperity is a thing to cause fear and trembling. As many as God tenderly loves he rebukes and chastens: those for whom he has no esteem he allows to fatten themselves without fear, like bullocks for the slaughter. It is in love that our heavenly Father uses the rod upon his children.

Yet see, the correction is " in measure ": he gives us love without measure, but chastisement " in measure." As under the old law no Israelite could receive more than the " forty stripes save one," which ensured careful counting and limited suffering, so is it with each afflicted member of the household of faith—every stroke is counted. It is the measure of wisdom, the measure of sympathy, the measure of love, by which our chastisement is regulated. Far be it from us to rebel against appointments so divine. Lord, if thou standest by to measure the bitter drops into my cup, it is for me cheerfully to take that cup from thy hand, and drink according to thy directions, saying " Thy will be done."

"He shall save his people from their sins."—Matt. i. 21.

LORD, save me from my sins. By thy name of Jesus I am encouraged thus to pray. Save me from my past sins, that the habit of them may not hold me captive. Save me from my constitutional sins, that I may not be the slave of my own weaknesses. Save me from the sins which are continually under my eye that I may not lose my horror of them. Save me from secret sins; sins unperceived by me from my want of light. Save me from sudden and surprising sins: let me not be carried off my feet by a rush of temptation. Save me, Lord, from every sin. Let not any iniquity have dominion over me.

Thou alone canst do this. I cannot snap my own chains or slay my own enemies. Thou knowest temptation, for thou wast tempted. Thou knowest sin, for thou didst bear the weight of it. Thou knowest how to succour me in my hour of conflict. Thou canst save me from sinning, and save me when I have sinned. It is promised in thy very name that thou wilt do this, and I pray thee let me this day verify the prophecy. Let me not give way to temper, or pride, or despondency, or any form of evil; but do thou save me unto holiness of life, that thy name of Jesus may be glorified in me abundantly.

"A little one shall become a thousand, and a small one a strong nation: I the Lord will hasten it in his time."
Isa. lx. 22.

WORKS for the Lord often begin on a small scale, and they are none the worse for this. Feebleness educates faith, brings God near, and wins glory for his name. Prize promises of increase. Mustard seed is the smallest among seeds, and yet it becomes a tree-like plant, with branches which lodge the birds of heaven. We may begin with one, and that "a little one," and yet it will "become a thousand." The Lord is great at the multiplication table. How often did he say to his lone servant, "I will multiply thee"! Trust in the Lord, ye ones and twos; for he will be in the midst of you if you are gathered in his name.

"A small one." What can be more despicable in the eyes of those who count heads and weigh forces! yet this is the nucleus of a great nation. Only one star shines out at first in the evening, but soon the sky is crowded with countless lights.

Nor need we think the prospect of increase to be remote, for the promise is, "I Jehovah will hasten it in his time." There will be no premature haste, like that which we see at excited meetings; it will be all in due time; but yet there will be no delay; When the Lord hastens, his speed is glorious.

"Thou, O Lord God, hast spoken it: and with thy blessing let the house of thy servant be blessed for ever."
2 Sam. vii. 29.

THIS is a promise pleaded, and so it yields double instruction to us. Anything which the Lord God has spoken we should receive as surely true, and then plead it at the throne.

Oh, how sweet to quote what our own God has spoken! How precious to use a "therefore" which the promise suggests, as David does in this verse!

We do not pray because we doubt, but because we believe. To pray unbelievingly is unbecoming in the Lord's children. No, Lord, we cannot doubt thee: we are persuaded that every word of thine is a sure foundation for the boldest expectation. We come to thee and say, "Do as thou hast said." Bless thy servants' house. Heal our sick; save our hesitating ones; restore those who wander; confirm those who live in thy fear. Lord, give us food and raiment according to thy word. Prosper our undertakings; especially succeed our endeavours to make known thy gospel in our neighbourhood. Make our servants thy servants, our children thy children. Let the blessing flow on to future generations, and as long as any of our race remains on earth may they remain true to thee. O Lord God "let the house of thy servant be blessed."

"Light is sown for the righteous, and gladness for the upright in heart."—Ps. xcvii. 11.

RIGHTEOUSNESS is often costly to the man who keeps to it at all hazards, but in the end it will bear its own expenses, and return an infinite profit. A holy life is like sowing seed: much is going out, and apparently it is buried in the soil, never to be gathered up again. We are mistaken when we look for an immediate harvest; but the error is very natural, for it seems impossible to bury light. Yet light is "sown," says the text. It lies latent: none can see it, it is sown. We are quite sure that it must one day manifest itself.

Full sure are we that the Lord has set a harvest for the sowers of light, and they shall reap it, each man for himself. Then shall come their gladness. Sheaves of joy for seeds of light. Their heart was upright before the Lord, though men gave them no credit for it, but even censured them: they were righteous, though those about them denounced them as censorious. They had to wait, as husbandmen wait for the precious fruits of the earth: but the light was sown for them, and gladness was being prepared on their behalf by the Lord of the harvest.

Courage, brothers! we need not be in a hurry. Let us in patience possess our souls, for soon shall our souls possess light and gladness.

"And I will make thee unto this people a fenced brazen wall: and they shall fight against thee, but they shall not prevail against thee: for I am with thee to save thee and to deliver thee, saith the Lord."—Jer. xv. 20.

STABILITY in the fear and faith of God will make a man like a wall of brass, which no one can batter down or break. Only the Lord can make such; but we need such men in the church, and in the world, but specially in the pulpit.

Against uncompromising men of truth this age of shams will fight tooth and nail. Nothing seems to offend Satan and his seed like decision. They attack holy firmness even as the Assyrians besieged fenced cities. The joy is that they cannot prevail against those whom God has made strong in his strength. Carried about with every wind of doctrine, others only need to be blown upon, and away they go; but those who love the doctrines of grace, because they possess the grace of the doctrines, stand like rocks in the midst of raging seas.

Whence this stability? "I am with thee, saith the Lord": that is the true answer. Jehovah will save and deliver faithful souls from all the assaults of the adversary. Hosts are against us, but the Lord of hosts is with us. We dare not budge an inch; for the Lord himself holds us in our place, and there we will abide for ever.

"But seek ye first the kingdom of God, and his righteousness; and all these things shall be added unto you."
Matt. vi. 33.

SEE how the Bible opens: "In the beginning God." Let your life open in the same way. Seek with your whole soul, first and foremost, the kingdom of God, as the place of your citizenship, and his righteousness as the character of your life. As for the rest, it will come from the Lord himself without your being anxious concerning it. All that is needful for this life and godliness "shall be added unto you."

What a promise this is! Food, raiment, home, and so forth, God undertakes to add to you while you seek him. You mind his business, and he will mind yours. If you want paper and string, you get them given in when you buy more important goods; and just so all that we need of earthly things we shall have thrown in with the kingdom. He who is an heir of salvation shall not die of starvation; and he who clothes his soul with the righteousness of God cannot be left of the Lord with a naked body. Away with carking care. Set all your mind upon seeking the Lord. Covetousness is poverty, and anxiety is misery: trust in God is an estate, and likeness to God is a heavenly inheritance. Lord, I seek thee, be found of me.

"For the elect's sake those days shall be shortened."
Matt. xxiv. 22.

FOR the sake of his elect the Lord withholds many judgments, and shortens others. In great tribulations the fire would devour all were it not that out of regard to his elect the Lord damps the flame. Thus, while he saves his elect for the sake of Jesus, he also preserves the race for the sake of his chosen.

What an honour is thus put upon saints! How diligently they ought to use their influence with their Lord! He will hear their prayers for sinners, and bless their efforts for their salvation. He blesses believers that they may be a blessing to those who are in unbelief. Many a sinner lives because of the prayers of a mother, or wife, or daughter, to whom the Lord has respect.

Have we used aright the singular power with which the Lord entrusts us? Do we pray for our country, for other lands, and for the age? Do we, in times of war, famine, pestilence, stand out as intercessors, pleading that the days may be shortened? Do we lament before God the outbursts of infidelity, error, and licentiousness? Do we beseech our Lord Jesus to shorten the reign of sin by hastening his own glorious appearing? Let us get to our knees, and never rest till Christ appeareth.

"His servants shall serve him: and they shall see his face; and his name shall be in their foreheads."—Rev. xxii. 3, 4.

THREE choice blessings will be ours in the glory land.

"His servants shall serve him." No other lords shall oppress us, no other service shall distress us. We shall serve Jesus always, perfectly, without weariness, and without error. This is heaven to a saint: in all things to serve the Lord Christ, and to be owned by him as his servant is our soul's high ambition for eternity.

"And they shall see his face." This makes the service delightful : indeed, it is the present reward of service. We shall know our Lord, for we shall see him as he is. To see the face of Jesus is the utmost favour that the most faithful servant of the Lord can ask. What more could Moses ask than— " Let me see thy face " ?

"And his name shall be in their foreheads." They gaze upon their Lord till his name is photographed upon their brows. They are acknowledged by him, and they acknowlege him. The secret mark of inward grace develops into the public sign-manual of confessed relationship.

O Lord, give us these three things in their beginnings here, that we may possess them in their fulness in thine own abode of bliss !

"And it shall be forgiven them ; for it is ignorance."
Num. xv. 25.

BECAUSE of our ignorance we are not fully aware of our sins of ignorance. Yet we may be sure they are many, in the form both of commission and omission. We may be doing in all sincerity, as a service to God, that which he has never commanded, and can never accept.

The Lord knows these sins of ignorance every one. This may well alarm us, since in justice he will require these trespasses at our hand ; but on the other hand, faith spies comfort in this fact, for the Lord will see to it that stains unseen by us shall yet be washed away. He sees the sin that he may cease to see it by casting it behind his back.

Our great comfort is that Jesus, the true priest, has made atonement for all the congregation of the children of Israel. That atonement secures the pardon of unknown sins. His precious blood cleanses us from all sin. Whether our eyes have seen it and wept over it, or not, God has seen it, Christ has atoned for it, the Spirit bears witness to the pardon of it, and so we have a threefold peace.

O my Father, I praise thy divine knowledge, which not only perceives my iniquities, but provides an atonement which delivers me from the guilt of them, even before I know that I am guilty.

"And I will put a division between my people and thy people: to-morrow shall this sign be."—Ex. viii. 23.

PHARAOH has a people, and the Lord has a people. These may dwell together, and seem to fare alike, but there is a division between them, and the Lord will make it apparent. Not for ever shall one event happen alike to all, but there shall be great difference between the men of the world and the people of Jehovah's choice.

This may happen in the time of judgments, when the Lord becomes the sanctuary of his saints. It is very conspicuous in the conversion of believers when their sin is put away, while unbelievers remain under condemnation. From that moment they become a distinct race, come under a new discipline, and enjoy new blessings. Their homes, henceforth, are free from the grievous swarms of evils which defile and torment the Egyptians. They are kept from the pollution of lust. the bite of care, the corruption of falsehood, and the cruel torment of hatred, which devour many families.

Rest assured, tried believer, that though you have your troubles you are saved from swarms of worse ones, which infest the homes and hearts of the servants of the world's Prince. The Lord has put a division; see to it that you keep up the division in spirit, aim, character and company.

"Then will I sprinkle clean water upon you, and ye shall be clean: from all your filthiness, and from all your idols, will I cleanse you."—Ez. xxxvi. 25.

WHAT an exceeding joy is this! He who has purified us with the blood of Jesus will also cleanse us by the water of the Holy Spirit. God hath said it, and so it must be, "Ye shall be clean." Lord, we feel and mourn our uncleanness, and it is cheering to be assured by thine own mouth that we shall be clean. Oh that thou wouldst make a speedy work of it!

He will deliver us from our worst sins. The uprisings of unbelief, and the deceitful lusts which war against the soul, the vile thoughts of pride, and the suggestions of Satan to blaspheme the sacred name—all these shall be so purged away as never to return.

He will also cleanse us from all our idols, whether of gold or of clay: our impure loves, and our excessive love of that which in itself is pure. That which we have idolized shall either be broken from us, or we shall be broken off from it.

It is God who speaks of what he himself will do. Therefore is this word established and sure, and we may boldly look for that which it guarantees to us. Cleansing is a covenant blessing, and the covenant is ordered in all things and sure.

"I shall not die, but live, and declare the works of the Lord."—Ps. cxviii. 17.

A FAIR assurance this! It was no doubt based upon a promise, inwardly whispered in the Psalmist's heart, which he seized upon and enjoyed. Is my case like that of David? Am I depressed because the enemy insults over me? Are there multitudes against me, and few on my side? Does unbelief bid me lie down and die in despair—a defeated, dishonoured man? Do my enemies begin to dig my grave?

What then? Shall I yield to the whisper of fear, and give up the battle, and with it give up all hope? Far from it. There is life in me yet: "I shall not die." Vigour will return and remove my weakness: "I shall live." The Lord lives, and I shall live also. My mouth shall again be opened: "I shall declare the works of Jehovah." Yes, and I shall speak of the present trouble as another instance of the wonder-working faithfulness and love of the Lord my God. Those who would gladly measure me for my coffin had better wait a bit; for "the Lord hath chastened me sore, but he hath not given me over unto death." Glory be to his name for ever! I am immortal till my work is done. Till the Lord wills it no vault can close upon me.

"Faithful is he that calleth you, who also will do it."
1 Thess. v. 24.

WHAT will he do? He will sanctify us wholly. See the previous verse. He will carry on the work of purification till we are perfect in every part. He will preserve our "whole spirit, and soul, and body, blameless unto the coming of our Lord Jesus Christ." He will not allow us to fall from grace, nor come under the dominion of sin. What great favours are these! Well may we adore the giver of such unspeakable gifts.

Who will do this? The Lord who has called us out of darkness into his marvellous light, out of death in sin into eternal life in Christ Jesus. Only he can do this : such perfection and preservation can only come from the God of all grace.

Why will he do it? Because he is "faithful"— faithful to his own promise which is pledged to save the believer; faithful to his Son, whose reward it is that his people shall be presented to him faultless ; faithful to the work which he has commenced in us by our effectual calling. It is not their own faithfulness, but the Lord's own faithfulness, on which the saints rely.

Come, my soul, here is a grand feast to begin a dull month with. There may be fogs without, but there should be sunshine within.

"No good thing will he withhold from them that walk uprightly."—Ps. lxxxiv. 11.

MANY pleasing things the Lord may withhold, but "no good thing." He is the best judge of what is good for us. Some things are assuredly good, and these we may have for the asking through Jesus Christ our Lord.

Holiness is a good thing, and this he will work in us freely. Victory over evil tendencies, strong tempers, and evil habits, he will gladly grant, and we ought not to remain without it.

Full assurance he will bestow, and *near communion* with himself, and *access* into all truth, and *boldness* with prevalence at the mercy seat. If we have not these, it is from want of faith to receive, and not from any unwillingness of God to give. A calm, a heavenly frame, *great patience*, and *fervent love*—all these will he give to holy diligence.

But note well that we must "walk uprightly." There must be no cross purposes and crooked dealings; no hypocrisy nor deceit. If we walk foully God cannot give us favours, for that would be a premium upon sin. The way of uprightness is the way of heavenly wealth—wealth so large as to include every good thing.

What a promise to plead in prayer! Let us get to our knees.

"For the vision is yet for an appointed time, but at the end it shall speak, and not lie: though it tarry, wait for it; because it will surely come, it will not tarry."—Hab. ii. 3.

MERCY may seem slow, but it is sure. The Lord in unfailing wisdom has appointed a time for the outgoings of his gracious power, and God's time is the best time. We are in a hurry; the vision of the blessing excites our desire, and hastens our longings; but the Lord will keep his appointments. He never is before his time; he never is behind.

God's word is here spoken of as a living thing which will speak, and will come. It is never a dead letter, as we are tempted to fear when we have long watched for its fulfilment. The living word is on the way from the living God, and though it may seem to linger, it is not in reality doing so. God's train is not behind time. It is only a matter of patience, and we shall soon see for ourselves the faithfulness of the Lord. No promise of his shall fail; "it will not lie." No promise of his will be lost in silence; "it shall speak." What comfort it will speak to the believing ear! No promise of his shall need to be renewed like a bill which could not be paid on the day in which it fell due—"it will not tarry."

Come, my soul, canst thou not wait for thy God? Rest in him and be still in unutterable peacefulness.

"And he said, Thus saith the Lord, Make this valley full of ditches. For thus saith the Lord, Ye shall not see wind, neither shall ye see rain; yet that valley shall be filled with water, that ye may drink, both ye, and your cattle, and your beasts."—2 Kings iii. 16, 17.

THREE armies were perishing of thirst, and the Lord interposed. Although he sent neither cloud nor rain, yet he supplied an abundance of water. He is not dependent upon ordinary methods, but can surprise his people with novelties of wisdom and power. Thus are we made to see more of God than ordinary processes could have revealed. Although the Lord may not appear for us in the way we expect, or desire, or suppose, yet he will in some way or other provide for us. It is a great blessing for us to be raised above looking to secondary causes, so that we may gaze into the face of the great First Cause.

Have we this day grace enough to make trenches into which the divine blessing may flow? Alas! we too often fail in the exhibition of true and practical faith. Let us this day be on the outlook for answers to prayer. As the child who went to a meeting to pray for rain took an umbrella with her; so let us truly and practically expect the Lord to bless us. Let us make the valley full of ditches and expect to see them all filled.

"I will not contend for ever, neither will I be always wroth: for the spirit should fail before me, and the souls which I have made."—Isa. lvii. 16.

OUR heavenly Father seeks our instruction, not our destruction. His contention *with* us has a kind intention *towards* us. He will not be always in arms against us. We think the Lord is long in his chastisements, but that is because we are short in our patience. His compassion endureth for ever, but not his contention. The night may drag its weary length along, but it must in the end give place to cheerful day. As contention is only for a season, so the wrath which leads to it is only for a small moment. The Lord loves his chosen too well to be always angry with them.

If he were to deal with us always as he does sometimes we should faint outright, and go down hopelessly to the gates of death. Courage, dear heart! the Lord will soon end his chiding. Bear up, for the Lord will bear you up, and bear you through. He who made you knows how frail you are, and how little you can bear. He will handle tenderly that which he has fashioned so delicately. Therefore, be not afraid because of the painful present, for it hastens to a happy future. He that smote you will heal you; his little wrath shall be followed by great mercies.

"Delight thyself also in the Lord ; and he shall give thee the desires of thine heart."—Ps. xxxvii. 4.

DELIGHT in God has a transforming power, and lifts a man above the gross desires of our fallen nature. Delight in Jehovah is not only sweet in itself, but it sweetens the whole soul, till the longings of the heart become such that the Lord can safely promise to fulfil them. Is not that a grand delight which moulds our desires till they are like the desires of God ?

Our foolish way is to desire, and then set to work to compass what we desire. We do not go to work in God's way, which is to seek him first, and then expect all things to be added unto us. If we will let our heart be filled with God till it runs over with delight, then the Lord himself will take care that we shall not want any good thing. Instead of going abroad for joys let us stay at home with God, and drink waters out of our own fountain. He can do for us far more than all our friends. It is better to be content with God alone than to go about fretting and pining for the paltry trifles of time and sense. For a while we may have disappointments; but if these bring us nearer to the Lord, they are things to be prized exceedingly, for they will in the end secure to us the fulfilment of all our right desires.

"He that humbleth himself shall be exalted."—Luke xviii. 14.

IT ought not to be difficult for us to humble ourselves, for what have we to be proud of? We ought to take the lowest place without being told to do so. If we are sensible and honest we shall be little in our own eyes. Especially before the Lord in prayer we shall shrink to nothing. There we cannot speak of merit, for we have none: our one and only appeal must be to mercy: " God be merciful to me a sinner."

Here is a cheering word from the throne. We shall be exalted by the Lord if we humble ourselves. For us the way upward is downhill. When we are stripped of self we are clothed with humility, and this is the best of wear. The Lord will exalt us in peace and happiness of mind; he will exalt us into knowledge of his Word and fellowship with himself; he will exalt us in the enjoyment of sure pardon and justification. The Lord puts his honours upon those who can wear them to the honour of the giver. He gives usefulness, acceptance, and influence to those who will not be puffed up by them, but will be abased by a sense of greater responsibility. Neither God nor man will care to lift up a man who lifts up himself; but both God and good men unite to honour modest worth.

O Lord, sink me in self that I may rise in thee.

"My grace is sufficient for thee: for my strength is made perfect in weakness."—2 Cor. xii. 9.

OUR weakness should be prized as making room for divine strength. We might never have known the power of grace if we had not felt the weakness of nature. Blessed be the Lord for the thorn in the flesh, and the messenger of Satan, when they drive us to the strength of God.

This is a precious word from our Lord's own lip. It has made the writer laugh for joy. God's grace enough for me! I should think it is. Is not the sky enough for the bird, and the ocean enough for the fish? The All-sufficient is sufficient for my largest want. He who is sufficient for earth and heaven is certainly able to meet the case of one poor worm like me.

Let us, then, fall back upon our God and his grace. If he does not remove our grief he will enable us to bear it. His strength shall be poured into us till the worm shall thresh the mountains; and a nothing shall be victor over all the high and mighty ones. It is better for us to have God's strength than our own; for if we were a thousand times as strong as we are, it would all amount to nothing in the face of the enemy; and if we could be weaker than we are, which is scarcely possible, yet we could do all things through Christ.

> "*Thus shall they know that I the Lord their God am with them, and that they, even the house of Israel, are my people, saith the Lord God.*"—Ez. xxxiv. 30.

TO be the Lord's own people is a choice blessing, but to know that we are such is a comfortable blessing. It is one thing to *hope* that God is with us, and another thing to *know* that he is so. Faith saves us, but assurance satisfies us. We take God to be our God when we believe in him; but we get the joy of him when we know that he is ours, and that we are his. No believer should be content with hoping and trusting, he should ask the Lord to lead him on to full assurance, so that matters of hope may become matters of certainty.

It is when we enjoy covenant blessings, and see our Lord Jesus raised up for us as a plant of renown, that we come to a clear knowledge of the favour of God towards us. Not by law, but by grace, do we learn that we are the Lord's people. Let us always turn our eyes in the direction of free grace. Assurance of faith can never come by the works of the law. It is an evangelical virtue, and can only reach us in a gospel way. Let us not look within. Let us look to the Lord alone. As we see Jesus we shall see our salvation.

Lord, send us such a flood-tide of thy love that we shall be washed beyond the mire of doubt and fear.

"He will not suffer thy foot to be moved."—Ps. cxxi. 3.

IF the Lord will not suffer it, neither men nor devils can do it. How greatly would they rejoice if they could give us a disgraceful fall, drive us from our position, and bury us out of memory! They could do this to their heart's content were it not for one hindrance, and only one : the Lord will not suffer it ; and if *he* does not suffer it, *we* shall not suffer it.

The way of life is like travelling among the Alps. Along mountain paths one is constantly exposed to the slipping of the foot. Where the way is high the head is apt to swim, and then the feet soon slide : there are spots which are smooth as glass, and others that are rough with loose stones, and in either of these a fall is hard to avoid. He who throughout life is enabled to keep himself upright and to walk without stumbling has the best of reasons for gratitude. What with pitfalls and snares, weak knees, weary feet, and subtle enemies, no child of God would stand fast for an hour were it not for the faithful love which will not suffer his foot to be moved.

> "Amidst a thousand snares I stand
>   Upheld and guarded by thy hand ;
>   That hand unseen shall hold me still,
>   And lead me to thy holy hill."

"For sin shall not have dominion over you : for ye are not under the law, but under grace."—Rom. vi. 14.

SIN will reign if it can : it cannot be satisfied with any place below the throne of the heart. We sometimes fear that it will conquer us, and then we cry unto the Lord, "Let not any iniquity have dominion over me." This is his comforting answer, "Sin shall not have dominion over you." It may assail you, and even wound you ; but it shall never establish sovereignty over you.

If we were under the law, our sin would gather strength and hold us under its power ; for it is the punishment of sin that a man comes under the power of sin. As we are under the covenant of grace, we are secured against departing from the living God by the sure declaration of the covenant Grace is promised to us, by which we are restored from our wanderings, cleansed from our impurities, and set free from the chains of habit.

We might lie down in despair and be "content to serve the Egyptians" if we were still as slaves working for eternal life ; but since we are the Lord's free men, we take courage to fight with our corruptions and temptations, being assured that sin shall never bring us under its sway again. God himself giveth us the victory through our Lord Jesus Christ, to whom be glory for ever and ever. Amen.

"My people shall be satisfied with my goodness, saith the Lord."—Jer. xxxi. 14.

NOTE the " my " which comes twice : " *My* people shall be satisfied with *my* goodness." The kind of people who are satisfied with God are marked out as God's own. He is pleased with them, for they are pleased with him. They call him their God, and he calls them his people ; he is satisfied to take them for a portion, and they are satisfied with him for their portion. There is a mutual communion of delight between God's Israel and Israel's God.

These people are satisfied. This is a grand thing. Very few of the sons of men are ever satisfied, let their lot be what it may ; they have swallowed the horse-leech, and it continually cries, " Give ! give ! " Only sanctified souls are satisfied souls. God himself must both convert us and content us.

It is no wonder that the Lord's people should be satisfied with the goodness of their Lord. Here is goodness without mixture, bounty without stint, mercy without chiding, love without change, favour without reserve. If God's goodness does not satisfy us, what will ? What ! are we still groaning ? Surely there is a wrong desire within if it be one which God's goodness does not satisfy.

Lord, I am satisfied. Blessed be thy name.

"Behold, he that keepeth Israel shall neither slumber nor sleep."—Ps. cxxi. 4.

JEHOVAH is "the Keeper of Israel." No form of unconsciousness ever steals over him, neither the deeper slumber nor the slighter sleep. He never fails to watch the house and the heart of his people. This is a sufficient reason for our resting in perfect peace. Alexander said that he slept because his friend Parmenio watched ; much more may we sleep because our God is our guard.

"Behold" is here set up to call our attention to the cheering truth. Israel, when he had a stone for his pillow, fell asleep ; but his God was awake, and came in vision to his servant. When we lie defenceless, Jehovah himself will cover our head.

The Lord keeps his people as a rich man keeps his treasure, as a captain keeps a city with a garrison, as a sentry keeps watch over his sovereign. None can harm those who are in such keeping. Let me put my soul into his dear hands. He never forgets us, never ceases actively to care for us, never finds himself unable to preserve us.

O my Lord, keep me, lest I wander and fall and perish. Keep me, that I may keep thy commandments. By thine unslumbering care prevent my sleeping like the sluggard, and perishing like those who sleep the sleep of death.

"If ye shall ask anything in my name, I will do it."
John xiv. 14.

WHAT a wide promise! Anything! Whether large or small, all my needs are covered by that word "anything." Come, my soul, be free at the mercy seat, and hear thy Lord saying to thee, "Open thy mouth wide, and I will fill it."

What a wise promise! We are always to ask in the name of Jesus. While this encourages *us*, it also honours *him*. This is a constant plea. Occasionally every other plea is darkened, especially such as we could draw from our own relation to God, or our experience of his grace; but at such times the name of Jesus is as mighty at the throne as ever, and we may plead it with full assurance.

What an instructive prayer! I may not ask for anything to which I cannot put Christ's hand and seal. I dare not use my Lord's name to a selfish or wilful petition. I may only use my Lord's name to prayers which he would himself pray if he were in my case. It is a high privilege to be authorized to ask in the name of Jesus as if Jesus himself asked; but our love to him will never allow us to set that name where he would not have set it.

Am I asking for that which Jesus approves? Dare I put his seal to my prayer? Then I have that which I seek of the Father.

"My God shall supply all your need according to his riches in glory by Christ Jesus."—Phil. iv. 19.

PAUL'S God is our God, and will supply all our need. Paul felt sure of this in reference to the Philippians, and we feel sure of it as to ourselves. God will do it, for it is like him : he loves us, he delights to bless us, and it will glorify him to do so. His pity, his power, his love, his faithfulness, all work together that we be not famished.

What a measure doth the Lord go by : " According to his riches in glory by Christ Jesus." The riches of his grace are large, but what shall we say of the riches of his glory ? His " riches of glory by Christ Jesus," who shall form an estimate of this ? According to this immeasurable measure will God fill up the immense abyss of our necessities. He makes the Lord Jesus the receptacle and the channel of his fulness, and then he imparts to us his wealth of love in its highest form. Hallelujah !

The writer knows what it is to be tried in the work of the Lord. Fidelity has been recompensed with anger, and liberal givers have stopped their subscriptions ; but he whom they sought to oppress has not been one penny the poorer, nay, rather he has been the richer ; for this promise has been true, " My God shall supply all your need." God's supplies are surer than the Bank of England.

*"No weapon that is formed against thee shall prosper;
and every tongue that shall rise against thee in judgment
thou shalt condemn."*—Isa. liv. 17.

THERE is great clatter in the forges and
smithies of the enemy. They are making
weapons wherewith to smite the saints. They
could not even do as much as this if the Lord of
saints did not allow them; for he has created the
smith that bloweth the coals in the fire. But see
how busily they labour! How many swords and
spears they fashion! It matters nothing, for on
the blade of every weapon you may read this
inscription: *It shall not prosper.*

But now listen to another noise: it is the strife
of tongues. Tongues are more terrible instruments
than can be made with hammers and anvils, and
the evil which they inflict cuts deeper and spreads
wider. What will become of us now? Slander,
falsehood, insinuation, ridicule—these are poisoned
arrows; how can we meet them? The Lord God
promises us that, if we cannot silence them, we shall,
at least, escape from being ruined by them. They
condemn us for the moment, but we shall condemn
them at last, and for ever. The mouth of them
that speak lies shall be stopped, and their falsehoods shall be turned to the honour of those good
men who suffered by them.

"For the Lord will not cast off his people, neither will he forsake his inheritance."—Ps. xciv. 14.

NO, nor will he cast off even so much as one of them. Man has his cast-offs, but God has none; for his choice is unchangeable, and his love is everlasting. None can find out a single person whom God has forsaken after having revealed himself savingly to him.

This grand truth is mentioned in the psalm to cheer the heart of the afflicted. The Lord chastens his own; but he never forsakes them. The result of the double work of the law and the rod is our instruction, and the fruit of that instruction is a quieting of spirit, a sobriety of mind, out of which comes rest. The ungodly are let alone till the pit is digged into which they will fall and be taken; but the godly are sent to school to be prepared for their glorious destiny hereafter. Judgment will return and finish its work upon the rebels, but it will equally return to vindicate the sincere and godly. Hence we may bear the rod of chastisement with calm submission; it means not anger, but love.

> " God may chasten and correct,
>   But he never can neglect;
>   May in faithfulness reprove,
>   But he ne'er can cease to love."

"In that day shall the Lord defend the inhabitants of Jerusalem; and he that is feeble among them at that day shall be as David; and the house of David shall be us God, as the angel of the Lord before them."—Zech. xii. 8.

ONE of the best methods of the Lord's defending his people is to make them strong in inward might. Men are better than walls, and faith is stronger than castles.

The Lord can take the feeblest among us and make him like David, the champion of Israel. Lord, do this with me! Infuse thy power into me, and fill me with sacred courage that I may face the giant with sling and stone, confident in God.

The Lord can make his greatest champions far mightier than they are : David can be as God, as the angel of Jehovah. This would be a marvellous development, but it is possible, or it would not be spoken of. O Lord, work thus with the best of our leaders! Show us what thou art able to do— namely, to raise thy faithful servants to a height of grace and holiness which shall be clearly supernatural!

Lord, dwell in thy saints, and they shall be as God ; put thy might into them, and they shall be as the living creatures who dwell in the presence of Jehovah. Fulfil this promise to thine entire church in this our day, for Jesus' sake. Amen.

"From this day will I bless you."—Haggai ii. 19.

FUTURE things are hidden from us. Yet here is a glass in which we may see the unborn years. The Lord says, "From this day will I bless you."

It is worth while to note the day which is referred to in this promise. There had been failure of crops, blasting, and mildew, and all because of the people's sin. Now, the Lord saw these chastened ones commencing to obey his word, and build his temple, and therefore he says, "From the day that the foundation of the Lord's temple was laid, consider. From this day will I bless you." If we have lived in any sin, and the Spirit leads us to purge ourselves of it, we may reckon upon the blessing of the Lord. His smile, his Spirit, his grace, his fuller revelation of his truth will all prove to us an enlarged blessing. We may fall into greater opposition from man because of our faithfulness, but we shall rise to closer dealings with the Lord our God, and a clearer sight of our acceptance in him.

Lord, I am resolved to be more true to thee, and more exact in my following of thy doctrine and thy precept ; and I pray thee, therefore, by Christ Jesus, to increase the blessedness of my daily life henceforth and for ever.

"For he satisfieth the longing soul, and filleth the hungry soul with goodness."—Ps. cvii. 9.

IT is well to have longings, and the more intense they are the better. The Lord will satisfy soul-longings, however great and all-absorbing they may be. Let us greatly long, for God will greatly give. We are never in a right state of mind when we are contented with ourselves, and are free from longings. Desires for more grace, and groanings which cannot be uttered, are growing pains, and we should wish to feel them more and more. Blessed Spirit, make us sigh and cry after better things, and for more of the best things!

Hunger is by no means a pleasant sensation. Yet blessed are they that hunger and thirst after righteousness. Such persons shall not only have their hunger relieved with a little food, but they shall be filled. They shall not be filled with any sort of rough stuff, but their diet shall be worthy of their good Lord, for they shall be filled with goodness by Jehovah himself.

Come, let us not fret because we long and hunger, but let us hear the voice of the Psalmist as he also longs and hungers to see God magnified. "Oh, that men would praise the Lord for his goodness, and for his wonderful works to the children of men."

"Look unto me, and be ye saved, all the ends of the earth: for I am God, and there is none else."—Isa. xlv. 22.

THIS is a promise of promises. It lies at the foundation of our spiritual life. Salvation comes through a look at him who is "a just God and a Saviour." How simple is the direction! "Look unto me." How reasonable is the requirement! Surely the creature should look to the Creator. We have looked elsewhere long enough, it is time that we look alone to him who invites our expectation, and promises to give us his salvation.

Only a look! Will we not look at once? We are to bring nothing in ourselves, but to look outward and upward to our Lord on his throne, whither he has gone up from the cross. A look requires no preparation, no violent effort: it needs neither wit nor wisdom, wealth nor strength. All that we need is in the Lord our God, and if we look to him for everything, that everything shall be ours, and we shall be saved.

Come, far-off ones, look hither! Ye ends of the earth, turn your eyes this way! As from the furthest regions men may see the sun and enjoy his light, so you who lie in death's borders at the very gates of hell may by a look receive the light of God, the life of heaven, the salvation of the Lord Jesus Christ, who is God, and therefore able to save.

> "*In those days, and in that time, saith the Lord, the iniquity of Israel shall be sought for, and there shall be none; and the sins of Judah, and they shall not be found: for I will pardon them whom I reserve.*"—Jer. l. 20.

A GLORIOUS word indeed! What a perfect pardon is here promised to the sinful nations of Israel and Judah! Sin is to be so removed that it shall not be found, so blotted out that there shall be none. Glory be unto the God of pardons!

Satan seeks out sins wherewith to accuse us, our enemies seek them that they may lay them to our charge, and our own conscience seeks them even with a morbid eagerness. But when the Lord applies the precious blood of Jesus, we fear no form of search, for "there shall be none," "they shall not be found." The Lord hath caused the sins of his people to cease to be : he hath finished transgression, and made an end of sin. The sacrifice of Jesus has cast our sins into the depths of the sea. This makes us dance for joy.

The reason for the obliteration of sin lies in the fact that Jehovah himself pardons his chosen ones. His word of grace is not only royal, but divine. He speaks absolution, and we are absolved. He applies the atonement, and from that hour his people are beyond all fear of condemnation. Blessed be the name of the sin-annihilating God!

"The Lord thy God will put out those nations before thee by little and little."—Deut. vii. **22**.

WE are not to expect to win victories for the Lord Jesus by a single blow. Evil principles and practices die hard. In some places it takes years of labour to drive out even one of the many vices which defile the inhabitants. We must carry on the war with all our might, even when favoured with little manifest success.

Our business in this world is to conquer it for Jesus. We are not to make compromises, but to exterminate evils. We are not to seek popularity, but to wage unceasing war with iniquity. Infidelity, Popery, drink, impurity, oppression, worldliness, error ; these are all to be "put out."

The Lord our God can alone accomplish this. He works by his faithful servants ; and, blessed be his name, he promises that he will so work. "Jehovah thy God will put out those nations before thee." This he will do by degrees, that we may learn perseverance, may increase in faith, may earnestly watch, and may avoid carnal security. Let us thank God for a little success, and pray for more. Let us never sheathe the sword till the whole land is won for Jesus.

Courage, my heart! Go on little by little, for many littles will make a great whole.

"He will not always chide: neither will he keep his anger for ever."—Ps. ciii. 9.

HE will chide sometimes, or he would not be a wise father for such poor erring children as we are. His chiding is very painful to those who are true, because they feel how sadly they deserve it, and how wrong it is on their part to grieve him. We know what this chiding means, and we bow before the Lord, mourning that we should cause him to be angry with us.

But what a comfort we find in these lines! "Not always" will he chide. If we repent and turn to him with hearts broken *for* sin and broken *from* sin, he will smile upon us at once. It is no pleasure to him to turn a frowning face towards those whom he loves with all his heart: it is his joy that our joy should be full.

Come, let us seek his face. There is no reason for despair, nor even for despondency. Let us love a chiding God, and before long we shall sing: "Thine anger is turned away, and thou comfortest me." Begone, ye dark forebodings, ye ravens of the soul! Come in, ye humble hopes and grateful memories, ye doves of the heart! He who pardoned us long ago as a judge, will again forgive us as a father, and we shall rejoice in his sweet, unchanging love.

"Who art thou, O great mountain? before Zerubbabel thou shalt become a plain: and he shall bring forth the headstone thereof with shoutings, crying, Grace, grace unto it."—Zech. iv. 7.

AT this hour a mountain of difficulty, distress, or necessity, may be in our way, and natural reason sees no path over it, or through it, or round it. Let faith come in, and straightway the mountain disappears and becomes a plain. But faith must first hear the word of the Lord—"Not by might, nor by power, but by my Spirit, saith the Lord of hosts." This grand truth is a prime necessity for meeting the insurmountable trials of life.

I see that I can do nothing, and that all reliance on man is vanity. "Not by might." I see that no visible means can be relied on, but the force is in the invisible Spirit. God alone must work, and men and means must be nothing accounted of. If it be so, that the Almighty God takes up the concerns of his people, then great mountains are nothing. He can remove worlds as boys toss balls about, or drive them with their foot. This power he can lend to me. If the Lord bids me move an Alp I can do it through his name. It may be a great mountain, but even before my feebleness it shall become a plain; for the Lord hath said it What can I be afraid of with God on my side?

"Your sorrow shall be turned into joy."—John xvi. 20.

THEIR particular sorrow was the death and absence of their Lord, and it was turned into joy when he rose from the dead and showed himself in their midst. All the sorrows of saints shall be thus transmuted; even the worst of them, which look as if they must for ever remain fountains of bitterness.

Then the more sorrow the more joy. If we have loads of sorrow, then the Lord's power will turn them into tons of joy. Then the bitterer the trouble the sweeter the pleasure: the swinging of the pendulum far to the left will cause it to go all the farther to the right. The remembrance of the grief shall heighten the flavour of the delight: we shall set the one in contrast with the other, and the brilliance of the diamond shall be the more clearly seen because of the black foil behind it.

Come, my heart, cheer up! In a little while I shall be as glad as I am now gloomy. Jesus tells me that by a heavenly alchemy my sorrow shall be turned into joy. I do not see how it is to be, but I believe it, and I begin to sing by way of anticipation. This depression of spirit is not for long, I shall soon be up among the happy ones who praise the Lord day and night, and there I shall sing of the mercy which delivered me out of great afflictions.

"And he said, My presence shall go with thee, and I will give thee rest."—Ex. xxxiii. 14.

PRECIOUS promise! Lord, enable me to appropriate it as all my own.

We must go at certain times from our abode, for here we have no continuing city. It often happens that when we feel most at home in a place, we are suddenly called away from it. Here is the antidote for this ill. The Lord himself will keep us company. His presence, which includes his favour, his fellowship, his care, and his power, shall be ever with us in every one of our marchings. This means far more than it says; for, in fact, it means all things. If we have God present with us, we have possession of heaven and earth. Go with me, Lord, and then command me where thou wilt!

But we hope to find a place of rest. The text promises it. We are to have rest of God's own giving, making, and preserving. His presence will cause us to rest even when we are on the march, yea, even in the midst of battle. *Rest!* Thrice blessed word. Can it ever be enjoyed by mortals? Yes, there is the promise, and by faith we plead it. Rest comes from the Comforter, from the Prince of Peace, and from the glorious Father who rested on the seventh day from all his works. To be with God is to rest in the most emphatic sense.

"The Lord shall command the blessing upon thee in thy storehouses, and in all that thou settest thine hand unto."
Deut. xxviii. 8.

IF we obey the Lord our God he will bless that which he gives us. Riches are no curse when blessed of the Lord. When men have more than they require for their immediate need, and begin to lay up in store-houses, the dry rot of covetousness, or the blight of hard-heartedness is apt to follow the accumulation; but with God's blessing it is not so. Prudence arranges the saving, liberality directs the spending, gratitude maintains consecration, and praise sweetens enjoyment. It is a great mercy to have God's blessing in one's iron safe, and on one's banking account.

What a favour is made ours by the last clause! "The Lord shall bless thee in all that thou settest thine hand unto." We would not put our hand to anything upon which we dare not ask God's blessing, neither would we go about it without prayer and faith. But what a privilege to be able to look for the Lord's help in every enterprise! Some talk of a lucky man: the blessing of the Lord is better than luck. The patronage of the great is nothing to the favour of God. Self-reliance is all very well, but the Lord's blessing is infinitely more than all the fruit of talent, genius, or tact.

"He that believeth shall not make haste."—Isa. xxviii. 16.

HE shall make haste to keep the Lord's commandments; but he shall not make haste in any impatient or improper sense.

He shall not haste to run away, for he shall not be overcome with the fear which causes panic. When others are flying hither and thither as if their wits had failed them, the believer shall be quiet, calm, and deliberate, and so shall be able to act wisely in the hour of trial.

He shall not haste in his expectations, craving his good things at once and on the spot; but he will wait God's time. Some are in a desperate hurry to have the bird in the hand; for they regard the Lord's promise as a bird in the bush, not likely to be theirs. Believers know how to wait.

He shall not haste by plunging into wrong or questionable action. Unbelief must be doing something, and thus it works its own undoing; but faith makes no more haste than good speed, and thus it is not forced to go back sorrowfully by the way which it followed heedlessly.

How is it with me? Am I believing, and am I therefore keeping to the believer's pace, which is walking with God? Peace, fluttering spirit! Oh, rest in the Lord, and wait patiently for him! Heart, see that thou do this at once!

"The Lord, he it is that doth go before thee; he will be with thee, he will not fail thee, neither forsake thee: fear not, neither be dismayed."—Deut. xxxi. 8.

IN the presence of a great work or a great warfare, here is a text which should help us to buckle on our harness. If Jehovah himself goes before us, it must be safe to follow. Who can obstruct our progress if the Lord himself is in the van? Come, brother soldiers, let us make a prompt advance! Why do we hesitate to pass on to victory?

Nor is the Lord before us only; he is with us. Above, beneath, around, within is the omnipotent, omnipresent One. In all time, even to eternity, he will be with us even as he has been. How this should nerve our arm! Dash at it boldly, ye soldiers of the cross, for the Lord of hosts is with us!

Being before us and with us, he will never withdraw his help. He cannot fail in himself, and he will not fail towards us. He will continue to help us according to our need, even to the end. As he cannot fail us, so he will not forsake us. He will always be both able and willing to grant us strength and succour till fighting days are gone.

Let us not fear nor be dismayed; for the Lord of hosts will go down to the battle with us, will bear the brunt of the fight, and give us the victory.

" He that walketh uprightly walketh surely."—Prov. x. 9.

HIS walk may be slow, but it is sure. He that
hasteth to be rich shall not be innocent nor
sure; but steady perseverance in integrity, if it do
not bring riches, will certainly bring peace. In
doing that which is just and right we are like one
walking upon a rock, for we have confidence that
every step we take is upon solid and safe ground.
On the other hand, the utmost success through
questionable transactions must always be hollow
and treacherous, and the man who has gained it
must always be afraid that a day of reckoning will
come, and then his gains will condemn him.

Let us stick to truth and righteousness. By
God's grace let us imitate our Lord and Master, in
whose mouth no deceit was ever found. Let us not
be afraid of being poor, nor of being treated with
contempt. Never, on any account whatever, let us
do that which our conscience cannot justify. If we
lose inward peace, we lose more than a fortune can
buy. If we keep in the Lord's own way, and never
sin against our conscience, our way is sure against
all comers. Who is he that can harm us if we
be followers of that which is good? We may be
thought fools by fools if we are firm in our integrity;
but in the place where judgment is infallible we
shall be approved.

"I have set the Lord always before me: because he is at my right hand, I shall not be moved."—Ps. xvi. 8.

THIS is the way to live. With God always before us, we shall have the noblest companionship, the holiest example, the sweetest consolation, and the mightiest influence. This must be a resolute act of the mind, "I have set," and it must be maintained as a set and settled thing. Always to have an eye to the Lord's eye, and an ear for the Lord's voice—this is the right state for the godly man. His God is near him, filling the horizon of his vision, leading the way of his life, and furnishing the theme of his meditation. What vanities we should avoid, what sins we should overcome, what virtues we should exhibit, what joys we should experience if we did indeed set the Lord always before us! Why not?

This is the way to be safe. The Lord being ever in our minds, we come to feel safety and certainty because of his being so near. He is at our right hand to guide and aid us; and hence we are not moved by fear, nor force, nor fraud, nor fickleness. When God stands at a man's right hand, that man is himself sure to stand. Come on, then, ye foemen of the truth! Rush against me like a furious tempest, if ye will. God upholds me. God abides with me. Whom shall I fear?

"I will make with them a covenant of peace, and will cause the evil beasts to cease out of the land: and they shall dwell safely in the wilderness, and sleep in the woods."
Ez. xxxiv. 25.

IT is the height of grace that Jehovah should be in covenant with man, a feeble, sinful and dying creature. Yet the Lord has solemnly entered into a faithful compact with us, and from that covenant he will never turn aside. In virtue of this covenant we are safe. As lions and wolves are driven off by shepherds, so shall all noxious influences be chased away. The Lord will give us rest from disturbers and destroyers; the evil beasts shall cease out of the land. O Lord, make this thy promise good even now!

The Lord's people are to enjoy security in places of the greatest exposure: wildernesses and woods are to be as pastures and folds to the flock of Christ. If the Lord does not change the place for the better, he will make us the better in the place. The wilderness is not a place to dwell in, but the Lord can make it so; in the woods one feels bound to watch rather than to sleep, and yet the Lord giveth his beloved sleep even there. Nothing without or within should cause any fear to the child of God. By faith the wilderness can become the suburbs of heaven, and the woods the vestibule of glory.

"He shall cover thee with his feathers, and under his wings shalt thou trust: his truth shall be thy shield and buckler."—Ps. xci. 4.

A CONDESCENDING simile indeed! Just as a hen protects her brood and allows them to nestle under her wings, so will the Lord defend his people, and permit them to hide away in him. Have we not seen the little chicks peeping out from under the mother's feathers? Have we not heard their little cry of contented joy? In this way let us shelter ourselves in our God, and feel overflowing peace in knowing that he is guarding us.

While the Lord covers us we trust. It would be strange if we did not. How can we distrust when Jehovah himself becomes house and home, refuge and rest to us?

This done, we go out to war in his name and enjoy the same guardian care. We need shield and buckler, and when we implicitly trust God, even as the chick trusts the hen, we find his truth arming us from head to foot. The Lord cannot lie; he must be faithful to his people; his promise must stand. This sure truth is all the shield we need. Behind it we defy the fiery darts of the enemy.

Come, my soul, hide under those great wings, lose thyself among those soft feathers! How happy thou art!

"He shall dwell on high: his place of defence shall be the munitions of rocks: bread shall be given him; his waters shall be sure."—Isa. xxxiii. 16.

THE man to whom God has given grace to be of blameless life dwells in perfect security.

He dwells on high, above the world, out of gunshot of the enemy, and near to heaven. He has high aims and motives, and he finds high comforts and company. He rejoices in the mountains of eternal love, wherein he has his abode.

He is defended by munitions of stupendous rock. The firmest things in the universe are the promises and purposes of the unchanging God, and these are the safe-guard of the obedient believer.

He is provided for by this great promise, "Bread shall be given him." As the enemy cannot climb the fort, nor break down the rampart, so the fortress cannot be captured by siege and famine. The Lord, who rained manna in the wilderness, will keep his people in good store even when they are surrounded by those who would starve them.

But what if water should fail? That cannot be, "his waters shall be sure." There is a never-failing well within the impregnable fortress. The Lord sees that nothing is wanting. None can touch the citizen of the true Zion. However fierce the enemy, the Lord will preserve his chosen.

> "*When thou passest through the waters, I will be with thee; and through the rivers, they shall not overflow thee: when thou walkest through the fire, thou shalt not be burned; neither shall the flame kindle upon thee.*"
>
> Isa. xliii. 2.

BRIDGE there is none: we must go through the waters, and feel the rush of the rivers. The presence of God in the flood is better than a ferry-boat. Tried we must be, but triumphant we shall be; for Jehovah himself, who is mightier than many waters, shall be with us. Whenever else he may be away from his people, the Lord will surely be with them in difficulties and dangers. The sorrows of life may rise to an extraordinary height, but the Lord is equal to every occasion.

The enemies of God can put in our way dangers of their own making, namely, persecutions and cruel mockings, which are like a burning fiery furnace. What then? We shall walk through the fires. God being with us, we shall not be burned; nay, not even the smell of fire shall remain upon us.

Oh, the wonderful security of the heaven-born and heaven-bound pilgrim! Floods cannot drown him, nor fires burn him. Thy presence, O Lord, is the protection of thy saints from the varied perils of the road. Behold, in faith I commit myself unto thee, and my spirit enters into rest.

"The Lord will give strength unto his people; the Lord will bless his people with peace."—Ps. xxix. 11.

DAVID had just heard the voice of the Lord in a thunderstorm, and had seen his power in the hurricane whose path he had described; and now, in the cool calm after the storm, that overwhelming power by which heaven and earth are shaken is promised to be the strength of the chosen. He who wings the unerring bolt will give to his redeemed the wings of eagles; he who shakes the earth with his voice will terrify the enemies of his saints, and give his children peace. Why are we weak when we have divine strength to flee to? Why are we troubled when the Lord's own peace is ours? Jesus, the mighty God, is our strength; let us put him on and go forth to our service. Jesus, our blessed Lord, is also our peace; let us repose in him this day, and end our fears. What a blessing to have him for our strength and peace both now and for ever!

That same God who rides upon the storm in days of tempest will also rule the hurricane of our tribulation, and send us, before long, days of peace. We shall have strength for storms, and songs for fair weather. Let us begin to sing at once unto God our strength and our peace. Away, dark thoughts! Up, faith and hope!

"If any man serve me, let him follow me; and where I am, there shall also my servant be: if any man serve me, him will my Father honour."—John xii. 26.

THE highest service is imitation. If I would be Christ's servant I must be his follower. To do as Jesus did is the surest way of bringing honour to his name. Let me mind this every day.

If I imitate Jesus I shall have his company: if I am like him I shall be with him. In due time he will take me up to dwell with him above, if, meanwhile, I have striven to follow him here below. After his suffering our Lord came to his throne, and even so, after we have suffered a while with him here below, we also shall arrive in glory. The issue of our Lord's life shall be the issue of ours: if we are with him in his humiliation we shall be with him in his glory. Come, my soul, pluck up courage, and put down thy feet in the blood-marked footprints which thy Lord has left thee.

Let me not fail to note that the Father will honour those who follow his Son. If he sees me true to Jesus he will put marks of favour and honour upon me for his Son's sake. No honour can be like this. Princes and emperors bestow the mere shadows of honour; the substance of glory comes from the Father. Wherefore, my soul, cling thou to thy Lord Jesus more closely than ever.

"Jesus said unto him, If thou canst believe, all things are possible to him that believeth."—Mark ix. 23.

OUR unbelief is the greatest hindrance in our way; in fact, there is no other real difficulty as to our spiritual progress and prosperity. The Lord can do everything; but when he makes a rule that according to our faith so shall it be unto us, our unbelief ties the hands of his omnipotence.

Yes, the confederacies of evil shall be scattered if we can but believe. Despised truth shall lift its head if we will but have confidence in the God of truth. We can bear our load of trouble, or pass uninjured through the waves of distress, if we can gird our loins with the girdle of peace, that girdle which is buckled on by the hands of trust.

What can we not believe? Is everything possible except believing in God? Yet he is always true; why do we not believe him? He is always faithful to his word; why can we not trust him? When we are in a right state of heart faith costs no effort: it is then as natural for us to rely upon God as for a child to trust its father.

The worst of it is, that we can believe God about everything except the present pressing trial. This is folly. Come, my soul, shake off such sinfulness, and trust thy God with the load, the labour, the longing of this present. This done, all is done.

*"But if thou shalt indeed obey his voice, and do all that
I speak; then I will be an enemy unto thine enemies, and
an adversary unto thine adversaries."*—Ex. xxiii. 22.

THE Lord Christ in the midst of his people is
to be acknowledged and obeyed. He is the
vicegerent of God, and speaks in the Father's
name, and it is ours implicitly and immediately to
do as he commands. We shall lose the promise
if we disregard the precept.

To full obedience how large the blessing! The
Lord enters into a league with his people, offensive
and defensive. He will bless those who bless us,
and curse those who curse us. God will go heart
and soul with his people, and enter in deepest
sympathy into their position. What a protection
this affords us! We need not concern ourselves
about our adversaries, when we are assured that
they have become the adversaries of God. If
Jehovah has taken up our quarrel we may leave
the foemen in his hands.

So far as our own interest is concerned we have no
enemies; but for the cause of truth and righteousness we take up arms and go forth to conflict. In
this sacred war we are allied with the eternal God,
and if we carefully obey the law of our Lord Jesus,
he is engaged to put forth all his power on our
behalf. Wherefore we fear no man.

"Trust in the Lord, and do good; so shalt thou dwell in the land, and verily thou shalt be fed."—Ps. xxxvii. 3.

TRUST and *do* are words which go well together, in the order in which the Holy Spirit has placed them. We should have faith, and that faith should work. Trust in God sets us upon holy doing: we trust God for good, and then we do good. We do not sit still because we trust, but we arouse ourselves, and expect the Lord to work through us and by us. It is not ours to worry and do evil, but to trust and do good. We neither trust without doing, nor do without trusting.

Adversaries would root us out, if they could ; but by trusting and doing we dwell in the land. We will not go into Egypt, but we will remain in Immanuel's land—the providence of God, the Canaan of covenant love. We are not so easily to be got rid of as the Lord's enemies suppose. They cannot thrust us out, nor stamp us out: where God has given us a name and a place, there we abide.

But what about the supply of our necessities ? The Lord has put a "verily" into this promise. As sure as God is true, his people shall be fed. It is theirs to trust and to do, and it is the Lord's to do according to their trust. If not fed by ravens, or fed by an Obadiah, or fed by a widow, yet they shall be fed somehow. Away, ye fears !

"In quietness and in confidence shall be your strength."
Isa. xxx. 15.

IT is always weakness to be fretting and worry-ing, questioning and mistrusting. What can we do if we wear ourselves to skin and bone? Can we gain anything by fearing and fuming? Do we not unfit ourselves for action, and unhinge our minds for wise decision? We are sinking by our struggles when we might float by faith.

Oh for grace to be quiet! Why run from house to house to repeat the weary story which makes us more and more heart-sick as we tell it? Why even stay at home to cry out in agony because of wretched forebodings which may never be fulfilled? It would be well to keep a quiet tongue, but it would be far better if we had a quiet heart. Oh to be still and know that Jehovah is God!

Oh for grace to be confident in God! The Holy One of Israel must defend and deliver his own. He cannot run back from his solemn declarations. We may make sure that every word of his will stand though the mountains should depart. He deserves to be confided in; and if we would dis-play confidence and consequent quietness, we might be as happy as the spirits before the throne.

Come, my soul, return unto thy rest, and lean thy head upon the bosom of the Lord Jesus.

"It shall come to pass, that at evening time it shall be light."—Zech. xiv. 7.

IT is a surprise that it should be so; for all things threaten that at evening time it shall be dark. God is wont to work in a way so much above our fears and beyond our hopes, that we are greatly amazed, and are led to praise his sovereign grace. No, it shall not be with us as our hearts are prophesying: the dark will not deepen into midnight, but it will on a sudden brighten into day. Never let us despair. In the worst times let us trust in the Lord who turneth the darkness of the shadow of death into the morning. When the tale of bricks is doubled Moses appears, and when tribulation abounds it is nearest its end.

This promise should assist our patience. The light may not fully come till our hopes are quite spent by waiting all day to no purpose. To the wicked the sun goes down while it is yet day: to the righteous the sun rises when it is almost night. May we not with patience wait for that heavenly light, which may be long in coming, but is sure to prove itself well worth waiting for?

Come, my soul, take up thy parable and sing unto him who will bless thee in life and in death, in a manner surpassing all that nature has ever seen when at its best.

"And he that sat upon the throne said, Behold, I make all things new."—Rev. xxi. 5.

GLORY be to his name! All things need making new, for they are sadly battered and worn by sin. It is time that the old vesture was rolled up and laid aside, and that creation put on her Sabbath suit. But no one else can make all things new except the Lord who made them at the first; for it needs as much power to make out of evil as to make out of nothing. Our Lord Jesus has undertaken the task, and he is fully competent for the performance of it. Already he has commenced his labour, and for centuries he has persevered in making new the hearts of men, and the order of society. By-and-by he will make new the whole constitution of human government, and human nature shall be changed by his grace; and there shall come a day when even the body shall be made new, and raised like unto his glorious body.

What a joy to belong to a kingdom in which everything is being made new by the power of its King! We are not dying out: we are hastening on to a more glorious life. Despite the opposition of the powers of evil, our glorious Lord Jesus is accomplishing his purpose, and making us, and all things about us, "*new*," and as full of beauty as when they first came from the hand of the Lord.

"And they shall beat their swords into plowshares, and their spears into pruninghooks: nation shall not lift up sword against nation, neither shall they learn war any more."—Isa. ii. 4.

OH, that these happy times were come! At present the nations are heavily armed, and are inventing weapons more and more terrible, as if the chief end of man could only be answered by destroying myriads of his fellows. Yet peace will prevail one day; yes, and so prevail that the instruments of destruction shall be beaten into other shapes and used for better purposes.

How will this come about? By trade? By civilization? By arbitration? We do not believe it. Past experience forbids our trusting to means so feeble. Peace will be established only by the reign of the Prince of Peace. He must teach the people by his Spirit, renew their hearts by his grace, and reign over them by his supreme power, and then will they cease to wound and kill. Man is a monster when once his blood is up, and only the Lord Jesus can turn this lion into a lamb. By changing man's heart, his blood-thirsty passions are removed. Let every reader of this book of promises offer special prayer to-day to the Lord and Giver of Peace, that he would speedily put an end to war, and establish concord over the whole world

"Thou shalt drive out the Canaanites, though they have iron chariots, and though they be strong."—Josh. xvii. 18.

IT is a great encouragement to valour to be assured of victory, for then a man goes forth to war in confidence, and ventures where else he had been afraid to go. Our warfare is with evil within us and around us, and we ought to be persuaded that we are able to get the victory, and that we shall do so in the name of the Lord Jesus. We are not riding for a fall, but to win; and win we shall. The grace of God in its omnipotence is put forth for the overthrow of evil in every form : hence the certainty of triumph.

Certain of our sins find chariots of iron in our constitution, our former habits, our associations, and our occupations. Nevertheless we must overcome them. They are very strong, and in reference to them we are very weak ; yet in the name of God we must master them, and we will. If one sin has dominion of us we are not the Lord's free men. A man who is held by only one chain is still a captive. There is no going to heaven with one sin ruling within us, for of the saints it is said, "Sin shall not have dominion over you." Up, then, and slay every Canaanite, and break to shivers every chariot of iron ! The Lord of hosts is with us, and who shall resist his sin-destroying power ?

"So shall we ever be with the Lord."—1 Thess. iv. 17.

WHILE we are here the Lord is with us, and when we are called away we are with him. There is no dividing the saint from his Saviour. They are one, and they always must be one: Jesus cannot be without his own people, for he would be a head without a body. Whether caught up into the air, or resting in Paradise, or sojourning here, we are with Jesus; and who shall separate us from him?

What a joy is this! Our supreme honour, rest, comfort, delight, is to be with the Lord. We cannot conceive of anything which can surpass or even equal this divine society. By holy fellowship we must be with him in his humiliation, rejection, and travail, and then we shall be with him in his glory. Before long we shall be with him in his rest and in his royalty, in his expectation and in his manifestation. We shall fare as he fares, and triumph as he triumphs.

O my Lord, if I am to be for ever with thee, I have a destiny incomparable. I will not envy an archangel. To be for ever with the Lord is my idea of heaven at its best. Not the harps of gold, nor the crowns unfading, nor the light unclouded, is glory to me; but Jesus, Jesus himself, and myself for ever with him in nearest and dearest fellowship.

"As birds flying, so will the Lord of hosts defend Jerusalem."
Isa. xxxi. 5.

WITH hurrying wing the mother bird hastens up to the protection of her young. She wastes no time upon the road when coming to supply them with food, or guard them from danger. Thus as on eagle's wings will the Lord come for the defence of his chosen ; yea, he will ride upon the wings of the wind.

With outspread wing the mother covers her little ones in the nest. She hides them away by interposing her own body. The hen yields her own warmth to her chicks, and makes her wings a house, in which they dwell at home. Thus doth Jehovah himself become the protection of his elect. He himself is their refuge, their abode, their all.

As birds flying, and birds covering (for the word means both), so will the Lord be unto us : and this he will be repeatedly and successfully. We shall be defended and preserved from all evil : the Lord who likens himself to birds will not be like them in their feebleness, for he is Jehovah of hosts. Let this be our comfort, that almighty love will be swift to succour, and sure to cover. The wing of God is more quick and more tender than the wing of a bird, and we will put our trust under its shadow henceforth and for ever.

"He keepeth all his bones: not one of them is broken."
Ps. xxxiv. 20.

THIS promise by the context is referred to the
much afflicted righteous man : " Many are
the afflictions of the righteous, but the Lord delivereth him out of them all." He may suffer skin-
wounds and flesh-wounds, but no great harm shall
be done, "not a bone of him shall be broken."

This is great comfort to a tried child of God,
and comfort which I dare accept ; for up to this
hour I have suffered no real damage from my many
afflictions. I have neither lost faith, nor hope, nor
love. Nay, so far from losing these bones of
character, they have gained in strength and energy.
I have more knowledge, more experience, more
patience, more stability than I had before the trials
came. Not even my joy has been destroyed. Many
a bruise have I had by sickness, bereavement, depression, slander, and opposition ; but the bruise
has healed, and there has been no compound
fracture of a bone, nor even a simple one. The
reason is not far to seek. If we trust in the Lord,
he keeps all our bones ; and if he keeps them, we
may be sure that not one of them is broken.

Come, my heart, do not sorrow. Thou art smart-
ing, but there are no bones broken. Endure hardness, and bid defiance to fear.

"I, even I, am he that comforteth you: who art thou, that thou shouldest be afraid of a man that shall die, and of the son of man which shall be made as grass; and forgettest the Lord thy maker, that hath stretched forth the heavens, and laid the foundations of the earth; and hast feared continually every day because of the fury of the oppressor, as if he were ready to destroy? and where is the fury of the oppressor?"—Isa. li. 12, 13.

LET the text itself be taken as the portion for to-day. There is no need to enlarge upon it. Trembling one, read it, believe it, feed on it, and plead it before the Lord. He whom you fear is only a man after all; while he who promises to comfort you is God, your Maker, and the Creator of heaven and earth. Infinite comfort more than covers a very limited danger.

"Where is the fury of the oppressor?" It is in the Lord's hand. It is only the fury of a dying creature; fury which will end as soon as the breath is gone from the nostril. Why, then, should we stand in awe of one who is as frail as ourselves? Let us not dishonour our God by making a god of puny man. We can make an idol of a man by rendering to him excessive fear as well as by paying him inordinate love. Let us treat men as men, and God as God; and then we shall go calmly on in the path of duty, fearing the Lord, and fearing nobody else.

"He will turn again, he will have compassion upon us; he will subdue our iniquities; and thou wilt cast all their sins into the depths of the sea."—Micah vii. 19.

GOD never turns from his love, but he soon turns from his wrath. His love to his chosen is according to his nature, his anger is only according to his office: he loves because he is love, he frowns because it is necessary for our good. He will come back to the place in which his heart rests, namely, his love to his own, and then he will take pity upon our griefs and end them.

What a choice promise is this—" He will subdue our iniquities"! He will conquer them. They try to enslave us, but the Lord will give us victory over them by his own right hand. Like the Canaanites, they shall be beaten, put under the yoke, and ultimately slain.

As for the guilt of our sins, how gloriously is that removed! "All their sins,"—yes, the whole host of them; "thou wilt cast"—only an almighty arm could perform such a wonder; "into the depths of the sea"—where Pharaoh and his chariots went down. Not into the shallows out of which they might be washed up by the tide, but into the 'depths" shall our sins be hurled. They are all gone. They sank into the bottom like a stone. Hallelujah! Hallelujah!

"God is our refuge and strength, a very present help in trouble."—Ps. xlvi. i.

A HELP that is not present when we need it is of small value. The anchor which is left at home is of no use to the seaman in the hour of storm ; the money which he used to have is of no worth to the debtor when a writ is out against him. Very few earthly helps could be called "very present": they are usually far in the seeking, far in the using, and farther still when once used. But as for the Lord our God, he is present when we seek him, present when we need him, and present when we have already enjoyed his aid.

He is more than "present," he is *very* present. More present than the nearest friend can be, for he is in us in our trouble ; more present than we are to ourselves, for sometimes we lack presence of mind. He is always present, effectually present, sympathetically present, altogether present. He is present now if this is a gloomy season. Let us rest ourselves upon him. He is our refuge, let us hide in him ; he is our strength, let us array ourselves with him ; he is our help, let us lean upon him ; he is our very present help, let us repose in him now. We need not have a moment's care, or an instant's fear. "The Lord of hosts is with us : the God of Jacob is our refuge."

"And of Joseph he said, Blessed of the Lord be his land, for the precious things of heaven, for the dew, and for the deep that coucheth beneath."—Deut. xxxiii. 13.

WE may be rich in such things as Joseph obtained, and we may have them in a higher sense. Oh for "the precious things of heaven"! Power with God, and the manifestation of power from God, are most precious. We would enjoy the peace of God, the joy of the Lord, the glory of our God. The benediction of the three divine Persons in love, and grace, and fellowship we prize beyond the most fine gold. The things of earth are as nothing in preciousness compared with the things of heaven.

"The dew." How precious is this! How we pray and praise, when we have the dew! What refreshing, what growth, what perfume, what life there is in us when the dew is about! Above all things else, as plants of the Lord's own right hand planting, we need the dew of his Holy Spirit.

"The deep that coucheth beneath." Surely this refers to that unseen ocean underground which supplies all the fresh springs which make glad the earth. Oh to tap the eternal fountains! This is an unspeakable boon; let no believer rest till he possesses it. The all-sufficiency of Jehovah is ours for ever. Let us resort to it now.

"Thine enemies shall be found liars unto thee."
Deut. xxxiii. 29.

THAT arch-enemy, the devil, is a liar from the beginning; but he is so very plausible that, like mother Eve, we are led to believe him. Yet in our experience we shall prove him a liar.

He says that we shall fall from grace, dishonour our profession, and perish with the doom of apostates; but, trusting in the Lord Jesus, we shall hold on our way and prove that Jesus loses none whom his Father gave him. He tells us that our bread will fail, and we shall starve with our children; yet the Feeder of the ravens has not forgotten us yet, and he will never do so, but will prepare us a table in the presence of our enemies.

He whispers that the Lord will not deliver us out of the trial which is looming in the distance, and he threatens that the last ounce will break the camel's back. What a liar he is! For the Lord will never leave us, nor forsake us. "Let him deliver him now!" cries the false fiend: but the Lord will silence him by coming to our rescue.

He takes great delight in telling us that death will prove too much for us. "How wilt thou do in the swelling of Jordan?" But there also he shall prove a liar unto us, and we shall pass through the river singing psalms of glory.

"This same Jesus, which is taken up from you into heaven, shall so come in like manner as ye have seen him go into heaven."—Acts i. 11.

MANY are celebrating our Lord's first coming this day; let us turn our thoughts to the promise of his second coming. This is as sure as the first advent, and derives a great measure of its certainty from it. He who came as a lowly man to serve will assuredly come to take the reward of his service. He who came to suffer will not be slow in coming to reign.

This is our glorious hope, for we shall share his joy. To-day we are in our concealment and humiliation, even as he was while here below; but when he cometh it will be our manifestation, even as it will be his revelation. Dead saints shall live at his appearing. The slandered and despised shall shine forth as the sun in the kingdom of their Father. Then shall the saints appear as kings and priests, and the days of their mourning shall be ended. The long rest and inconceivable splendour of the Millennial reign will be an abundant recompense for the ages of witnessing and warring.

Oh that the Lord would come! He is coming! He is on the road and travelling quickly. The sound of his approach should be as music to our hearts! Ring out, ye bells of hope!

> *"Peter answered and said unto him, Though all men shall be offended because of thee, yet will I never be offended."*
> Matt. xxvi. 33.

"*WHY*," cries one, "*this is no promise of God.*" Just so, but it was a promise of man, and therefore it came to nothing. Peter thought that he was saying what he should assuredly carry out ; but a promise which has no better foundation than a human resolve will fall to the ground. No sooner did temptation arise than Peter denied his Master, and used oaths to confirm his denial.

What is man's word ? An earthen pot broken with a stroke. What is your own resolve ? A blossom, which, with God's care, may come to fruit, but which, left to itself, will fall to the ground with the first wind that moves the bough.

On man's word hang only what it will bear.

On thine own resolve depend not at all.

On the promise of thy God hang time and eternity, this world and the next, thine all and the all of all thy beloved ones.

This volume is a cheque-book for believers, and this page is meant as a warning as to what bank they draw upon, and whose signature they accept. Rely upon Jesus without limit. Trust not thyself nor any born of woman, beyond due bounds ; but trust thou only and wholly in the Lord.

"For the mountains shall depart, and the hills be removed; but my kindness shall not depart from thee, neither shall the covenant of my peace be removed, saith the Lord that hath mercy on thee."—Isa. liv. 10.

ONE of the most delightful qualities of divine love is its abiding character. The pillars of the earth may be moved out of their places, but the kindness and the covenant of our merciful Jehovah never depart from his people. How happy my soul feels in a firm belief of this inspired declaration! The year is almost over, and the years of my life are growing few, but time does not change my Lord. New lamps are taking the place of the old, perpetual change is on all things; but our Lord is the same. Force overturns the hills, but no conceivable power can affect the eternal God. Nothing in the past, the present, or the future can cause Jehovah to be unkind to me.

My soul, rest in *the eternal kindness* of the Lord, who treats thee as one near of kin. Remember also *the everlasting covenant*. God is ever mindful of it—see that thou art mindful of it too. In Christ Jesus the glorious God has pledged himself to thee to be thy God, and to hold thee as one of his people. Kindness and covenant—dwell on these words as sure and lasting things which eternity itself shall not take from thee.

"He hath said, I will never leave thee, nor forsake thee." —Heb. xiii. 5.

SEVERAL times in the Scriptures the Lord hath said this. He has often repeated it, to make our assurance doubly sure. Let us never harbour a doubt of it. In itself the promise is specially emphatic. In the Greek it has five negatives, each one definitely shutting out the possibility of the Lord's ever leaving one of his people so that he can justly feel forsaken of his God. This priceless Scripture does not promise us exemption from trouble, but it does secure us against desertion. We may be called to traverse strange ways, but we shall always have our Lord's company, assistance, and provision. We need not covet money, for we shall always have our God, and God is better than gold, his favour is better than fortune.

We ought surely to be content with such things as we have, for he who has God has more than all the world besides. What can we have beyond the Infinite? What more can we desire than Almighty Goodness.

Come, my heart; if God says he will never leave thee, nor forsake thee, be thou much in prayer for grace, that thou mayest never leave thy Lord, nor even for a moment forsake his ways.

"And even to your old age I am he; and even to hoar hairs will I carry you: I have made, and I will bear; even I will carry, and will deliver you."—Isa. xlvi. 4.

THE year is very old, and here is a promise for our aged friends ; yes, and for us all, as age creeps over us. Let us live long enough, and we shall all have hoar hairs ; therefore we may as well enjoy this promise by the foresight of faith.

When we grow old our God will still be the I AM, abiding evermore the same. Hoar hairs tell of our decay, but he decayeth not. When we cannot carry a burden, and can hardly carry ourselves, the Lord will carry us. Even as in our young days he carried us like lambs in his bosom, so will he in our years of infirmity.

He made us, and he will care for us. When we become a burden to our friends, and a burden to ourselves, the Lord will not shake us off, but the rather he will take us up and carry and deliver us more fully than ever. In many cases the Lord gives his servants a long and calm evening. They worked hard all day and wore themselves out in their Master's service, and so he said to them, "Now rest in anticipation of that eternal Sabbath which I have prepared for you." Let us not dread old age. Let us grow old graciously, since the Lord himself is with us in fulness of grace.

"Having loved his own which were in the world, he loved them unto the end."—John xiii. 1.

THIS fact is essentially a promise; for what our Lord was he is, and what he was to those with whom he lived on earth, he will be to all his beloved so long as the moon endureth.

"*Having loved:*" here was the wonder! That he should ever have loved men at all is the marvel. What was there in his poor disciples that he should love them? What is there in me?

But when he has once begun to love, it is his nature to continue to do so. Love made the saints "*his own*"—what a choice title! He purchased them with blood and they became his treasure. Being his own, he will not lose them. Being his beloved, he will not cease to love them. My soul, he will not cease to love thee!

The text is well as it stands: "*to the end,*" even till his death the ruling passion of love to his own reigned in his sacred bosom. It means also *to the uttermost.* He could not love them more: he gave himself for them. Some read it, *to perfection.* Truly he lavished upon them a perfect love, in which there was no flaw nor failure, no unwisdom, no unfaithfulness, and no reserve.

Such is the love of Jesus to each one of his people. Let us sing to our Well-beloved a song.

" Thou shalt guide me with thy counsel, and afterward receive me to glory."—Ps. lxxiii. 24.

FROM day to day and from year to year my faith believes in the wisdom and love of God, and I know that I shall not believe in vain. No good word of his has ever failed, and I am sure that none shall ever fall to the ground.

I put myself into his hand for guidance. I know not the way that I should choose: the Lord shall choose mine inheritance for me. I need counsel and advice; for my duties are intricate, and my condition is involved. I seek to the Lord, as the High Priest of old looked to his Urim and Thummim. The counsel of the infallible God I seek in preference to my own judgment or the advice of friends. Glorious Jehovah, thou shalt guide me!

Soon the end will come: a few more years, and I must depart out of this world unto the Father. My Lord will be near my bed. He will meet me at heaven's gate: he will welcome me to the glory-land. I shall not be a stranger in heaven: my own God and Father will receive me to its endless bliss.

GLORY BE TO HIM WHO WILL GUIDE ME HERE,

AND RECEIVE ME HEREAFTER. AMEN.

INDEX OF SCRIPTURE TEXTS.

Other devotional books
from Marshall Morgan & Scott

Great Verses from the Psalms

Charles H. Spurgeon

For today's readers, *Great Verses from the Psalms* contains selections carefully chosen from Charles Spurgeon's classic work, *The Treasury of David*, skilfully edited in the form of devotional readings. Here are Spurgeon's own comments on the best-known and best-loved verses from the Psalter. At least one verse is included from each of the 150 Psalms; from most of them several of the more familiar verses are included.

Talking about the value of the Psalms for daily living, Spurgeon said, 'In these busy days it would be greatly to the spiritual profit of Christian men if they were more familiar with the Book of Psalms, in which they would find a complete armoury for life's battles, and perfect supply for life's needs. Here we have both delight and usefulness, consolation and instruction. The Book supplies the babe in grace with penitent cries, and the perfected saint with triumphant songs. He who is acquainted with the marches of the Psalm-country knows that the land floweth with milk and honey, and he delights to travel therein.'

Daily Thoughts on Holiness

Andrew Murray

Holiness and the deepening of the spiritual life were constant themes in the writings and preaching of Andrew Murray. In the course of his long life (1828–1917) he wrote a great many books, most of which have remained in print up to the present day.

This compilation of daily devotional readings contains the essence of Andrew Murray's message, and includes selections from such established classics as *With Christ in the School of Prayer*, *The Full Blessing of Pentecost*, *The Spirit of Christ* and *Waiting on God*.

The key to the continued popularity of Andrew Murray's books is the timelessness of their central theme—the relationship of the disciple with his Lord, and its practical outworking in the common circumstances of everyday life.